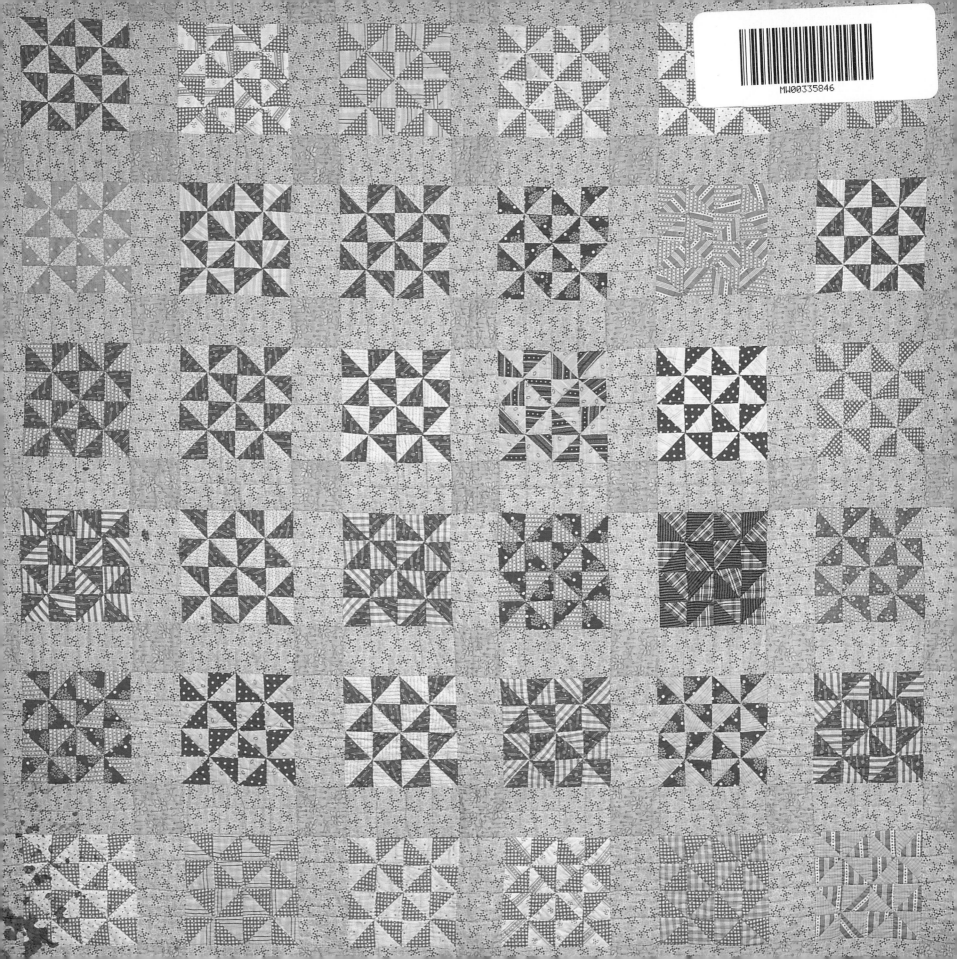

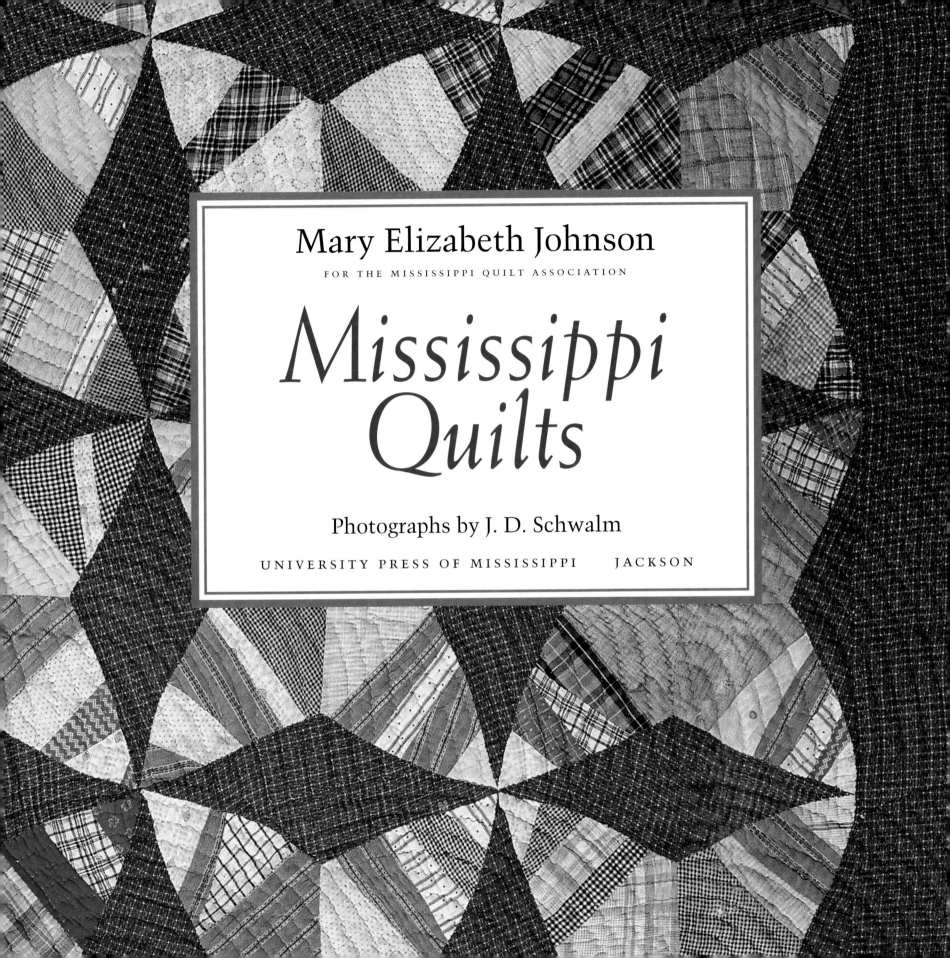

Mary Elizabeth Johnson

FOR THE MISSISSIPPI QUILT ASSOCIATION

Mississippi Quilts

Photographs by J. D. Schwalm

UNIVERSITY PRESS OF MISSISSIPPI   JACKSON

www.upress.state.ms.us

Printed in Hong Kong

04   03   02   01   4   3   2   1

Title page spread: "String Star," set in the "Rocky Road to Kansas" pattern, made by Sallie Brown Wilson of Caile, Sunflower County, Mississippi, circa 1900. MQA quilt no. H-51. Collection of Nancy Sykes, great-granddaughter. See figure 5.2, page 99.

Library of Congress Cataloging-in-Publication Data
Johnson, Mary Elizabeth.
  Mississippi quilts / Mary Elizabeth Johnson for the Mississippi Quilt Association ; photography by J. D. Schwalm.
    p. cm.
  Includes bibliographical references and index.
  ISBN 1-57806-357-4 (cloth : alk. paper) – ISBN 1-57806-358-2 (pbk. : alk.paper)
   1. Quilts–Mississippi–History–19th century. 2. Quilts–Mississippi–History–20th century. I. Mississippi Quilt Association. II. Title.

NK9112 .J64 2001
746.46'09762–dc21

                                                        00-050371

British Cataloging-in-Publication Data available

Dedicated to Martha Skelton,

Whose lifelong dedication to the art of quilting

has brought recognition and honor

to the state of Mississippi

CONTENTS

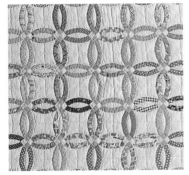

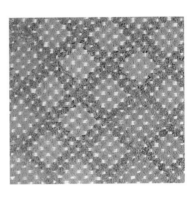

Eudora Welty, Honorary Chairperson,
Mississippi Quilt Association Hertiage Quilt Search

ACKNOWLEDGMENTS

The Mississippi Quilt Association's Heritage Quilt Search Project would not have been possible without the quiltmakers and quilt owners who so generously shared their quilts, photographs, and stories. Our most sincere thanks for making *Mississippi Quilts* a reality.

The Heritage Quilt Search board had to depend on many to accomplish its objectives. We give heartfelt thanks for six years of time and energy so graciously given by the Heritage Quilt Search Project's board of directors, committee chairs, and members. We extend our appreciation for their time and energy in planning, organizing fund-raising events, arranging facilities, publicizing events, directing volunteers, and carrying out quilt search days. We are greatly indebted to them for all they contributed, but especially for never losing sight of our goal.

We extend a special thanks to Carol Vickers. Without her dedication and perseverance this project might never have been completed. She not only chaired this project throughout its entirety, but also undertook research beyond that attained in the quilt search days. Carol sought out additional quilts to be included in this book, resulting in a more complete story of quilting in Mississippi. After the documentation had been gathered, she spent many days sorting, editing, and making sense of the data. It is only fitting that she write the introduction to this book.

A special thanks to members and their husbands who made quilts, doll beds, and other fundraising items that helped provide funds for the documentation process.

We are grateful to the Mississippi governor's mansion, museums, churches, and organizations that offered the use of their facilities for quilt search and photography days. We offer our deepest appreciation to the hundreds of devoted volunteers who worked endless hours to accomplish the thankless tasks necessary to making these days successful.

Words cannot express our feelings of gratitude to J. D. Schwalm, photographer, for his efforts in capturing the realism of the quilts for this book. His artistic ability and talented eye brought out the best in each quilt. His constant devotion to the art of photography enhanced the finished product. His efforts to accommodate were phenomenal.

Gratitude and thanks are extended to the following individuals, organizations, and corporations for their special and unique contributions:

Eudora Welty, Pulitzer prize–winning author, for serving as honorary chairperson of our project, for allowing the use of quotes from her writings, and for the use of photographs from the Eudora

Welty collection housed at the Mississippi Department of Archives and History;

Individual donations and gifts given in the form of memorials from members of Mississippi Quilt Association and other interested parties;

Quilt guilds across the state for their donations and their continuous support and encouragement;

La-Z-Boy South, the Bank of Mississippi, Union Planters Bank, Trustmark National Bank, National Bank of Commerce, and Wal-Mart for their financial support;

Governor William Winter, who advocates the preservation of Mississippi history, for his advice and encouragement when we were at our lowest point, for without his guidance we would not have succeeded in our efforts to obtain funding to publish our book;

Elbert Hilliard, director of Mississippi Archives and History, for working with us and for presenting our request to the Joint Legislative Budget Committee for funds to cover publication costs;

The Joint Legislative Budget Committee for recommending that the appropriation of funds for the publication of *Mississippi Quilts* be included in the Department of Archives and History's budget;

Governor Ronnie Musgrove, Lieutenant Governor Amy Tuck, Speaker of the House of Representatives Tim Ford, and the members of the Mississippi legislature for approving the funds to publish *Mississippi Quilts*;

Mary Elizabeth Johnson, for her outstanding efforts in interpreting our raw data into a finished product in which MQA takes great pride;

The University Press of Mississippi, Craig Gill, Senior Editor, and staff for support and guidance throughout this project and the publication of this book.

The Board of Directors of the Mississippi
Quilt Association Heritage Quilt Search Project

INTRODUCTION

The Mississippi Heritage Quilt Search Project

A study of quilts and quiltmakers can provide keen insight into the life of any group at any given time in a country's history. Just as an archaeologist can look at a campsite occupied thousands of years ago and tell us many things about the people who built the fire and cooked the food, a quilt researcher can look at a quilt, talk with its owner, and make interesting, fascinating, and sometimes poignant observations about the time in which the quilt was made and the person who made it. An awareness of this fact spurred the Mississippi Quilt Association, in 1994, to appoint a documentation committee to explore the possibilities of conducting a statewide search for historic Mississippi quilts.

The Mississippi Quilt Association was formed in 1991 with the expressed purpose of providing a network and forum for quilters and quilt enthusiasts to grow technically, artistically, and historically. From its inception, a quilt search had been a priority with the members, and by early 1995 this aspect of the association's purpose began to take shape. With the publication of this book, the search has come full circle.

It was, and is, the dream of the Mississippi Quilt Association to leave a legacy which will reflect not on those women who conducted the search, but on the women and men who made the quilts—oftentimes under the most trying of circumstances. It was the conviction of the search team that every quilt has a story to tell, and that story deserves to be told.

How does a group begin such a formidable task, with no money and limited knowledge of what the job entails? The work must begin with unbounded enthusiasm, determination, and the same "can do" attitude which quilters have traditionally exhibited!

On January 5, 1995, the Executive Board of the Mississippi Quilt Association approved a proposal, presented by an exploratory committee, to establish a documentation project. In retrospect, what has been accomplished seems nothing short of phenomenal. At the time, the prospect of traveling the state to look at hundreds of quilts seemed exciting. Little thought was given to the toll that the work ahead would take.

At the first search day, a photograph of the search's core team was taken. At the end of the search, a final photograph was made. As one member commented, "When we began, we all looked thinner, younger, and more naive." Had the individuals involved thought of the hundreds of hours required, the time spent away from families, the frustrations and sometimes backbreaking work, the project might never have been undertaken.

However, at the end of the final search day on October 17, 1997, amid hugs and tears, members of the search team were reluctant to let go of the camaraderie, bonding, and cooperative spirit which had developed among members of the team and which permeated the entire project. The group had seen one another through marriages, births, divorces, illnesses, and deaths. They saw personal quilting projects begun, abandoned, taken up again, finished, and hung in major shows. And most importantly, they helped build a database about Mississippi quilts and quiltmakers, one which will stand in the future as a point of pride and a significant research contribution to the history of quilts and quilting. As one of the volunteers with the search project stated, "We want the quilt owners, along with all Mississippians, to feel the same excitement about these quilts and their histories that we felt when we first unfolded them."

The purpose of the search was never to look only for beautiful quilts. Rather, it was the goal of the group to discover and record a cross section of the quilts made by Mississippi women. Many utilitarian quilts, made expressly to provide warmth, were expected, and they appeared at every search day. There was, for example, a denim quilt made of scraps from the legs of overalls altered to fit a very short man. And there were many quilts backed with fertilizer sacks, on which the print was still visible; often, the string from feed sacks had been used to quilt the piece.

At the other end of the spectrum, exquisite pieces of work appeared. Workers could usually tell when a *broderie perse* quilt or a magnificent red-and-green four-block quilt was hung to be photographed—everyone in the room turned to admire the quilt.

Proper organization was imperative to the success of the project. Everyone was aware that there had to be specific tasks with specific persons assigned to each task. With that in mind, the following positions were established: documentation chair, documentation vice-chair (and chair of fundraising), coordinator of operations, local site coordinator, photography chair, sites committee chair, publicity chair, financial manager, and records manager.

Following the appointment of the documentation committee, one of the early decisions made by the committee was to record only those quilts made prior to 1946. This date seemed a logical cutoff, since quilts made prior to that time contain no polyester. Documenting all quilts up to the present somehow seemed an unmanageable task. This challenge is left to future Mississippi Quilt Association members who will experience the thrill of unfolding a quilt, lovingly presented for documentation by a granddaughter, a great-grandson, or a nephew of the quilt's maker.

As a beginning step toward learning more about the tasks facing them, the committee invited quilt author and historian Bets Ramsey of Chattanooga, Tennessee, to come to Jackson and conduct a workshop on documentation. Using information provided by Ms. Ramsey, the committee organized itself with specific duties assigned various members. Probably the greatest piece of advice given to the search team by Ms. Ramsey was, "Don't make it your goal to document every quilt in the state. What you want is a cross-section of quilts from each region of the state and from every segment of the population."

One of the major considerations during the early days of organizing for the search was the documentation form which would be used to record information about each quilt. A three-page form was devised to include information about the quilt, its maker, and its provenance. These forms include information about the quilt owner, the quiltmaker (or makers), and physical information about each of the 1,769 quilts documented.

Between August 1995 and October 1997, nineteen quilt search days were held in towns covering the state geographically (see map, p. 201). The first search day was held in Ridgeland, Mississippi, a suburb of Jackson, the state capital. This was a controlled search day with members of the search team bringing in their own quilts and those of people they knew. This procedure was decided upon so that committee members could test the system they had formulated, the documentation form, and the photography.

Each quilt was presented at the check-in table. The owner filled in basic information on the form and was interviewed concerning the quilt's history. While this was being done, the quilt was photographed hanging on special frames which were moved to each site as the search traveled the state.

What was a typical search day for members of the search team? It usually meant driving for some distance, or arriving the evening before. Since the schedule called for one search day every five or six weeks, this alone placed strains on individuals and their families. The search day began with volunteers arriving before 8 A.M. to set up frames for photography, to arrange tables for all the various stations the quilts went through, and to orient local volunteers. A number was assigned to each quilt, and a system of checks and balances was used to assure that no quilt would be lost.

Search days were busy, but never frantic. Each person knew her job and did it. Eight or nine members of the core team went to almost every search day; then local volunteers were utilized for such tasks as registration and check-in, interview, check-out, and scribe. Local hostesses always provided typical Mississippi-style lunches. It is estimated that approximately three hundred volunteers worked at least one day during the search.

The core team had originally committed to traveling to each site, and within the team four volunteers had extensive knowledge of the history of fabric, dyes, quilt patterns, batting, quilting styles, and such. These women were assigned the daunting task of identifying patterns and recording some thirty-five pieces of information about each quilt, including the approximate date of construction if no date was known by the owner. They spread each quilt on a table and recorded the information, including such things as pattern, stitches per inch, type of batting, and fabric used. (See copy of the documentation form on pp. 202–06.)

As word of the search project spread, more and more quilts were presented for documentation. On some days, more than 175 quilts were brought to the site. Publicity prior to the search days indicated that each quilt owner was limited to five finished quilts, made in Mississippi prior to 1946 or brought to the state before that date; however, that rule was not strictly adhered to. Some owners brought in unquilted tops, framed pieces of quilts, and woven coverlets. The search team tried to give each quilt equal attention—whether it was an elaborate "Sunday" quilt that had been lovingly cared for or a ragged utility quilt. Volunteers knew that the quilts reflected the lives of the women who made them and that the work of these women deserved respect.

The most interesting aspect of the quilt search was, of course, the stories told by the quilt owners; and many of these stories are retold in this book. For example, the owner of a quilt made for competition in the 1933 Chicago World's Fair told of how her mother, an artist as well as a quilter, made the quilt, then died a year later at the age of thirty-nine.

Another quilt owner told of how the quiltmaker, her great-grandmother, had the quilt hidden in a hollow tree near her home when she heard the Federal troops were approaching during the Civil War (see page 41-43). This same story was also attached to a quilt found in another part of the state and is possibly one of those oral stories which expand with the passing of time. Interviewers knew that the owner of a quilt made many years ago was relating a story which he or she had heard from a family member of a previous generation, and they encouraged the owner to record the story in writing on the documentation form.

Some interesting observations were made by the search team. When the team held a search day in Meridian, in the east central part of the state, it was noted that a larger than expected number of quilts had wool bats in the middle. This finding remained a puzzle until an interview with a quilt owner revealed the fact that during the 1920s this section of the state was overrun by cypress weed, commonly known as "dog fennel," and the only animals which would eat the weed were sheep. Being the pragmatists that women had to be to survive, they used the wool from these sheep in their quilts.

By far, the most common batting in quilts was cotton. Over and over, the search team heard the story of how women went to the field after the cotton had been picked and "scrapped" enough cotton to make a quilt. The women and children sat around the fire at night and picked the seeds from the cotton until there was enough for the quilter to "card a bat."

An unusual construction, which the search team called an "envelope edge," was noted in several areas of the state. Another observation concerned the elaborately embroidered crazy quilts, made of silks, satins, and brocades, which the search team had expected to find in locations along the Mississippi River (the French influence should have been felt more strongly along the river). However, crazy quilts of equal beauty were documented in every section of the state.

As expected, a proliferation of "Sunbonnet Sue" and "Overall Sam" quilts, "Double Wedding Ring" quilts, and "Dresden Plate" quilts appeared. However, Mississippi quilters in the thirties seemed to prefer a myriad of star patterns. There were eight-pointed stars, six-pointed stars, "Seven Sister Stars," "Feathered Stars," "Lone Stars," Touching Stars, "Broken Stars," and as many as fifty other star patterns.

It is interesting to speculate on this obsession with star patterns. Perhaps women spent only a few minutes alone at night when they went outside to make sure a chicken coop was closed or to check on whether the young tomato plants were safe from the frost. These quiet moments under the stars were the only private times a woman could salvage from a busy day, and perhaps as she looked at the fabrics available to her, the beauty of the stars prompted her to choose that pattern. Whatever the case, the reader of this book will benefit from the fascination star quilt patterns have held for Mississippi quilters.

The attitudes of quilt owners, both present and past, were of interest to the search team. Several exquisite quilts which had been purchased in antique stores were documented, as were quilts which were purchased at yard sales and flea markets. This fact leads to the question of why owners disposed of their quilts. At one search site, an owner of five quilts asked for help in locating a buyer for her quilts. She said they had come to her from her mother but they meant little to her and she would like for someone who would enjoy them to have the quilts. Others presented their quilts, however tattered, with obvious affection and were eager to learn how best to care for these prized possessions.

One day a mother and daughter brought in a tacked (tied) crib quilt which had been made for the mother in the thirties when she was born. When the analysts suggested that there seemed to be another quilt inside the tacked quilt, the owners sat down and took the outer cover off, revealing a patchwork quilt. They had no idea it was there and probably would never have seen it had they not brought the quilt for documentation.

The attitude of an owner toward his or her quilts might also be related to the condition of the quilts. Some were in excellent condition, obviously having been well cared for. In many cases, these were (as expected) "Sunday" quilts. However, some of the utility quilts were well preserved while some quilts, even exquisite ones, had obviously not been cared for.

Often the poor condition of quilts was due to a lack of knowledge about how to care for them. With this in mind, the Heritage Quilt Search Project distributed a printed sheet on caring for older quilts, and owners were also given a label to attach to the quilt, indicating it had been documented.

When the search team visited Port Gibson, an owner brought some of her family's collection of fifty-three quilts to be documented. The importance of this collection lies not only in the number of quilts but in the high level of artistry of the makers and in the fact that the quilts were made over a period of four generations, beginning in the early 1800s and ending in the 1950s.

One of the goals of the search was to make its findings available to a wide audience. With that in mind, the group approached the Mississippi Department of Archives and History about the possibility of housing the information. With the availability of computer technology, it was decided that the Mississippi Quilt Association should commission a computer programmer to write a program containing all the information on the documentation form. All information has now been entered into the resulting program (Microsoft EXCEL), and it is anticipated that this information, along with the hard copies of the documentation forms, will be placed in the state archives.

As is true with any project of this nature, the search could have gone on indefinitely. However, it was obvious that a true representation of Mississippi quilts had been achieved, and after the nineteenth search day the Documentation Committee moved forward toward achieving its goals of mounting an exhibit to travel the state and of publishing a book of findings of the search. This, of course, entailed narrowing the nearly 1,800 quilts to a manageable number.

To that end, a jury committee was appointed with the following guidelines for selecting quilts for inclusion in either the exhibit or the book: a quilt should be representative of Mississippi quilting traditions, have a story of special interest attached to it, possess an appeal to an audience wider than just the owner or the search committee, offer some educational value, or be of historical interest to the state.

Following intensive review and discussion, approximately 250 quilts were identified for professional photography and further examination. Of these, more than 175 were brought to a central location to be photographed; and although some had to be eliminated for various reasons, most of those quilts appear in this book.

The Mississippi Quilt Association has made every effort to interpret documentation forms correctly in preparing the text for the book. Given the fact that forms were completed in the owner's handwriting, sometimes hurriedly, it is inevitable that errors might have occurred. The estimated date of a quilt's construction was based on information given by the owner and information gained from the quilt itself, including such things as period fabrics, pattern, fading, backing, and so on. Dates assigned are approximate and ordinarily refer to the decade in which the quilt was made rather than a specific year.

Funding for the quilt search proved to be a challenge. Anyone who has undertaken a volunteer project can appreciate the difficulty faced by the Mississippi Quilt Association in this matter. Early on, it was discovered that corporations had only a passing interest in quilts or quilt history; therefore, the Documentation Board relied upon its own ingenuity to fund the search.

The costs of film, film developing, and duplication were covered by offering the owner, for a small fee, a copy of the completed documentation form and a photograph of the quilt. Two major donation quilts, "Everything's Coming Up Roses" and "Mississippi Stars," were raffled, with much of the proceeds going toward the computer program and professional photography and for purposes of matching two grants from the Mississippi Arts Commission, which helped fund the exhibit. During the 2000 session of the Mississippi legislature, through the cooperation of the Mississippi Department of Archives and History, funding was made possible for publication of this book.

Quilting is an artistic tradition that holds deep meaning for Mississippians, and it is a tradition that transcends the boundaries of race, economic status, or social class. While the history of Mississippi has been recorded in books, the history of quilting, like that of many other traditions, has existed in a rather tenuous state. Hundreds of people volunteered their time and expertise to complete this project. It is their hope that the results will further enhance the history of the state as seen through the eyes of the thousands of women (and sometimes men) who quilted in the past and who continue the tradition today.

Carol Vickers, Chairman, Mississippi Quilt Association
Heritage Quilt Search Project

Mississippi Quilts

CHAPTER ONE

Mississippi Quiltmaking before 1825

. . . the quilt hung motionless, just clear of the ground. It was a bed-size square that looked rubbed over every inch with soft-colored chalk that repeated themselves, more softly than the voices sounding off on the porch.

—Eudora Welty, *Losing Battles*

LOST IN THE MISTS OF TIME—like much of the Native American culture, numerous houses both fancy and plain, and physical evidence of the colorful characters of territorial Mississippi—are the earliest beginnings of textile traditions in the state. The indigenous people sewed garments of finely tanned deerskin, using thread spun from the inner bark of trees, animal fur, or shredded sinew.[1] Cloth was one of the earliest items of trade brought into this rough frontier country, along with guns, powder, shots, beads, kettles, knives, and hatchets.[2] Whether bedcoverings were among the items the first Mississippians made with these materials is a question that may never be answered. Certainly, there is very little likelihood that any traces of such bedcoverings remain, as textiles are among the most fragile of all material made by human enterprise. The high humidity and wild swings in temperature, from broiling hot to freezing cold, which are typical environmental conditions statewide, are very damaging to textiles. So are the many insects, which thrive in this environment. Add the storms, floods, hurricanes, and other natural disasters that have visited Mississippi, and it is easy to see that the chances of finding a three-hundred-year-old textile are slim indeed. With no physical evidence, we must use our imagination, deductive reasoning, and what we know of quiltmaking in other parts of the country to get an idea about any quilts that might have been in the state when no written record is available. A review of the settlement patterns and economic conditions can provide clues and establish a base for the quilts that came in later years.

The area now known as the state of Mississippi was crossed and recrossed by explorers

Chintz appliqué, or *broderie perse*, quilt made by Catharine Crenshaw Holman in Rowan (now Davie) County, North Carolina, in the 1821–1835 period. MQA quilt no. C-100. Collection of Elizabeth Harden Aydelott, great-great-granddaughter.

from many European nations, and they variously claimed ownership prior to 1798. The first European explorer, Alonso de Pineda, came in 1519 from Spain. Twenty years later, a more famous Spaniard, Hernando De Soto, made it to what is now Coahoma County, where he built boats and crossed the Mississippi River. De Soto brought horses and hogs to North America, as well as diseases to which native populations had no resistance and to which at least half of those populations are estimated to have succumbed by 1650. The French came next, down the Mississippi River, looking for passage to the Pacific Ocean. Father Marquette and Louis Jolliet traveled to the location of present Rosedale in 1673; there they decided that the river flowed into the Gulf of Mexico, so they turned around and went back to Quebec. Other French explorers such as La Salle, Cadillac, and Bienville followed during the next fifty years. During this time, Great Britain was also trying to expand its colonization into this area; the British were after the abundant natural resources, such as fur-bearing animals, which were valuable for trade. Finally, after much push and pull between various nations, including the newly independent United States of America, the Mississippi Territory and Adams County were established on May 7, 1798, with Winthrop Sargent as the first territorial governor.

By this time, both sides of the Mississippi River were lined with plantations from New Orleans to Natchez and beyond. In the restless quest for land, men had purchased acreage from Spain, France, or Britain, whichever country claimed the area at the time. Only when the United States began to govern the area was it possible to begin to establish clear title to the huge tracts of land that beckoned the early entrepreneurs.

The early explorers brought no women with them, as their interest lay in discovery, not in settlement. There were, however, women in the plantations that were established by 1750; theirs must have been a primitive existence indeed, as the plantation lifeline, steamboats, did not regularly ply the river until more than fifty years later. The first steamboat, the *New Orleans*, did not begin cruising the Mississippi until 1811.[3]

Many planters were aware of the drawbacks of life on the plantation for women, writes Catherine Clinton in *The Plantation Mistress*. She quotes one cotton grower who complained in 1823 that he had given up on the idea of finding a wife because "it would be very difficult to find one who would be willing to go [to] the wilds of Mississippi and there spend the balance of her life [away] from her friends and relations."[4] One woman, Nancy Robinson, who made such a decision and traveled as a bride to Holmes County, Mississippi, in 1833 wrote, "I have ended my life of folly, gaiety and amusement. I [think] I will never be happy any more away from my family." Four months later, she was still unhappy: "I am sad tonight, sickness preys in my frame. I am alone and more than 150 miles from any near relative in the wilds of an Indian nation."[5] Such letters back to dearly beloved and much missed family members must have discouraged many women and girls from trying the life, as indicated by what an unnamed woman wrote: "In 1836 I came to this country. It was then a dense canebrake except immediately on the Mississippi River which was at that time known as Bachelor's Bend from the fact that most of the inhabitants were unmarried men."[6]

Despite these accounts of trials of life on the frontier, many women were persuaded to make the journey into early Mississippi and set up homes as best they could. Because it was land that their adventurous husbands sought, many women found themselves settled into rural accommodations in the beginning. It took many months to clear enough forest away to make fields for farming; this preoccupied the husband and meant that he was not, in most cases, able to provide an elegant home for his wife until long after their initial homesteading. But any cabin, however rough, could seem like a mansion to a woman who had been living in a wagon or a tent for many months. At least she could get out the things she had brought from back home, including her quilts, and settle into more permanent shelter.

Settlement of the Territory

The territory's development began around Natchez, which remains the county seat of Adams County. Merely three years after this first county's establishment, five others were in place: Jefferson (originally Pickering), organized in 1799; Washington, in 1800, and Claiborne and Wilkinson, in 1801. A new territorial governor, W. C. C. Claiborne, arrived in Natchez on November 23, 1801, and permission was granted by the Choctaw and Chickasaw Indians to build a road through their lands that would follow a trail they had used for centuries as a trading and hunting route. Mapmakers refused to use one of the names for this new byway: "Road From Nashville In The State of Tennessee To The Grindstone Ford of The Bayou Pierre In The Mississippi Territory." This road, of which a few stretches still remain, was the Natchez Trace; it had other names at the time, including "Mail Road" and "Cumberland Road."[7] It would become famous as a transit for boatmen returning home on foot after delivering their cargoes to Natchez and New Orleans from the northeast. Journeys along the Natchez Trace were often quite adventurous, at least in the retelling, punctuated with wild tales of highwaymen and fierce bears and other beasts. (Recent research has shown that there was actually very little crime on the Trace, according to the records kept by lawmen along the route.)

In time, overnight camping spots, or "stands," were established along the Trace. The only one of these remaining is Mount Locust, just north of Port Gibson, and it has been restored to reflect the living conditions of the family that would have been the innkeepers; one bedroom displays quilts on the beds. The Natchez Trace opened in 1803 but was already undergoing improvements in 1806, with federally funded "causeways over all marshes and bridges over all streams less than forty feet wide." If the streams were more than forty feet wide, they were to "have trees fallen across them so as to admit the passage of a mail carrier with his mail."[8]

For twenty years, all of present-day Mississippi and Alabama was known as the Mississippi Territory, encompassing an area that stretched south of Tennessee to the Gulf of Mexico and east to Georgia. The western boundary was the Mississippi River. Known to the Atlantic seaboard as the "Southwest," the area supported a population that was a mix of frontier farmers and landed planters; the latter brought with them an aristocratic heritage that included ownership of slaves.[9] However, the term "ranch" might have been better than "plantation" for some of the very early eighteenth-century operations.[10] It took many tries and repeated failures to establish profitable crops in the Mississippi Valley, and during the colonial period, cattle raising was the first really profitable and lasting agricultural industry in the Southwest. Although cotton would eventually become the primary crop, the one on which the antebellum economy of Mississippi was based, herding was probably the means by which most people sustained themselves, and it is surely from this group that much of the population of the state descended.

An Early Urban Scene

Yeomen farmers were part of the mix of settlers in frontier Mississippi. They practiced a more sedentary type of agriculture than the more numerous herders, sometimes achieving a measure of comfort and wealth. As Clark and Guice write in *The Old Southwest, 1795–1830*, "Life among the nobodies along the interior river valleys . . . could hardly have differed more from the life of the nabobs whose plantation homes stood high on the bluffs of the Mississippi River and on its broad, fertile delta. Because the social structure was not static, 'nobodies' sometimes became 'somebodies,' especially in the Natchez District where several patterns of life existed."[11]

Without question, the Natchez District was the most cosmopolitan region within the entire area known as "the old Southwest." As an early writer, William B. Hamilton, described it, it was "a lodestone which drew young and ambitious men from all parts of the United States and from other regions of the world, in the manner of New York City."[12] The resulting mix was of western Europeans living beside Africans, mulattos, and Indians of various tribes and blends of blood mixtures. However, the town was fundamentally English, reflecting the nationality of the settlers who had arrived during the American Revolution. It seems that the white population was not divided into fixed social classes, but was based on wealth. It must be noted that, although Natchez was the Mississippi Territory's premier urban commercial center, its population in 1810 was only fifteen hundred; even so, records from two years later show that it "supported artisans in twenty-four trades, eight attorneys, and an equal number of physicians. The fifty-six commercial establishments included twenty-four mercantile houses, a bank, and three

weekly papers. . . . There was a nursery for the growth of the Pride of China trees, which shaded the town's streets."[13]

Statehood Opens the Doors

On December 10, 1817, President James Monroe signed the congressional resolution that admitted Mississippi to the Union, "opening an era of population and political expansion in the southwestern cotton-slave kingdom [that would] eventually give rise to a significant sectional force in the Republic."[14] Settlers began to stream in from the Carolinas, where worn-out soil could not compete against the fertile "Black Belt" and delta soils of Mississippi. South Carolinians in particular left their state in the thousands around 1819 and 1820, and they were accompanied by their neighbors from North Carolina and Georgia. Virginians and Kentuckians joined this first westward migration, the movement over the Appalachians into Mississippi, Alabama, and Louisiana. Before 1810, only one out of every ten Americans lived west of the Appalachians; after 1820, it was one out of every four.[15] The Mississippi River acted as the final passageway for many who traveled by water: from the Ohio, Tennessee, and Cumberland Rivers and their tributaries, the Mississippi channeled some of the earliest families into the Natchez District.

The quilt documentation forms offer the story of Ada Louemma Moore, who came as a child with her family on a barge, riding the rivers from Tennessee to Tunica County in the northeastern corner of Mississippi; the final leg of the journey was on the Mississippi River. The Moores established a plantation and commissary in this delta county. Ada Louemma married a planter, J. W. Lake, lived most of her life in the hamlet of Maud, and died in

1934, having achieved her goal of making each of her grandchildren a quilt.[16] Even though her trip was made several years after the period of time under discussion, her story could be that of many early settlers of Mississippi who came before and after her—it was a model that was repeated many times.

Travel on the rivers was not without perils, but it was surely more comfortable than the overland routes. Passage on the "traces," especially through Alabama, opened up after the War of 1812, in which Andrew Jackson defeated the Creek Indians, who actively and persistently resisted the invasion of the white settlers. Overland trips were made in wagons and carriages, with overnight stays in private homes or taverns for the whites, and in outdoor camps for slaves. Large families could make quite a caravan, and sometimes they traveled with tents, under which they made camp every night. The migrations were often of six or seven hundred miles or more, with twenty miles a day considered a good speed. Records of wagon journeys indicate that quilts were handy items to have for packing china, lining the interiors of the wagons, making pallets for children, and providing a touch of home. Many of the people who brought quilts to the documentation days spoke with familiarity about their ancestors' arrivals in Mississippi. Some mentioned that a forefather had settled first in Alabama, then moved on to Mississippi. Some mentioned that the family moved several times before settling in a permanent location; this was apparently a commonplace practice when there was an abundance of available land. One quilt owner described his family's wanderings:

Mary Ardra Young [the quiltmaker] was born in 1811 in Abbeville District, S.C., a descendent of Scots-Irish immigrants who settled in South Carolina in the 1760s. Both grandfathers were patriots of the American Revolution. [Miss Young] moved with her parents to Wilcox County, Alabama, in 1829. In 1833, she married David A. Black. To this union was born ten children—eight daughters and two sons (both of whom would be killed in battle during the Civil War). The Blacks lived in Alabama for five years after their marriage, and then, in 1838, moved to Lincoln County, Tennessee, where they lived for ten years. In 1848, they returned to Alabama for one year before striking out for present-day Union County, Mississippi. They settled for good there, in the community of Cotton Plant, with Mrs. Black dying there in her 95th year, in 1906.[17]

Many told of their foremothers bringing quilts with them. A pair of quilts that now reside with their owner in Long Beach, Mississippi, are accompanied by family stories of their travel into the state. One quilt was thought to have been made before the family packed up in 1798 to move to Mississippi from Virginia, because it was said to have been used on the trip. The second quilt, in a similar design, is thought to have been made as the family traveled along the wagon trail.[18]

Few Quilts Survive

The oldest quilt discovered by the documentation project comes from these very early days of Mississippi's history (see fig. 1.1). The fabric from which the quilt is made can be dated with certainty, and the provenance of the quilt can be traced from its most recent private owner back through the generations to its original owner. Rarely does such an old quilt, in such good condition, with such an impeccable family history, come to public attention;

Fig. 1.1. Toile quilt from the family of Andrew Marschalk (1767–1837) of Natchez. It is cotton with linen backing and cotton batting. Fabric was manufactured circa 1785; quilt was made circa 1800; it is 88 inches wide by 105 inches long. MQA quilt no. F-80. Collection of the Mississippi State Historical Museum, donated by Mr. William E. Stewart, great-great-great-grandson of the original owner.

there is cause for celebration when one does. The generosity of the previous owners in placing it in a public institution, where it may be studied and enjoyed by numbers of people, is to be commended.

Since its documentation by the Mississippi Quilt Association's Heritage Quilt Search Project, this quilt has been placed in the collection of the Mississippi State Historical (Old Capitol) Museum, where it has undergone some minor conservation, primarily of the binding, which was frayed in some sections. The original red of the print has faded to pink, but other than some small holes near the center and some brownish stains here and there, this two-hundred-year-old textile is in remarkably good

shape. It has cotton batting, a linen backing, and is quilted in an overall "hanging diamond" design, with about eight stitches per inch.

The quilt is of the type known as "whole cloth," meaning that it is made from a broad expanse of fabric (which might have required the seaming together of several widths or sections to obtain the required size). This particular quilt is made from a scenic cotton print named "Apotheosis of Benjamin Franklin and George Washington." The fabric was used to decorate the bedroom of a home in New York, a fact confirmed by a letter written in 1785 by a guest in the room who described the allegorical figures of the bed hangings "and many more objects of a piece with them." The scene shows Minerva leading Benjamin Franklin and Liberty toward the Temple of Fame. Below them, Washington guides the Chariot of America drawn by leopards, with an unidentified female seated behind him. Various slogans, such as "Where Liberty Dwells, There Is My Country" and "American Independence 1776" are printed on banner-type shapes that female figures and cherubs hold. Also pictured is a globe illustrating the original thirteen colonies and the Atlantic Ocean.[19] American Independence became a subject for fabric printers about 1785, and although they were printed in England, Scotland, and France, the fabrics naturally found a popular market on this side of the Atlantic.[20]

The motif was designed for copperplate printing, a method of adding pattern to fabric, one that is easy to recognize because it is done with only one color—blue, red, purple, or black—on a cream or white background. Copperplate printing on fabric spanned the years from 1750 to about 1830. The monochromatic scenic prints became known as "toiles," and sometimes as "toiles de Jouy," meaning, literally, "fabrics of Jouy," a city of southern

France. In America, the fabric's popularity in wealthy southern homes led to it being called a "colonial print."

The designs of copperplate printing, which was done by hand, were adapted to the much faster machine roller-printing after about 1830. It is not easy to tell the older copperplate print from the newer roller print on a textile such as this quilt, but it is very likely that this example was copperplate printed. The Marschalk family was living in Natchez during the time that copperplate printing was at its height of popularity. Roller-printed reproductions were not yet available.

This example is typical of quilts that would have been found in wealthy homes of the area during this period. It is likely that the quilt is the only remaining piece of what was originally a set of bed hangings consisting of a bed skirt, draperies, and possibly valances that would have been hung from the stretchers between the bedposts. Window treatments may have duplicated the bed hangings in fabric and general style.

The subject matter depicted in toile fabrics ran the gamut from patriotic homages to quaint scenes of country life. Wine making, from the gathering of grapes to tasting the final product, was popular; mise-en-scénes of shepherds and shepherdesses with obvious interest in each other decorated many a bedroom; and exotic locales, with abundant tropical vegetation and animals, was another theme. The artists who drew the designs were quite talented, and the object seems to have been to transport the observer into a fantasy.

Other great favorites for whole-cloth quilts were blue-resist fabrics, identifiable by their color scheme, limited to a range of blues, and the motifs, which are usually floral in nature. Pillar prints, executed with many different colors, were a widespread choice: these printed fabrics had an architectural element as a primary motif. The column, or pillar, ran lengthwise on the fabric and was usually accompanied by twining plants, such as morning glories or ivy. Although no whole-cloth quilts made of these fabrics emerged during the quilt search, it is very likely that quilts like these were part of the furnishings of some of the grand houses of early Natchez and its surrounding plantations.

Toiles, blue-resists, and pillar prints were only a few of the very high fashion fabrics popular during Mississippi's territorial period and early statehood. Another fabric that was a favorite all across Europe (especially in France) and America (particularly in the Carolinas) was chintz. Chintz is a cotton fabric printed with no fewer than five colors, which were used originally to create only floral motifs. What sets it apart from other fabrics is the scale of the floral print, which is usually large, and the finish on the fabric, which is glossy and shiny. Homemakers at the turn of the eighteenth century, and into the first quarter of the nineteenth century, loved it, even though the fact that it was imported made it quite expensive. When chintz appears in early quilts, it is generally used sparingly, as a border or sometimes as a small part of a piecing design; if an antique quilt displays an abundant use of chintz, it generally indicates that it was from a wealthy household.

Chintz in two different patterns has been used to make hexagons in a patchwork design known to quilters as "Flower Garden" in a very old quilt documented in the search. The quilt was made by Catharine Crenshaw (born October 13, 1804), who married John Holman on January 8, 1821, in Newberry, South Carolina. The newlyweds began life together in Rowan (now Davie) County, North Carolina, then moved back to Newberry. In 1850, they immigrated to Winston County, Mississippi, near Yellow Creek. They brought this quilt with them;

Fig. 1.2. Chintz appliqué, or *broderie perse*, quilt made by Catharine Crenshaw Holman in Rowan (now Davie) County, North Carolina, in the 1821–1835 period, and brought to Mississippi in 1850. It is made of cotton, with chintz appliqués and thin cotton batting. It is 96 inches wide by 98 inches long. MQA quilt no. C-100. Collection of Elizabeth Harden Aydelott, great-great-granddaughter.

the family believes that it was made the year that Catharine Crenshaw married. The fabrics in the quilt were certainly available to her at that time; they would even have been available in Natchez, which was considered on the very frontier of civilization in 1821.

The quilt shows only two different types of hexagonal flowers, and they appear to have been made of two different chintzes. The second row of all flowers is pink, and the center and outer ring of the flower are the same in each flower. The border is a plaid with a tan background and stripes of red and black; the fabric is shattering along the black stripe.[21] A plaid border twelve inches wide is an unusual finishing detail, and it is probably handwoven; it would be a nod to the thrift of the maker

that she combined imported chintz with homemade fabric.

Chintz was the inspiration for a style of quilt that is commonly known as *broderie perse*, although no record has been found of this term being used during the first half of the nineteenth century, when the technique developed. The term means "Persian embroidery," and the method is actually a type of appliqué. It is accomplished by carefully cutting motifs out of chintz, then stitching them in a planned arrangement onto a background (almost always white or cream-colored linen or cotton). In the Carolinas, where the process is thought to have originated, the preferred arrangement began with a primary design in the center; it was surrounded by printed borders and flanked with secondary motifs of different sizes. This arrangement is known as a medallion set.

Many *broderie perse* quilts were made in North and South Carolina between 1815 and 1840, and quite a few of them incorporate chintz fabrics that had been printed specifically for use in such quilts. As the popularity of these quilts grew, fabric manufacturers began to print lengths that contained at least one border, possibly more, and several different-sized motifs, each meant for a different area of the quilt. One popular motif was the "Hunt Cornucopia," also known as "Trophy of Arms." This motif can be found in the center of a second quilt brought to Mississippi from South Carolina with the Holmans in their 1850 move (see fig. 1.2). The family believes the quilt was made during the Holmans' sojourn of 1821 to 1835 in North Carolina; the area in which they lived, near present-day Charlotte, was noted for its production of this type of quilt, and their stay coincided with the height of the fashion for such work.

The Holman quilt contains other motifs from specially printed *broderie perse* fabrics, although they are not the supporting motifs from the "Hunt Cornucopia" panel. (One can just imagine quilters exchanging motifs with one another, rather than staying exclusively with the ones that came on their printed panel of fabric.) The border print on the four sides of the quilt is a good example of those that were manufactured to imitate two different borders. (In some quilts, the two border motifs were cut apart and used in different areas of the piece.)

Restrained and elegant in its design, the Holman *broderie perse* quilt is an outstanding example of this very refined type of needlework. As Ellen Fickling Eanes writes about "chintz appliqué quilts" (the term she prefers) in *North Carolina Quilts*, "As style was dictated by tradition and fabric choices were somewhat limited, quiltmakers had to be ingenious to design quilts that were not duplicates of those being made by friends or sisters. Bed sizes had to be considered, and careful planning was necessary to use every snip of flower or leaf, balancing color and symmetry. The rewards were elegant treasures, which were preserved as showpieces by later generations. . . . Because these quilts were usually passed from one generation to another with their histories included, the present owners are apt to know the identities of the quiltmakers."[22]

Summary

The two quilts shown on these pages are very high style quilts, which is the reason they have survived for two hundred years. They were made as special quilts, or as one of the quilters said, "Sunday quilts—you put them out when the preacher came." In the case of the whole-cloth quilt, it was probably part of an elegant guest bedroom ensemble. Indeed, in the 1785 letter that records the details of this fabric, the writer was the guest in a room decorated with the fabric. The room would have been used for important people and closed off from regular household activities the majority of the time. Therefore, not only was the quilt spared normal, destructive wear and tear such as laundering, it was protected from harsh environmental conditions that could have damaged it.

In the case of the chintz appliqué piece, it was a serious undertaking that required skill and artistic talent, although made when many others of its type were, in a sort of early nineteenth-century fad. Each completed quilt of this type was considered a masterpiece by the quilter's family and given proper respect and care. Clearly, the oral traditions of the families to which each of these quilts belong have instilled a respect and reverence for the wonderful objects they are, as the quilts are both in remarkable condition, especially to have passed down through four generations.

Not many quilts have survived from this period of time, for the reasons mentioned in the introductory paragraph to this chapter. The everyday quilts, the utility quilts, those that went out with the herders, those that hung over the doorways and windows of rough log houses, those that wrapped bodies for burial, are gone. Too bad they were so useful.

CHAPTER TWO

Antebellum Quiltmaking in Mississippi

1825–1861

When the mire of roads had permitted, the aunts and girl-cousins had visited two and three
together and pieced it on winter afternoons. It was in the pattern of "Delectable Mountains,"
and measured eight feet square, the slanty red and white pieces running into the eight-pointed star
in the middle, with the called-for number of sheep spaced upon it. Then Aunt Beck had quilted
it with her bent needle.

—Eudora Welty, *Losing Battles*

ANTEBELLUM MISSISSIPPI was a time of prosperity—land was cheap and the price of cotton was high. "Flush times" was the catchword throughout the state, through all levels of society, and the good news spread back to Atlantic states, attracting even more pioneers. With the remainder of Indian lands being ceded to the United States in 1830 and 1832, the way was opened for a surge of white settlers into the state. (The Choctaw gave up more than ten million acres in the Treaty of Dancing Rabbit Creek alone.) In the four years between 1833 and 1837, land speculators and settlers bought seven million acres in north Mississippi, land which had been obtained from the Chickasaw. During the 1830s, the population of Mississippi grew more rapidly than the population of the nation.

The economy of the state during the antebellum period was of a colonial type, as in other parts of the South, in that Mississippi raised staple crops, such as cotton, for export as raw material, and it imported the finished goods, such as fabric, that its society required. Before the American Revolution, much of the South had traded mainly with England, but afterwards it began to depend more on the industries of the Northeast, and while the region as a whole became dependent on the port of New York, the state of Mississippi relied on New Orleans. It shipped its cotton either there or to Mobile, depending on which was closer. However, by 1860 a textile industry was getting started in the state, and there were six textile factories, employing 717 people.[1] (Quilters will remember that the

Appliqué work done by a slave shows souls in progress to heaven or hell. The object on which the work has been done is an apron, but its similarity to a quilt is unmistakable. Photograph by Eudora Welty, circa 1940. Photograph courtesy of the Eudora Welty Collection, Mississippi Department of Archives and History.

1820s to 1830s was a time of similar industrialization in New England. Those were the times of the "Lowell Mill girls," when young girls left their rural environments to earn salaries in the textile industries of Lowell, Massachusetts, and other mill towns.)

Cotton was produced on both small and large farms; there were about thirty-five thousand farms containing between twenty and one hundred acres; there were slightly over two thousand farms with five hundred acres or more. There is a correlation between the sizes of farms and numbers of slaveholders: in 1860, 3,500 slaveholders owned more than 30 slaves, and 27,391 slaveholders held fewer than 30 slaves. There were 332,426 white people in Mississippi who owned no slaves. Yet, of the nearly 800,000 people in the state, more than half (436,631) were black. (Free blacks numbered 773, one of the smallest populations of any southern state.)[2] There were also a substantial number of herdsmen in Mississippi who owned a home place but not much land (and few, if any, slaves); the free-range laws ensured plenty of grazing lands for their cattle.

Farmers and planters were hardworking businessmen with fieldwork to supervise, laborers to oversee, and books to balance. And their wives seldom conformed to the Southern-belle stereotype. Managing a large household required energy and intelligence as well as graceful manners. Home was more likely to be a modest frame cottage than a Tara or a Mount Vernon.[3] Nonetheless, there were men who made great fortunes—planter aristocrats who owned as many as 100 slaves and who wielded great political and social influence. Natchez, still the center of population of the state in 1860, had a population of 6,612; 11 of this number were millionaires. There were only 75 men with this kind of wealth in the entire nation at the time.[4]

Cotton money could buy almost anything from anywhere in the world, and there was plenty to choose from, as this visitor to Natchez in the mid-1830s wrote:

Here are all the banks and most of the dry goods and fancy stores. Here, consequently, is the center of business, and, to the ladies, that of attraction. . . . In passing up this street, . . . the stranger is struck with the extraordinary number of private carriages, clustered before the doors of the most fashionable stores, or millenaries, rolling through the street, or crossing and recrossing it from those by which it is intersected, nearly every moment, from eleven till two on each fair day. But few of these equipages are of the city: they are from the plantations in the neighborhood, which spread out from the town over richly cultivated "hill and dale,"—a pleasant and fertile landscape—far into the interior.[5]

We can take for granted that these dry goods stores of the 1830s carried all manner of fabrics, because they were situated on the best of all delivery routes, that of the Mississippi River. Even as early as 1808, a tourist had counted eighty-three boats of different types docked at Natchez-Under-the-Hill,[6] many of them bound from New Orleans with cargo from the Atlantic seaboard, indeed, with merchandise from all over the world.

Steamboats collected cotton for transport to the port of New Orleans, where it was shipped to Le Havre in France as well as to other European ports. On their return trips up the river, the paddle wheelers delivered merchandise bought and paid for with cotton money. Vicksburg and Natchez were the two important commercial ports, but there were also private landings along the Mississippi serving individual plantations, especially in the Delta.

Trains came into Mississippi in two stages: in the first one, the railroad was built to take cotton from the inland towns to a river port. Natchez and Vicksburg both realized that trains would be the way to obtain more cotton for their ports, and each tried to build a track to Jackson, where they could access the rich plantations of Hinds, Madison, and Rankin Counties. The Natchez line failed, but the Vicksburg and Jackson Railroad became the most successful railroad in the state. It started up in 1838 and carried passengers over the five miles of track east from Vicksburg; gradually the track was extended, and by 1840 it reached all the way to Jackson. Next, a bridge was built over the Pearl River, and by 1861 the track reached Meridian.[7]

The second stage was the linkage of the smaller railroads to bigger lines. New Orleans and Mobile both made connections to the North that doubled their importance as cotton centers, because now they could ship to national markets in the Northeast by train and to international markets by boat. By 1858, New Orleans and Jackson were connected by rail; so were Memphis and Jackson. Trains ran between Memphis and Charleston, providing a link to the Atlantic coast. Passengers as well as cargo traveled the rails. A stagecoach between Jackson and Vicksburg took twelve hours and cost ten dollars; the Vicksburg and Jackson railroad cut the time to two and a half hours and the cost to two dollars.[8]

The railroads improved the economy by making it easier to get products to market, and they also provided jobs for many men. Many of the respondents to the documentation questionnaires mentioned the railroad as an employer, from these early beginnings throughout the next century, but especially after the Civil War, when destroyed track had to be replaced and extended. Some of the documentation team have theorized that the woman of the house had more time for quilting with her "railroad man," as they were called, out of the house for long periods of time. The railroad was important to quilters as a delivery system for the fabrics they needed, as a place of employment for their menfolks, and, in at least one example, as inspiration for a quilt design (see fig. 2.1).

Fig. 2.1. "Railroad Crossing," a variation of "Rocky Mountain Road," probably made by a Mrs. Seale in the 1850–1860 period (possibly earlier, according to owner) in Neshoba County, Mississippi. Made of all-cotton materials, it is quilted by the piece, also stippled with 10 to 11 stitches per inch, and is 74 inches wide by 82 inches long. MQA quilt no. I-41. Collection of Frances Williams, great-granddaughter.

Women's Lives

When Gideon Lincecum lifted his wife down off the wagon at a spot near present-day Columbus, Mississippi, in 1825, having just finished their ox-and-wagon migration from South Carolina, he must have been overjoyed to hear her remark— "with one of her sweetest and most satisfied-looking smiles"—as she assured him of her happiness at her new home, "Who could look at this fat game, so easily obtained, this beautiful river with its handsome dry bluff, and gushing spring water and be otherwise?"[9] We can only hope that she remained as happy throughout the time it took to establish a life in what was still a man's country.

It is a tribute to Mississippi women that they were able to find the time to make quilts—even after the initial settlement period was over, with its unimaginable hardships and lack of creature comforts, most women did not live in the lap of luxury. It is really surprising to see on the quilt documentation forms that many of them lived to be eighty or ninety years old—perhaps the hardships of life toughened them up. Many labored alongside their men in the fields and also ran the home, doing laundry and cooking and taking care of the children. Historians often note that few diaries were kept by working women, because there was simply no time in their lives for reflection and recording daily events. The few firsthand records from the working women of this period of time generally take the form of household accounts.

It is frequently remarked in quilt literature that only the women of privilege had time to keep diaries, and, indeed, women who lived in households with slaves were spared some of the more exhausting work, such as hauling water and firewood and washing clothes. However, the life of even the privileged was not easy. Simply coping with the environment was exhausting. No matter how much money one had, there was always the heat or the cold, and the bugs and the snakes. Although it is difficult for us to imagine life without running water, electricity, and, most of all, air conditioning, it was all they knew; and the women made the best of it, even thrived and found happiness. While the majority of the quilts from this period of time come from women who lived on farms of all sizes, the term "antebellum" always makes us think of plantations, so let us visit one in Hinds County, Mississippi.

Down on the Plantation

A thrilling glimpse of what life was really like on an early plantation is provided by the following notes written on a quilt documentation form by the great-great-great-great-granddaughter of a plantation mistress:

Lucy Hatch was born August 5, 1805, in North Carolina. She attended a good school in Alabama, and was married at 16 to Benjamin Whitfield, a Hinds County plantation owner who was also a minister and eventually a trustee of Mississippi College. When Lucy Hatch became Mrs. Benjamin Whitfield, she also became the mistress of Magnolia Plantation. One family story describes her as "a tyrant when she was pregnant. She thought no one should be idle. After the servants finished their regular work, she had them make quilts."

Her son described her energy and activities in creating a productive farm on the frontier: "She rose at three o'clock in the morning, and by four o'clock everything was in full movement about the house. Breakfast was served promptly at six o'clock the year round. She made her own carpets, netted curtains for her windows, prepared all the ordinary supplies for the table. She had all the cloth for the servants woven on her looms, and the thread spun on her own wheels; the clothes made by her own seamstresses. She superintended all the improvements about the house, yard, and garden. She marketed incessantly, though living twelve miles from town. . . . Sometimes her energy was fierce; she would scold and punish until it seemed a reign of terror. And yet she was in general so kind to her servants, and so provident of their welfare, that they all held her in reverence and grateful regard, even after their liberation."[10]

It is obvious that Mrs. Whitfield took her job quite seriously, and, indeed, it is very likely that without her supervisory function in the domestic realm the plantation would not have prospered. Not only was she bearing the children for her husband, thereby ensuring that his lineage would continue, she was seeing to the growing and preservation of the vegetables and fruits that went on their table, she was making the fabric and thread for the servants and overseeing the production of their clothing, and she also manufactured many of the household textiles. We can only imagine what she had to do to "make her own carpets." No wonder she was a bit of a tyrant at times—and, just possibly, not only when she was pregnant. How many of us could have handled this kind of responsibility when we were barely out of our sixteenth year?

All the early plantations are not "gone with the wind." An account of the establishment of an early Mississippi plantation came to the quilt documentation effort from the family who still owns and lives on the land. The property is now known as Hamer Hills Farm, and it was established in Mont-gomery County in 1837 by James Cochran Hamer of Anson County, North Carolina. A popular Mississippi travel magazine in 1998 described this still-functioning plantation:

When James Hamer bought the first parcel of land in frontier Mississippi, he had never seen his new farm. The Treaty of Dancing Rabbit Creek, 1830, marked the purchase of North Mississippi land by the United States from the peaceful, agrarian Choctaw Indians. Before Hamer could make the journey, tragedy struck when his wife Ann died following complications from childbirth. A few months later James packed up provisions, the farm implements he needed to turn wilderness into a farm, and his four motherless sons, ranging in age from two months to eight years, and headed to the newly-opened Choctaw Indian Territory.

Self-sufficiency on the frontier farm meant setting up a sawmill, a syrup mill, a cotton gin, and even a church and a school. Orchards and gardens were planted for food, herbs grown for medicine, livestock raised for transportation, farm work and food. Many artifacts from the farm's early years remain to teach today's generation about frontier life in Mississippi, including the millstone brought by James Hamer on that long wagon journey.

The farm, which grew to encompass 1424 acres, is today a Historic Centennial Farm. Direct descendants of that hardy pioneer live and work on the farm, producing cotton, corn, timber, wildlife, registered English shepherds, and, surprisingly, porcelain. The pride of the farm is the family farmhouse, circa 1870, filled with family furniture and works of art created by family forebears.[11]

A "summer spread" in the collection of Hamer Hills Farm was made in the 1850s by Mary Adeline

Fig. 2.3. The "Whig Rose" summer spread design graces a bed at Hamer Hills Farm, still owned and operated by the descendants of the original owner. A wreath done by the quiltmaker hangs above the bedside stand; it is made of hair from family members. On the other side of the bed is a painting, also by the quiltmaker. MQA quilt no. H-15. Photograph by Harold Head.

Fig. 2.2. Mary Adeline (Sweatman) Kelly, circa 1860, of Winston County, maker of the "Whig Rose" summer spread. Photograph courtesy of Alice Elizabeth Hamer Sanford and Alice Penelope (Penny) Sandford.

Fig. 2.4. "Whig Rose" summer spread, called "Rose of Sharon" by the family, made by Mary Adeline Sweatman Kelly. It is appliqué with solid cotton fabrics and hemmed edges and has the original finish on fabrics. It is 86.5 inches wide by 92 inches long. MQA quilt no. H-15. Collection of Alice Elizabeth Hamer Sanford, great-granddaughter, and Alice Penelope (Penny) Sanford, great-great-granddaughter.

Sweatman Kelly, who was born in Harrison County, Mississippi (see fig. 2.2). After spending part of her childhood in Greene County, Alabama, where her mother moved upon Mary Adeline's father's death, she accompanied her brother, David Sweatman, back to Mississippi in 1852 to settle in Winston County. She perhaps taught school in Winston County, as that was her profession. She had attended finishing school, probably in Alabama at the famed Judson College for Women, and she was proficient in many artistic disciplines. She became engaged to Charles Duncan Kelly, a merchant and the mayor of Winona, Mississippi; the family believes that she made this quilt as part of her hope chest. The wedding took place on November 5, 1856. Mary Adeline bore four children and died of complications from the fourth delivery in 1868, at the age of thirty-eight. The quilt top (see fig. 2.4) has passed from Mary Adeline to her daughter, Alice Penelope Kelly Hamer, then to *her* daughter, Alice Elizabeth Hamer Sanford, and finally to the current generation, represented by Alice Penelope (Penny) Sanford, who is Mary Adeline's great-great-granddaughter.[12]

A summer spread is exactly what the name says—a spread to put on the bed in summer, when warmth is not desired. Summer spreads are often mistaken for unfinished quilt tops. This coverlet has, however, been hemmed on all four sides, indicating that it was to be used as is (fig. 2.4). Summer spreads make a case for the belief that women often made quilts to satisfy their need for artistic expression. A summertime bed could have been adequately made up with any of several choices; instead, Mrs. Kelly went to the trouble to appliqué an interesting, colorful design. Because there are so many warm months in Mississippi, she probably got more use out of it year-round than she would have if it had been quilted.

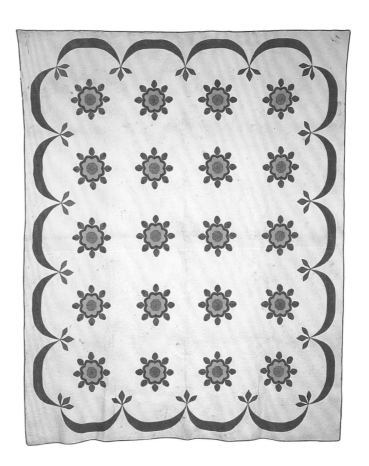

What Does "Whig" Mean?

Three quilts in this chapter are named either "Whig Rose" (figs. 2.4 and 2.5) or "Whig's Defeat" (fig. 2.6). The term "Whig" was originally applied to those who opposed the British monarchy, and during the American Revolution it was the term for rebel colonists. (All members of the DAR, Daughters of the American Revolution, would be daughters of Whigs.) However, the term was used slightly differently during Andrew Jackson's second term as president.

By 1830 or so, "Old Hickory's" supporters, the Jacksonians, had solidified a central core of beliefs that would more or less define the Democratic par-

Fig. 2.5. "Whig Rose" by unknown quilter, although quilt is signed in ink on one edge with the name "Ann Wilkerson." Found in a trunk in the attic of the home of the owner in Vicksburg, it was made in the 1850–1875 period. It is made of all-cotton materials, with quilting at 10 stitches per inch, and is 78 inches wide by 94 inches long. MQA quilt no. E-75. Collection of Christi Bounds.

Fig. 2.6. "Whig's Defeat" made by Martha Wiseman McBryde in Cotton Plant, Union County, Mississippi, in the 1855–1860 period. The quilt is made of all-cotton materials, with hand quilting at 12 stitches to the inch, and is 96 inches wide by 97 inches long. MQA quilt no. O-85. Collection of Catherine King, great-granddaughter.

If a quilt carries the term "Whig" in its name, it could either be from the years of the American Revolution and afterward, 1775 to 1800, when the term was first used, or it could be from the Jacksonian era and several years after, from 1834 to 1852. The name of the quilt will make it abundantly clear which side of the fence the maker was on: there's no doubt when it's called "Whig's Defeat."

To make everything more confusing, at one time the pattern known as the "Whig Rose" was claimed by both Democrats and Whigs! The Democrats just called it the "Democrat Rose." And, because we are discussing the names of quilt patterns, it will surprise no one to learn that there is more than one design known as the "Whig Rose." One may be seen in figure 2.5; the other was the summer spread pictured in figure 2.4. The summer spread consists of four motifs surrounded by a border of green scalloped swags and red appliqués that are probably supposed to represent bunting or ribbons and could be interpreted as political motifs. Both of these "Whig Roses" were made in the 1850s, so it's a good guess that neither of the makers was a supporter of Andrew Jackson. On the other hand, maybe they were Democrats and *did* support him! (The second option is more likely the case in Mississippi—the capital is named for him, and his military accomplishments in the state, from the Battle of New Orleans through the final removal of the Indians to Oklahoma, made him quite a hero to many Mississippians. The documentation effort listed a red-and-white Mississippi quilt made of touching "Stars of Bethlehem" with the name "Stonewall Jackson."[15])

The design known as "Whig's Defeat" evolved during the second quarter of the nineteenth century. It is an abstract geometric design that is both pieced and appliquéd (see fig. 2.6). Its name would indicate that the maker was a supporter of Presi-

ty for many years; this was the party "of the farmers, mechanics, and laborers," as Jackson claimed. He was supported by southern planters who looked to him to protect their interests concerning slavery and state's rights. The more successful President Jackson's policies became, the more opposition he garnered; his opponents began calling him "King Andrew." Because they "rebelled against the monarch" they were labeled "Whigs."[13]

The use of the name "Whig" by opponents of Jackson and Jacksonianism became widespread by 1834. The Whigs became an active political force, putting their candidate, William Henry Harrison, into the office of president of the United States in 1840. (Harrison was a retired national hero who had defeated Chief Tecumseh at Tippecanoe; a slogan of the campaign was "Tippecanoe and Tyler Too.")[14]

dent Andrew Jackson and his policies. The very idea that a quilt could be given a political name demonstrates the notion that women often spoke with their needles. Even by the time of the second go-round of the term "Whig," women had little public voice in matters of government or politics. They could make their opinions known through quilts, though!

Slave-Made Quilts

Any discussion of quilts made in a plantation economy must include the contribution made by the slave seamstresses who worked alongside their white mistresses. There are surely many slave-made quilts in Mississippi, but documenting them is impossible. There are almost never any written records that tell the story of a slave and her needlework. (We will probably learn even less about the participation of black men in quilting, although Roland Freeman has recorded the oral history of a descendant of Isaac Phipps, who was taught to sew by his mother, a plantation seamstress named Thomasie; Isaac Phipps sometimes joined his wife and daughters at the quilting frame.[16]) Even when a mention is made in a diary or a letter of servants who were especially skilled in sewing or quilting, the name of the individual is rarely given. In the rare instances that a name is used, it is almost always just the first or given name; no family names are attached.

Inevitably, any recognition of a servant's contribution to a quilt depends on oral history, which is told and retold as it travels down through the generations with the piece. As Mary Lorenz and Anita Stamper wrote in *Mississippi Homespun: Nineteenth-Century Textiles and the Women Who Made Them*, "The role of the historian must be to chronicle the oral history of an object and then try to reconcile or elaborate that history through a physical examination of the object and through a study of any available written records."[17] In other words, when all that is available is oral history, the quilt must be examined in light of other things that can be known for certain. Some substantiating facts would include knowing where the quilt was made, when it was made, whether or not the fabrics in the particular quilt were available to the quilter at that time, whether or not the style of quilt was one that was in the repertoire of quiltmaking at the time the quilt was supposed to have been made, and any number of other factors such as type of binding and so on.

With these qualifying statements in place, we present two quilts that very well could have been made by slaves in Mississippi. One is from the Lake family of Grenada, in Yalobusha County, and the other is from the Whitfield family of Magnolia Plantation in Hinds County.

The first is believed to have been made in the 1840s by Millies Lake, a slave who was later freed by her owners, William and Clementine Lake. A search of census records for Yalobusha County by Mary Lorenz and Anita Stamper revealed that William Lake in 1840 owned six slaves, four of them female. By 1860 he owned ten slaves, six of them females, according to the slave census for that year; no names are given. In 1866, according to the Yalobusha County marriage records, a freedwoman named Mary Ann Lake married a freedman, Ben Butler. Lorenz and Stamper wondered if Mary Ann Lake could be Millies Lake, but, as they say, there is no way to know for sure. "The Millies Lake quilt is symbolic of the many untold histories of slave-made textiles and their makers," they write.[18]

The quilt attributed to Millies Lake is an impressive object done in a very formal arrange-

Fig. 2.7. This quilt is thought to have been made by a slave, Millies Lake, in the 1840s. Measurements are not available. Lake collection, 87.48.1, Mississippi State Historical Museum (Old Capitol), donated in 1987 by Barbara Daigre of Grenada.

Family Shirting/Improved/Bleached and Finished." Quilting follows the shape of the hexagons, with a row on both sides of the seamline, and the border is quilted in straight parallel rows.

The slave makers of the second quilt (fig. 2.8) are not named. Family tradition holds that it was made by a slave or slaves under the direction of Mistress Lucy Whitfield, whose daily activities were detailed earlier in this chapter. A letter written by Richard Griffith (son-in-law of Lucy Whitfield) in 1848 refers to the plantation seamstress who was training a young girl to sew. For some reason, the girl had been taken from the house back to the slave quarters, and the seamstress wanted her returned. This letter provides more than an amusing glimpse of an antebellum household's tug-of-war; it documents the existence of a tradition of "sewing slaves," where an experienced seamstress taught younger women how to stitch.

The family believes that Lucy Hatch Whitfield may have given a chintz appliqué quilt to her daughter, Sallie Ann, upon the occasion of her marriage to Richard Griffith in 1848. The groom was born in Pennsylvania and educated in Ohio. He eventually served two terms as the treasurer of the state of Mississippi. He was also a soldier and served in the Mexican War, where he met and became a close friend of Jefferson Davis. He was a brigadier general at the time of his death during the Seven Day's Battle at Richmond, Virginia, in 1862. A year later the Griffith home in Jackson was invaded by Yankees during the battle of Jackson, but somehow the quilt was not destroyed.[19]

Sallie Ann later married Stephen P. Baley, a prominent business and civic leader in Jackson. She gave the quilt to their granddaughter, and it remained in the family until recently, when it was donated to the Old Capitol Museum. Susan Miller, the great-great-great-great-granddaughter of Lucy

ment of motifs and colors (fig. 2.7). Red, gold, and green solid-color fabrics (probably obtained from William and Clementine Lake's dry-goods store) have been cut into hexagons and diamonds, then hand-pieced into the pattern known to quilters as "Martha Washington's Flower Garden" or "Field of Diamonds." In truth, the quilt looks more like a design for an intricate tile floor than a flower garden, partly because of the geometric pattern of squares in the intricately pieced border. It is backed in a white cotton fabric stamped with scattered bird and flower motifs and the legend "Superior

Hatch Whitfield, has paid it homage by using it as a departure point for some of her own work, an example of which was featured in the February 2000 issue of *American Patchwork and Quilting* magazine.

Quilters who are familiar with the technique of *broderie perse* (discussed in the previous chapter) will recognize this quilt as an unusual example. There are two major differences between the Griffiths quilts and typical quilts of this type. First, in the Griffiths quilt, the same motif is repeated nine times, in three rows of three, rather than using a central medallion setting pattern. Second, templates have been used to cut the parts of the primary motif; a pattern shape has been imposed on the fabric, rather than using the outer edges of the printed fabric design as a cutting guide. In outline, the primary motif closely resembles the "Ohio Rose," with its scalloped edges and halo of bud shapes. In contrast, the many chintz cutouts interspersed between the nine main motifs have all been cut carefully along their design lines so that distinct petals and leaves show against the quilt's white background, in the traditional method associated with *broderie perse*.

The quilt is in excellent condition and has never been washed, meaning that the chintz is in its original state, with the glazed, polished surface emblematic of this fabric type. The suggestion has been made that the distance from the origin of the *broderie perse* quilt, in both time and miles, is the reason for these peculiar deviations. We will never know exactly what influenced the designer of this quilt, anymore than we will know for sure whose hands did the actual stitching—whether it was by slaves at the Whitfield plantation, or by the indefatigable Lucy.

The connection between plantation mistresses and their quilts has always been a point of disagree-

ment among quilt scholars. One camp believes that much of the work attributed to the white mistress was performed by the slaves at her command; the other camp holds that the making of a quilt was work a lady could do while the slaves took care of the more labor-intensive aspects of running a plantation house, such as cooking, cleaning, child-rearing, and so on. In this one instance, at least, there is proof that sewing help was available to the plantation mistress; how she used it is not so easily known.

Fig. 2.8. Chintz quilt, thought to have been made by slaves at Magnolia Plantation, Hinds County, about 1840. It is 105 inches square. Collection of Mississippi State Historical Museum (Old Capitol), donated by the descendants of Lucy Hatch Whitfield. Photograph by Steve Struse.

One other quilt submitted for documentation was said to have been made by a slave, whose name had been lost in the passage of time, for her mistress, Winnie Grisham. The quilt and its oral history have been passed down through generations of the family.[20] The quilt is from the 1850–1860 period, and so it fits within a time frame that supports the family history. It is done in a pattern, "Flying Geese," which was not particularly popular in the South before the most recent quilt revival, except for use in borders of quilts. The colors in the quilt are soft beiges and tans, with a few grays, making a very subtle and pleasing blend. The points on all the triangles that make up the entire quilt top are sharp, the sign of a skilled hand at work; novices will often blunt the tips of the triangle. However, without more information, it is impossible to know whether the quilt is slave-made or not.

A Time of Great Creativity in Quiltmaking

During the second quarter of the nineteenth century, new forms of quilts began to be developed, and familiar styles were refined and adapted to new applications. Wide availability of fabrics, advanced transportation systems, which also afforded new and easier opportunities for travel, and a general prosperity all combined to create an environment that nurtured the making of quilts. The block style of quilt was becoming a part of quiltmakers' repertoires, in part because the smaller confines of log cabins and trail wagons prohibited the making of large, whole cloth pieces. However, quilters kept the styles to which they were accustomed; they just built on those basic forms.

Broderie perse became more popular than ever, especially in the South. A typical example of a medallion-style *broderie perse* piece came to light

in the documentation effort (fig. 2.9). It employs a motif that was very popular for this type of quilt, the "Tree of Life." The quiltmaker fashioned a branched tree laden with leaves and blossoms from bits of chintz, omitting the chintz birds and butterflies that were favorites of many women working in this form. Instead, this maker confined her theme to unusual flowers and chose to expose the roots at the base of the tree, making a very unusual interpretation of the "Tree of Life" motif. Most other examples show the tree planted in a basket or on a pile of stones. As in other quilts of this type, multiple borders have been used to take the quilt to bed size.

The first border around the central medallion is of a chintz that appears to have been block-printed (see fig. 2.10); this would make the fabric very old, pre-dating machine methods of fabric production. Block printing all but disappeared around 1770. (Family history holds that some of the fabrics in the quilt may have come from mourning dresses worn by some of their Huguenot ancestors when they left France in the mid-1600s.) The third border from the center is pieced with triangles in white and a muted two-color print; it is in borders such as this that the very beginnings of the patchwork tradition can be observed. Two white borders are used as spacers between the decorative borders, and a wide green border finishes the quilt. White borders were often where quilters exhibited their skill at producing fine cables and other fancy designs, and this quilter used a number of quilting designs for her very fine work. The green border is an unusual finish for a quilt of this type; it seems a bit heavy for such a delicate design.

The maker, Eliza Ann Spigener, spent the first thirty-eight years of her life near Charleston, South Carolina, then moved to Buyck, Alabama, which is in Elmore County (nearer to Georgia than Missis-

Fig. 2.9. *Broderie perse* quilt in the "Tree of Life" design, made by Eliza Ann Spigener in Alabama, in the 1840–1858 period. It is made of all-cotton materials, hand-pieced and appliquéd, with the original finish on fabrics. Hand-quilted in various designs with fine, close quilting at 8 stitches per inch, it is 92 inches wide by 102 inches long. MQA quilt no. M-15. Collection of Susan Peterson.

Fig. 2.10. The fabric of the innermost border appears to have been block-printed.

sippi), where she made this quilt and four others as part of her daughter's trousseau. Her daughter, Eliza Mary Margaret Spigener, married in 1858. The present owner, the great-great-great-granddaughter of the maker, believes that Mrs. Spigener made the quilt in 1858, when she was fifty-two years old; the documentation team estimated that it could possibly have been made somewhat earlier, perhaps in the 1840s. Actually, since this quilt is known to be one of five "sister" quilts, it could be that the work spanned several years before the wedding date. Two more of the five are still in the family, making a total of three that survive.[21] It is entirely conceivable that Mrs. Spigener became familiar with the technique of *broderie perse* while she lived in Charleston. Many lovely quilts of this type were made there during the period in which she was a resident of the city.

The fact that there was a great population shift going on in the nation gave rise to a special style of quilt that was commemorative in nature. It was the friendship, or signature, quilt, which a group of friends would make and present to one of their own who was "headed west," that is, into Mississippi, Alabama, or Louisiana. The making of signature quilts did not really flower in Mississippi until the twentieth century, when they were used mostly as fund-raisers and gifts, but it can be assumed that the tradition had been established in this earlier period of time and passed down through the generations as oral history, sometimes accompanying an artifact, as in the following example.

The quilt search documented a signature quilt in Natchez with the date of 1858 embroidered on it in several places; the piece was made in Sicily Island, Louisiana (in Catahoula Parish), by members of the Lovelace family, who were early (1770s) settlers. All the names on the quilt are of Lovelace women or women who married into the family.[22]

The pattern of the quilt is the familiar "Autograph Cross," a pieced design in which the center "cross" is made of light-colored fabric so that a name might be inscribed. Although its history alone makes it interesting and unique, the quilt is made even more unusual by the use of "Garden Maze" sashing in red. This type of sashing is rare on signature quilts, and, in this case, it is the most distinctive feature remaining on a quilt that is in very poor condition. (It is too frayed to be photographed; the quilt was discovered by one of the present owners between the springs of a bed which had been passed down through generations of her family.)

Chintz remained a favorite fabric for quilts, and it was used in quilts other than those of the *broderie perse* style. The documentation effort recorded a chintz child's quilt made by the mistress of Auburn, one of the great antebellum houses of Natchez that still stands. Carolyn Williams, plantation mistress and mother, made what she called a "child's pallet quilt" sometime around 1830. She pieced tiny bits of brown chintz with white to make a small quilt, thirty-six inches wide and forty-one inches long, in the "Broken Dishes" pattern. She quilted it beautifully, with eight stitches to the inch. The quilt is in very poor condition, probably the result of hard wear. There were nine Williams children, one of whom grew up to marry Dr. Haller Nutt and become mistress of the famous unfinished mansion called Longwood. The quilt is now in the possession of Carolyn Williams' great-great-granddaughter.[23]

A charming star design known as "Darting Minnows" (figs. 2.11 and 2.12) has squares of a rose-colored chintz as the center square of the motif. The points of the star, which are actually included in the sashing strips of the quilt, are made with a navy pin-dot. The motif is formed when the sashing strips join with the rose-colored chintz corner blocks; the block of the quilt is actually solid white and filled with quilting in interlocking circles. A star motif is formed by this ingenious setting pattern and is repeated 120 times over the surface of the quilt. According to the present owner, it was brought into the state "during the Civil War when the fighting got too bad, and the family moved to Luxahoma, Mississippi, from Kentucky."[24]

This quilt is an excellent example of the way that the repeat-block quilt developed. As illustrated in the "Tree of Life" *broderie perse* quilt, pieced borders were frequently incorporated as a design element in early quilts. In fact, many of the star patterns that became standard in every quiltmaker's repertoire, such as the "Ohio Star" and the "Variable Star" (of which this "Darting Minnows" design is a variation), first made their appearance in the pieced borders of medallion-style quilts. It was a short step to take these little blocks that worked so nicely as a border and line them up next to one another in rows to make a complete quilt. This quilt nicely ties up two trends of the second quarter of the eighteenth century—a favoritism for chintz and the emerging style of repeated blocks.

The second quarter of the century was a great time for star patterns. This was when the well-loved "Lone Star" made its appearance. The design, which consists of one big eight-pointed star that fills the whole quilt top, is pieced of many diamonds. It offers the opportunity for wonderful color schemes, and the empty corners and triangles of the eight-point design were often filled with chintz appliqués, intricate quilting, or smaller stars. Many other star designs emerged during this time, including the "Variable Star" and the "Ohio Star" as well as smaller versions of the diamond-pieced star, known as "Star of Bethlehem." All these examples could be turned into "Feathered Stars" with the

Fig. 2.11. "Darting Minnows" made by Minnie Love Murphy Still in Kentucky, circa 1840. It is made of all-cotton materials, hand-pieced and hand-quilted with very fine, close stitching at 12 stitches per inch, and is 78.5 inches wide by 97 inches long. MQA quilt no. P-152. Collection of Monica A. Kirk Bristow, great-great-granddaughter of the maker.

Fig. 2.12. Detail of "Darting Minnows"

Fig. 2.13. "Feathered Star" made in Kokomo, Indiana, circa 1830, probably by Rosa Burns. The quilt is made of all-cotton materials, hand-pieced and appliquéd, and is hand-quilted with very fine, close stitching at 12 stitches per inch; it is 87 inches square. MQA quilt no. D-129. Collection of JoAnn Goldman, great-great-great-granddaughter.

addition of a sawtooth border around the points. A spectacular example of the "Feathered Star" design was brought into Mississippi from Indiana in 1940 (fig. 2.13). Family tradition holds that the quilt goes to the youngest girl in each generation and that the stains on it are from wounds suffered by a Civil War soldier.

Many other pieced patterns appeared in Mississippi during the years 1825 through 1861, from the simple "Four-Patch" and "Nine-Patch" to the complicated "Pinwheel" (see section on "Wheel" quilts in chapter 7). In some patterns, piecing was combined with appliqué to create wonderful new designs such as "Whig's Defeat" (also known as "Grandmother's Engagement Ring"). There were inventive and wonderful appliqué designs, some of which seem to have come straight from the imagination of the maker.

Such is the case with a curious leitmotif chosen by Martha Frances Gray York (fig. 2.14) of Pontotoc County, Mississippi, for the quilt she made in the 1850–1860 period. It has all the signs of a "best" quilt: a planned color scheme with fabric probably purchased especially for making it; solid color fabrics and no prints; a difficult and unusual pattern; and exquisite quilting (fig. 2.15). The owner believes this to have been one of four quilts in Martha Frances's dowry; that may explain the heart shapes that are formed by the two large plume forms. Martha Frances York had four sons; she gave this quilt to one of them, William, as a wedding gift in 1917, the same year she would celebrate fifty years of her own marriage. William's wife, Eveann Baird York, the mother of the present owner, used the quilt as a bedspread on special occasions, sometimes turning it upside down on the bed to enjoy the beautiful quilting.

There were a number of very appealing floral appliqués produced in the years between 1825 and

Fig. 2.14. Martha Frances Gray York, the maker of MQA quilt no. M-85, is thought to have originated the design of her quilt, which she made several years before this photograph was taken.

Fig. 2.15. Original appliqué design by Martha Frances Gray York, Pontotoc County, Mississippi, in the 1850–1860 period. Quilt is made of all-cotton materials, appliqué is done with a blind stitch, quilting is at 8 to 10 stitches per inch, and the piece is 76 inches wide by 85 inches long. MQA quilt no. M-85. Collection of Charlotte Y. Swearengen, granddaughter.

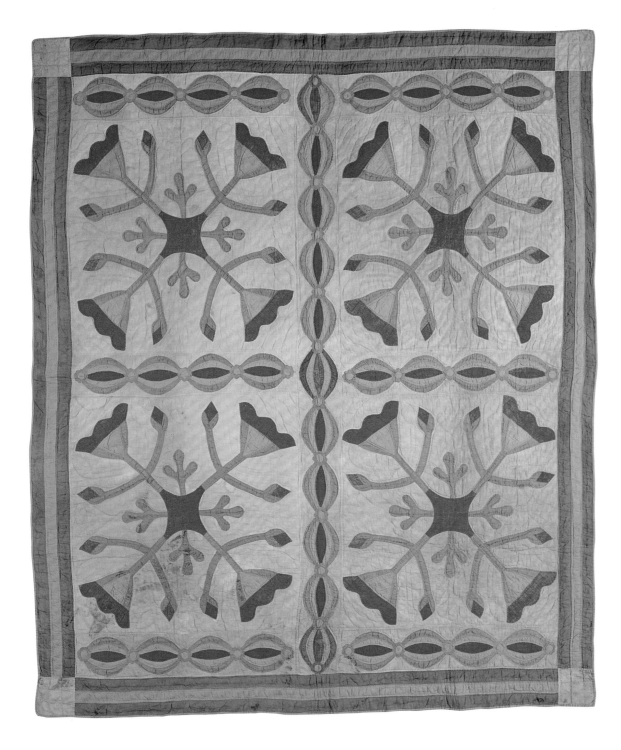

Fig. 2.16. "Tulip" with "Pomegranate" sashing and borders, maker unknown, Pike County, Mississippi, circa 1850. Quilt is made of all-cotton materials, appliquéd with a blind stitch, hand-quilted at 6 stitches per inch by the piece, also with supplemental botanical designs, and is 75 inches wide by 88 inches long. MQA quilt no. Q-75. Collection of Mr. and Mrs. Lowery T. Martin, great-grandson.

1861. It was a time for women to express their sense of beauty, their refinement, and their skill through their needlework. Girls of a certain social standing were expected to demonstrate their abilities with the needle by making a number of quilts for their hope chest or, as it is sometimes expressed, their dowry, or their trousseau—the personal outfitting of a bride. Flowers were a favored motif because they are universally equated with beauty and grace. A noteworthy piece is "The Love Rose," a quilt made by Mary Temperance Chilcoat as "one of her wedding quilts when she married Isham N. Hellums in late 1860s or 1870" in Pontotoc County, according to an indirect descendant. (Mary Hellums died in 1871 during the birth of her first child.)[25] Although the background of the quilt is now gray, instead of the original white, the colors of the flowers are so clear and bright they almost have a Day-Glo quality. There are nine identical motifs, which actually look more like tulips than roses, each composed of a stem with four leaves topped by a bell-shaped blossom of two colors—bright yellow and fuchsia. The flowers are arranged so that within the center row all three blossoms point toward the top of the quilt; the flowers in each of the side rows point toward the middle. It is a quilt obviously made with love, covered with fine, close quilting at seven stitches per inch, and, surely, part of its attraction had to be its name.

Many floral appliqué quilts came into the state with new brides as they accompanied their husbands to find land in Mississippi. There is a lovely coxcomb quilt said to have been made by Frances Minter Hawkins (1806–1861), who came from North Carolina with her husband, a doctor, to Hernando, where he established a farm still in the possession of his descendants (which is also a Centennial Farm, like Hamer Hills Farm.)[26]

The familiar appliquéd tulip, made of three petals with the middle one usually of a different color, made its appearance during this time. One example was made in Alabama (and brought later into Mississippi) by Caroline Murphy Henderson for her son when he was a baby. He was born in 1861.[27] Another popular tulip design, that of four flowers whose stems meet in the center of the block, where a bird's-eye view of the blossom is shown (as opposed to the silhouette or side views of the other four), was worked by Elizabeth Berry, who stitched her name and the phrase "was born October 183_ [sic]" onto the quilt. Although the documentation form does not say where she was born, she spent most of her life in Yalobusha County and made many other quilts.[28] This one was heavily quilted.

A different kind of tulip with a distinctive shape and secondary branches emerged in the 1850s. Two almost identical quilts of this design were found in the documentation effort, both from the southwestern corner of the state. One, from Lincoln County, was made by Roberta Jones Hope of Bogue Chitto. Its color scheme is medium brown, dark green, bright yellow, and white. Four full blocks and two half-blocks are set together with stripped sashing in yellow and brown, with white-and-brown nine-patch blocks at the intersections of the sashing.[29]

The second quilt (fig. 2.16) is well traveled. It belonged to Jackson F. Williams, who lived in Pike County, around the Summit area. Sometime in the second quarter of the century, he and his brother decided to move to Texas, into Red River County, where other Mississippians were settling. The Williamses loaded all their possessions, including this quilt, into a covered wagon and made the trip to Texas.[30] The quilt was carefully placed in a box built of "heart" pine; vines, split so there would be a flat side, were attached to the bottom of the box

Fig. 2.17. Jackson F. and Anna Williams, owners of the "Tulips with Pomegranates" quilt, in front of their home in Franklin County, Mississippi, in the 1860–1870 period. Courtesy of Mr. and Mrs. Lowery T. Martin.

of cool water and a dipper, probably made from a gourd, always rested. There was also a metal bowl, used as a sink for hand and face washing, that sat in a hole cut in the shelf. A towel for drying up can be seen hanging nearby on the wall. The "Tulip" quilt would have made a colorful addition to the interior of the house, but it was probably kept in storage except for special occasions, as it is in excellent condition 150 years after being made.

Many more Mississippi families would move to Texas in the years to come, initially to avoid the battleground the state would become during the Civil War, and afterwards to start afresh in a land not scarred by war. One quilt brought in for documentation was said to have been in a covered wagon that crossed both the Mississippi and the Red Rivers, somehow getting wet in both streams; the quilt, still carrying the stains from the muddy rivers, is now back in Mississippi, where it was made.[31]

A wreath quilt about which little is known, except that it looks to have been made in the 1850s, has nine wreaths over the white background of the top. There are two different kinds of flowers in each wreath and a marvelous five-lobed leaf that could be a sweetgum. It is very pretty and different from any of the other quilts of this time.[32]

Another unusual floral design, identified as "Rose of Sharon" by the documentation team, was made about 1850 and brought into Mississippi from Arkansas. It contains nine motifs that are meant to represent a flowering bush or branch, with flowers in different stages of maturity, from buds to full-blown blossoms. This quilt is heavily stitched in beautiful patterns— a feathered cable trims one edge. A similar quilt (fig. 2.18), made in Mississippi, has three-dimensional flowers created with ruching and accents of wool embroidery and was purchased by the current owner for a mere fifty dol-

so that it was raised off the floor and less vulnerable to the dampness of the wagon floor.

It is not clear how long Jackson Williams stayed in Texas, but in 1860 he returned, without his brother, to Amite County and settled in the Smithdale area. A photograph of him with his wife, Anna Young, shows them at the home they built practically on top of the Franklin-Amite county line (fig. 2.17). Although this particular house was built after the war, it is of the antebellum style used by successful farmers all over southern Mississippi and Alabama. There is a breezeway, a nice deep front porch, a brick sidewalk up to the steps from the front fence, and several tall cedar trees. The roof is wooden shakes, split from longleaf pine—all wood in the house was heart longleaf pine. The lattice-enclosed box at the end of the porch contained the "water shelf," where a bucket

lars. The technique of ruching, which is the gathering up of fabric and stitching in place so that a three-dimensional result is accomplished, was not often used on quilts. It is a dressmaking technique, used to add decoration to a bodice front or to make an interesting textured panel in a skirt, for example. There are documented examples of quilts from this period of time that incorporate ruching, but they are rare. In this quilt, as in other examples in which ruching is used, the color scheme of all the blocks is identical, and the blocks are set together without sashing, the better to provide ample background for the breathtaking quilting designs that fill all empty spaces.

Summary

There is a saying that "nothing succeeds like success," and this era of Mississippi history, when money was flowing through the state, engendered a time of great creativity and production in quiltmaking, as it did in architecture and decorative arts. The quilts show an inventiveness, a joyful approach to their making. They are surely a reflection of the flush times the state was enjoying.

The careful reader will have noticed that three of the finest quilts photographed for this period of time were brought into the state from elsewhere. There is a reason that relatively few Mississippi quilts from this era remain, and the following chapter, with its discussion of the ravages suffered by the state during the Civil War, will perhaps shed some light on this sad circumstance.

Fig. 2.18. "Appliquéd Flower Quilt" made by Sara Wilson Williams, Montgomery County, Mississippi, circa 1850. It has cotton fabrics and batting, wool embroidery for flower stems, and very fine hand quilting at 9 stitches per inch, with designs of triple diamonds, four-leaf clovers, and other motifs. It is 82.5 inches wide by 88.5 inches long. MQA quilt no. O-22. Collection of Tommy Covington.

CHAPTER THREE

Quiltmaking during the Civil War and Reconstruction
1861–1875

The pallet seemed thinner than paper, and was already the warmth of the floor underneath. Long since faded, blanched again tonight by moonlight, it showed a pattern as faint as one laid by wind over a field of broomsedge. It was the quilt that had baked on the line all day, and its old winter cleanness mixed with today's dust penetrated their very skins with a smell strong as medicine.

—Eudora Welty, *Losing Battles*

THERE IS NO WAY to overestimate the impact of the Civil War on Mississippians. It changed everyone's lives forever. Mississippi, more than many other states, was a terrible battleground, in part because of the importance of the Mississippi River at its western border. The state's resources and nearly all private property were damaged or destroyed. The loss is unfathomable to those of us who have never lived through such an experience.

Those who brought quilts to be documented remembered the losses in many ways. They often mentioned that a relative had been killed or injured during the war. Some recalled stories of their ancestors' resourcefulness, especially regarding quilts being hidden so they weren't stolen or destroyed.

In spite of all the tribulations and sorrow of the war and the years of recovery afterward, or maybe because of them, some people made quilts. Perhaps it was a way to restore a sense of calm, of order, a way to regain a modicum of control in a world where so much was torn apart.

From Abundance to Destitution in Three Years

At the beginning of 1861, Mississippi was the fifth wealthiest in a nation of thirty-four states. Its wealth was built on an economy consisting of a large number of independent farmers and planters who were doing very well growing cotton. Small farmers, whose own families provided most of the necessary labor, made up the majority of the white

Textile production was an everyday part of life for many women in Mississippi, even after "bought goods" were readily available. This woman, who is blind, might have helped to support herself by selling her hand-woven rag rugs. Photograph by Eudora Welty, 1935–1940. Photograph courtesy of the Eudora Welty Collection, Mississippi Department of Archives and History.

population of the state. And although the average small farmer would never achieve the true wealth of the large plantation owners, he was able take care of his family and look forward to a better future, *if things remained the same.* However, rumblings on the national front and in Washington indicated that changes were on the way; many of these small, successful farmers came to believe and agree with the large planters that the best way to preserve the status quo was to secede from the Union.

"Secessionist fever" fueled the optimism of many Mississippi residents who believed that life in the South could remain the same if it was a separate, independent nation. Accordingly, Mississippi was the second state to secede from the Union, on January 9, 1861, about three weeks after South Carolina. Approval for secession was not universal: one Mississippi planter predicted the time "when the northern soldier would tread [the Confederacy's] cotton fields, when the slave should be made *free* and the proud Southerner stricken to dust in his presence."[1] Although there were wealthy Mississippians who feared that secession would lead to war and destruction of their holdings, most who objected were small farmers who owned no slaves. The northeastern county of Tishomingo, with very few slaves, remained mainly Unionist, and to a lesser degree, so did its neighboring counties of Pontotoc and Itawamba. Jones County actually seceded from the Confederacy in 1862 and became the "Republic of Jones."[2]

As the war came to Mississippi, bloody battles were fought on land at Corinth and Holly Springs in the northern part of the state. Coastal and river areas were besieged with fire from federal warships; the railroads were targets for raiding parties bent on crippling transportation of goods and troops. The wealth of the state was gradually eroded, first by the expense of outfitting for war and then by the absence of new crops of cotton. As the war wore on, there was no one to work the fields; with the state under blockade, there was no way to market any crops that might have been harvested.

Vicksburg, a stronghold on the Mississippi, underwent an experience of war like no other American city, ever. Constant shelling by federal gunboats inspired much of the populace to seek protection in caves dug into the many hillsides of the town. Some residents referred to the caves as their "rat holes" and stayed inside them no more than was absolutely necessary, which was during periods of extreme shelling.

Several accounts of the time detail life in the caves and how they were made habitable, though by no means luxurious, with furnishings from owner's houses—carpets, tables, beds, candelabra, and so on. Quilts were taken into the caves, as evidenced in this excerpt from the diary of Lucy McRae, young daughter of a Vicksburg merchant who was settled into one of the city's largest caves, located on an exceptionally high hill in the northeastern part of the city (but uncomfortably close to federal land artillery). "It had four entrances, dug in the form of arched hallways, coming to a common center, at which point was dug a room which was curtained off. In this cave my mother took refuge with her three young children, my father having such an aversion for a cave that he would not enter one. . . . Mother took pillows, *comforts*, provisions, and clothing into the cave with her. . . . All along the ground in this cave planks were laid, that our beds might be made as comfortable as possible under the circumstances."[3]

A minister's wife, a Mrs. Lord, wrote this description of their new cave, built with help from "his own reverend hands": "Imagine to yourself in the first place a good-sized parapet, about six feet high, a path cut through and then the entrance to the cave—this is secured strongly with boards, it is dug the height of a man and about 40 feet under the hill. It communicates with the other cave which is about the same length opening out on the other side of the hill—this gives us good circulation of air. In this cave we sleep and live literally under ground. I have a little closet dug for provisions, and niches for flowers, lights and books—inside. Just by the little walk is our eating table with an arbor over it, and back of that our fireplace and kitchen with table."[4]

Other residents could not bear the thought of hiding underground in a cave and took to their basements, with the accompanying inconvenience: "The cellar is so damp and musty the bedding has to be carried out and laid in the sun every day, with the forecast that it may be demolished at any moment. . . . Clothing cannot be washed or anything else done. . . . People do nothing but eat what they can get, sleep when they can, and dodge the shells. There are three intervals when the shelling stops, either for the guns to cool or for the gunners' meals, I suppose—about eight in the morning, the same in the evening, and at noon. In that time we have both to prepare and eat ours."[5]

Ingenious Solutions to Vexing Shortages

As the war wore on, supplies became more and more difficult to obtain. Fortunes were made in blockade running, a euphemism for smuggling (the occupation of the fictional Rhett Butler during the War, if one chooses to remember). Prices for common staples such as flour doubled during the first year of the war. Soap, made with animal fat that became more and more scarce as time went on, went up 1000 percent in price. Imported coffee, which went for twelve cents a pound before the war, rose to five dollars in 1863;[6] people in Mississippi learned to drink a brew made from parched corn and okra or dried sweet potatoes. Tea was obtained from dried blackberry leaves. Inks and dyes came from natural sources such as berries and tree bark, and horse collars were made from corn shucks.[7] Some products, such as candles, were unavailable at any price. Farmers planted less cotton, switching instead to the food crops of wheat and corn.

Much of the tiresome, tedious work that women had gratefully turned over to commercial enterprises had to be resumed. Parthenia Antoinette Hague, who set down her memories of the time in *A Blockaded Family: Life in Southern Alabama during the Civil War*, recalled coming upon a woman doing her own threshing: "There she sat, a sheaf of wheat held with both hands, and with this she was vigorously belaboring the barrel, at every stroke a shower of wheat-grains raining down upon quilts and coverlets."[8] Similar labors were surely being repeated in Mississippi, as the lives of women all across the South were totally altered by the war.

As many different writers have observed, southern women of the middle and upper classes had always managed large households, and as the war progressed their administrative skills were put to running the plantations and businesses their husbands had left behind. Wives of ordinary farmers, too, took over managerial duties and kept the rhythm of planting and harvesting as best they could. Much of what women did was plain old back-breaking labor; however, in some instances, ingenious ways to get around shortages proved that a good mind was to be valued as much as a strong back. Women excelled in problem-solving perhaps most admirably in the production of clothing and other textiles.

As some of the worst battles of the war were being fought in Mississippi in 1862, the six textile mills of the state were humming along making fabric, using two thousand pounds of wool and twenty bales of cotton *per day*. By March of 1863, sewing factories were producing ten thousand garments a week as they furiously tried to keep up with the demands for clothing for Confederate soldiers.[9] These textile mills could not stop production of war material to spin and weave threads and fabrics for domestic use, and women had to find ingenious ways to supply themselves and their families with the textile products they had previously had in relative abundance. There are many accounts of carpets being cut up and their edges bound to function as blankets; draperies and sheets became garments. Parthenia Hague wrote, "It was really ridiculous, our way of making raids upon what remained of our fine bed-linen, pillow-shams, and slips, for garments of finer texture than our own home-woven cloth. I well remember that once, when I stepped into a friend's room, her very first words were, 'This is the last bleached, seamless bed-sheet I've got, and now I must cut it up for garments!' I doubt very much if a fine sheet could have been found in any house in our settlement when the war closed. Perhaps there was not one in the blockaded South."[10]

Women returned to the hand-manufacture of threads and fabrics. Labor-intensive practices such as spinning and weaving, long since sent out to be accomplished commercially or abandoned completely with a profusion of fabrics available for purchase, became part of the daily work of the household. Many writers, among them Elizabeth Fox-Genovese of Emory University, believe that white women, especially those of privilege, were taught to card and spin fibers into thread, and to weave those threads into fabrics, by their slaves. "It

is doubtful that the household would have had the tools—wheels, looms—of textile production at the outbreak of hostilities if some household members had not been using them all along. . . . In most slaveholding households during the entire antebellum period, slave women were regularly spinning, carding, and weaving. The evidence also suggests that many slave women had a sophisticated knowledge of dyes, which they used primarily in making their families' Sunday clothes."[11]

Although they may have lost any fabric production knowledge they could have had, plantation women were not lacking in sewing skills. They regularly cut, from purchased fabric, the garments for their slaves, which they would either sew themselves or have done by a sewing slave. They also did fine, light sewing and quilting. They put these sewing skills to good use, not only producing what they required for themselves and their people, but helping as they could to provide necessary items for the Confederate troops. Groups of women at Natchez formed "Needle Regiments" to sew for the soldiers. A box that one of these regiments packed contained "sixty pairs of socks, twenty-five blankets, thirteen pairs of gloves, fourteen flannel shirts, sixteen towels, two handkerchiefs, five pairs of trousers, and one bushel of dried apples."[12] Emma Balfour, the wife of Dr. William T. Balfour and "a great favorite of General Pemberton," the "defender of Vicksburg," wrote in her diary on the fifth day of the siege, "I was up in my room sewing and praying in my heart, oh, so earnestly for our cause."[13]

Parthenia Hague describes a practice that was duplicated all over the South during the war: "Sewing societies were formed in every hamlet, as well as in our cities, to keep the soldiers of the Confederacy clothed as best we could. They met once every week, at some lady's house, if it was in the country. To such societies all the cloth that could be spared from each household was given and made into soldier's garments. Socks, gloves, blankets, woolen coverlets, and even home-made bedquilts were donated; wool scarfs, knitted on long oak or hickory-wood needles, were sent for our soldiers in the bitter cold of Virginia, to wrap around their necks and cover their ears."[14]

She goes on to describe "spinning bees":

Many women whose husbands were in the army found it uphill work to card and spin all that was necessary to clothe a numerous family. In such cases, as often as was needful, there would be a gathering of ladies of the settlement, both married and single, for the spinning bee. Wheels, cards, and cotton were all hauled in a wagon to the place appointed. On the way, as often as not, a long flexible twig would be cut from the woods, and attached to one of the spinning-wheels; from the top of such flagstaff would play loosely to the wind, and jolts of the wagon, a large bunch of lint cotton, as our ensign. Sometimes as many as six or eight wheels would be whirring at the same time in one house, and assistance was also given in weaving, cutting out, and making up clothing for such families.[15]

One of the first things that these industrious ladies ran out of was commercially spun sewing thread. "All sewing-machines in our settlement were at a stand-still during the period of the war, as our home-made thread was not suited to machines, and all sewing had to be done by hand," recalled Parthenia Hague.[16]

So, as the war wore on, and garments wore out, women could not use their beloved sewing machines to stitch up replacements. Neither could they buy fabric, unless a bolt had made its way through the blockade, in a rare combination of good luck and good fortune. Although they do not gloss over the real deprivations they were experiencing, women in their diaries of the period have a relatively "can-do" attitude toward "making-do," and they gamely recycled garments in all sorts of inventive ways. Silk dresses would be taken apart and "turned," or remade with the "wrong" side of the fabric out. When a turned dress could not be worn any longer, it was often cut down to a smaller size to fit someone else, or perhaps used to make a quilt, if there was not some more pressing need for the fabric. During the war years, silk dresses were gradually replaced with those made of homespun, which Confederate women wore with pride.

The diary of Narcissa Black (now in the Mississippi Department of Archives and History) contains a careful accounting of the articles she and her slave weaver, Chaney Scot Black, made and sold to various customers, not only during the war, but before and afterwards. Narcissa and Chaney lived in McNairy County, Tennessee, which borders Mississippi on Tennessee's southernmost edge, about three miles from Corinth. The two women sheared sheep, cleaned wool, spun yarn, dyed yarns and fabric, wove apparel fabric and coverlets, and sewed. They also produced such items as bed cords, well ropes, and plough lines.[17] One diary entry notes that on January 24, 1864, she sold a cloth coat for ten dollars. Six months later, on June 24, an entry records that her husband (whom she called Mr. Black) had come home from a shopping trip to Savannah (Tennessee) with "one lb. of indigo and madder, paid 7 dollars for it, bail [sic] of flax thread, five dollars." She also bartered: "cost of framing two comforts—3 yards of osnaburg" (13 Feb. 1862); "cost of a calico dress—making two shirts (14 July 1863)."[18]

War's End Finally Comes: A Cruel Aftermath

Battles continued to be fought all over Mississippi after the fall of Vicksburg and throughout the remainder of 1864. Sherman turned his attention to the capture of Meridian in February; it was an important railroad center. The town of Oxford was almost completely burned on August 22. Yankee raiders sought to destroy all railroad bridges, trestles, and rails and other vital property throughout the year. Jackson was burned twice, in May and July of 1863. The first burning of the city occurred as a result of a stroll taken by Sherman and Grant down a Jackson street shortly after they occupied the city. As they walked and discussed what they should do, they came upon a factory, run mostly by women, that was busily turning out fabric for tents. As the fabric rolled off the looms, the letters "C.S.A." were woven into the selvages. Bales of cotton were stacked outside. Grant, according to his diary, told Sherman that "the girls had done enough work." The two generals sent the girls home with all the fabric they could carry, then burned the place to the ground.[19]

The destruction went on all over the South. A group of four quilts brought into Mississippi from Kentucky in 1917 were said by the family to have survived Sherman's policy of burning everything in his path. "Family tradition says that the great-grandmother of the present owner made the quilts before the Civil War. In 1864 Sherman's troops burned their farm to the ground. Sherman allowed them to keep a cooking pot, the clothes on their backs, and one quilt for each family member."[20] (The family has also kept the cooking pot.)

At the end of the war, most of Mississippi was in ruins: the *New Orleans Times* reported soon after the end of the war that extreme poverty ruled in almost every household in Mississippi. The infrastructure of the state—roads, bridges, cities—was in shambles. Most farms and businesses were badly damaged or destroyed. The decimation of Mississippi's productive white men was appalling; the state had a larger percentage of fatalities than any in the Confederacy.

Reconstruction: A Failed Idea

The years from 1865 to 1869 were very tough ones for Mississippi, as the conditions just described would ensure. In addition, there was great uneasiness between blacks and whites, living as they did in a new and unaccustomed social order, one that had changed very swiftly. There was great resistance on the part of whites to accepting blacks as having equal rights; blacks, for their part, had to begin a new way of life with practically no economic foothold. Everybody, black and white, was poor; most were exhausted from years of war and deprivation. The state was occupied, beginning in the second half of 1865, by a military force of thirteen thousand men, nearly all of whom were former slaves and glad for the opportunity to earn a soldier's wages.

The majority in Congress in 1866 were in agreement about Reconstruction: new southern state governments should be created that included the black right to vote and excluded ex-Confederates. However, the Mississippi state legislature refused to ratify the Fourteenth and Fifteenth Amendments to the United States Constitution; the amendments guaranteed voting rights to black men and gave blacks full citizenship of the states in which they lived. In 1867 the state was placed under federal military rule, which lasted until February 23, 1870, when Mississippi was "redeemed"—readmitted to the Union. Three days later, military rule was suspended, and Governor James Alcorn was inaugurated. Senators Aldebert Ames and Hiram Revels (the first black United States senator) took their seats in Congress. (It is interesting to note that, in spite of all the upheaval in the state, the first ever Mississippi State Fair was held in Jackson in 1869.)

Views of Reconstruction have shifted as history has given it distance. The earliest critics condemned it as a cynical and brutal rape of southern society, a "blackout of honest government." This opinion held that the redeeming of the state represented a return to constitutional government and to proper race relations in the South. In the 1930s, historians began to look at Reconstruction as a plan controlled by northern business interests who were against the South regaining its economic base for fear that it would return to trading with Europe, where prices for consumer goods were often lower than those made in northeastern factories. More recently, the civil rights struggles of the 1950s and 1960s have cast Reconstruction as another phase in the black American search for justice.[21] No matter what spin is put on that era of Mississippi history, one thing is for sure: it was very difficult for those who lived through it.

Amazingly, Quilts Were Made during the War

It is a miracle that any quilts at all were made during the tough times of the Civil War and Reconstruction, but a surprising number were. The examples that came to light during the documentation effort show the same spirit of inventiveness and exploration as those of the antebellum period, but

they have an added twist that is not visible. Many of them had to be hidden from the armies that roamed back and forth across the countryside and took whatever they needed to maintain themselves. Quilts were very handy items for men in war. Bets Ramsey and Merikay Waldvogel document a story of a lovely *broderie perse* piece that was removed from a dead mule after having been used as a saddle blanket.[22] There are numerous accounts of quilts being sent away to war with husbands and sons; many of the quilts never came back, even if the men did. As the war lengthened into years, and supplies were harder and harder to obtain, quilts were cut up to serve where needed— as bandages, for example.

However, a few made it through the war, sometimes because they were so useful (and so highly valued by their makers). A story researched and written for the documentation project could be that of many resourceful Mississippi families:

Susan Powell was born on November 15, 1825 in South Carolina and moved with her family to Greene County, Alabama in the mid- to late-1830s. On September 4, 1845, she married William D. Watson, but by 1850 she was a widow, living with her mother and two brothers. In 1853, she married for a second time, to Dr. Jeremiah Prophit Davis. [She had another September wedding; the date of this one was the twenty-fourth.]

After living three years more in Greene County, Alabama, Susan, her husband, first-born daughter, and their "large group of slaves" moved with another family, William and Emma Davis and their children, to Newton County, Mississippi. They established a farm on several hundred acres of land, and were doing well when the Civil War broke out. Jeremiah and William joined the

Fig. 3.1. "Drunkard's Path" made by Susan Powell Watson Davis in the Battlefield community of Newton County, Mississippi, circa 1860. MQA quilt no. D-95. Collection of Lydia Smith Tucker, great-granddaughter.

Confederate Army, with Jeremiah taking the rank of First Lieutenant in Knox's Company of the Stonewall Rangers, Mississippi Calvary.

When the men went off to war, they left Susan and Emma with the children and slaves to tend to the large plantation. In April of 1863, neighbors brought word that federal troops, under the command of Colonel Benjamin H. Grierson, were between Philadelphia, Mississippi and their plantation. The Yankees were under orders from General Grant to take or destroy everything in their path as they made their way to meet General Sherman in Meridian. By April 23, they were encamped at the Davis homestead.

Because she knew that the soldiers would confiscate the farm animals and anything else they wanted, Susan called on a trusted slave, one whom she considered a friend, to take a few things down to the river "bottom" (swamp) and hide them in the tall cane. She gave the slave three quilts, a milk cow, and a mule. He stuffed the quilts into a hollow tree, tied up and muzzled the mule and cow to keep them quiet, and managed to stay hidden until the troops passed and went on southward toward Meridian.

The two women survived unharmed in the house. Because of Susan's quick thinking, the family was able to plant a crop that year with the mule, have milk from the cow for the children, and keep warm with the three quilts. The survival of her family is a testimony to the strong pioneer spirit of Susan Powell Davis, a spirit that she passed down to her descendants.

At the end of the war, Jeremiah Davis returned home, after having been imprisoned at Cairo, Illinois. William died at the Sandusky, Ohio prison on January 14, 1865. The Davis slaves were now freedmen, and Jeremiah deeded each one of the families on his property a parcel of land, and to this day, some of them remain there.[23]

Family members today retain with pride one of the three quilts hidden in the hollow tree (fig. 3.1). The quilt design is "Drunkard's Path." A different quilt from the same pattern, made about 1890, exhibits the same peculiar characteristic as this one: the cut-away portions are not used to create a design in the adjoining square (see fig. 4.3, p. 58). Instead, a second color is used, so the basic premise of the pattern has been overlooked by the quilter. In both quilts, it looks as though the quilter was more interested in making a three-color quilt than in conserving fabric.

Many quilts escaped destruction in the war because they were part of the household goods packed when families fled in front of invading federal troops. Parthenia Hague tells of a disabled Confederate veteran and his wife and five small children, who, upon hearing rumors that the Federals were coming through his town (near Mobile) packed the "best belongings of their house: wearing apparel, all their valuables in jewelry and plate, bed-quilts, counterpanes, a feather-bed and pillows, bandboxes, hatboxes, trunks, and many other articles of value. I saw the carriage unpacked, and stood amazed that such a quantity of stuff could be stowed in such a small space."[24]

One of the quilts documented came with the story that it had been thrown over some belongings in a wagon as the family was forced out of their home, which the Union army was taking over for a hospital. The maker of the quilt, Elizabeth Tillman, was married to Major Green Cumby, a stagecoach driver and saddler. They were living near Farmington, Mississippi, in 1862 when the Federal troops invaded. The troops insisted that the slaves remain to assist in the hospital, but finally allowed a mother and her daughter to accompany Mrs. Cumby, her children, and her mother as they were evacuated.

Quilts were not only saved, new ones were actually made during the war and Reconstruction years. There are several accounts of quilts being made in other southern states during the war to raise money for the cause, but none appeared in this documentation effort. That does not mean it didn't happen, though. Surely one or two of the good ladies in Natchez's "Needle Regiments" stitched a quilt. Supplies were hard to come by for making quilts, as might be expected in a state that not only was blockaded, but was the scene of many battles throughout the war. An account of Dora Miller, wife of a Vicksburg lawyer, tells of her scampering to her husband's office during the shelling of the city: "H. carried the bank box, I the case of matches, Martha the blankets and pillows, keeping an eye on the shells. We slept on piles of newspapers."[25] In this instance, newspapers were used more or less as mattresses; however, an account exists of a "confederate quilt" that was made from two homespun sheets filled with layers of newspaper—an extreme example, perhaps, of the creative solutions to problems of shortages created by the blockade.[26]

A way around the blockade was to make thread and fabric at home. A case in point is that of a group of women in Tippah County. The mother, Eunice Turner (1811–1881), her daughter Susan Turner (1838–1916), Susan's daughters Pearl (1885–1901) and Jennie (1891–1913) were a family of women well known for their quilts and coverlets. They grew the cotton and flax (for linen) from which they spun thread. They wove their own fabrics and dyed them with natural dyestuffs. From these materials they made garments and quilts. The proud owners

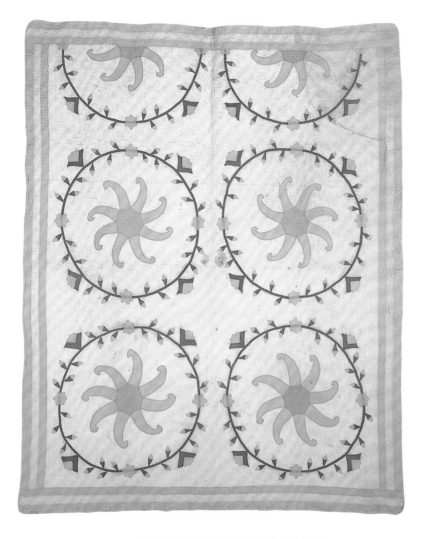

of one of the first sewing machines in the area, they learned how to use it to machine-appliqué their quilts. There was a family tradition that the oldest child in each branch of the family was given a quilt.[27]

One quilt, known to the current generation as "The Grandpa Quilt" (figs. 3.2 and 3.3), is done in a pattern that the documentation team could only describe as "Star Fish," although it might also pass as a daisy. Whatever it is, this motif is centered within a wreath of flowers. The wreath has a green vine and leaves, and the flowers and buds have faded from red to a pleasant cream color. The arms of the "starfish" or "daisy" have attained this same color, but the bright orange of the octagon which centers the design is not faded at all. These "arms" or "petals" are machine-appliquéd with a very tiny stitch in reddish-brown thread. Borders of three strips—two reds and a white—finish the quilt on all four sides. One can only imagine what a vivid statement the quilt made when its colors were new.

Several other very beautiful and unusual appliqué quilts were made across the state during the war. A "Pomegranate" design (fig. 3.4) was the pattern chosen by Josephine Smith Ruffin in 1865 when she decided to make a quilt to celebrate the birth of a child, who turned out to be a boy. She and her husband, William Henry, named the child, who was born on January 1, 1866, John Frederick Ruffin. William Henry Ruffin would not live to see his son grow up; a prisoner in the Civil War, he died on October 29, 1869. He and Josephine had been married only five years at his death.

Josephine Ruffin did her shopping for quilt materials in Columbus, Mississippi. She paid one dollar per yard for the fabric and twenty-five cents per spool for the thread. The colors are still very clear and pretty: gold, brown, and soft green, with a white background for the design of four

Fig. 3.2. "Star Fish," called "The Grandpa Quilt" by the family, made by Susan Turner of Tippah County, Mississippi, in the 1860s. It is made of all-cotton materials, machine- and hand-appliquéd, with fine hand quilting in the double clamshell design at 12 stitches per inch, and is 65 inches wide by 79 inches long. MQA quilt no. O-157. Collection of Sherra W. Owen, great-great-great-great-granddaughter.

Fig. 3.3. The original design of this Civil War–era quilt was machine-appliquéd in place.

Fig. 3.4. "Pomegranate" summer spread made by Josephine Ruffin, Oktibbeha County, Mississippi, 1865. It is cotton, appliquéd with a blind stitch. MQA quilt no. L-03. Collection of Lelia Ruffin Wilson, great-granddaughter.

Fig. 3.5. Mr. and Mrs. John Frederick Ruffin in a smart phaeton, circa 1890. Mr. Ruffin's mother made the "Pomegranate" summer spread to celebrate his birth.

Fig. 3.6. "Small Stars" made by Elizabeth Berry in Yalobusha County, Mississippi, signed and dated 1870. Quilt is of cotton fabrics with a wool batting; it is quilted by the piece in the stars, with cross-hatching elsewhere, and is 83.5 inches wide by 98 inches long. MQA quilt no. M-57. Collection of Jacqueline Tennyson.

pomegranates per motif. She had decided from the outset not to quilt it, as "it was the style then to use them as coverlets or bedspreads."[28] Although she made the quilt to celebrate the birth of her son, Josephine actually gave it to her daughter, Lelia Ruffin Henry, who passed it along to her granddaughter, Lelia Ruffin Wilson. Mrs. Wilson provided a picture of her great-uncle, John Frederick Ruffin, fashionably turned out in a single-horse carriage with his bride, Pearl Stevens Ruffin (fig. 3.5).

Other flowers and fruits were popular appliqué motifs: a design very similar to the pomegranate was called "Cotton Boll" by the Neshoba County family who own it. The quilt was in progress when the Civil War interrupted its making; the maker ran out of green fabric, and when she was finally able to get some to finish her project, the colors didn't match. There are wonderful variations on the "Carolina Lily" motif: an interesting example made in Mississippi contains solid reddish-brown setting blocks and a "Wild Goose Chase" border on two sides. An exquisitely beautiful "Peony" or "Lily" quilt, made in Brighton, Tennessee, and later brought to Mississippi, has thirty blocks with a red flower that is pieced of diamonds (MQA# E-060).

Pieced patterns started to proliferate across the entire country about this time, and quilters in Mississippi enthusiastically joined in the trend. One quilter who particularly enjoyed piecing was Jane Elizabeth Caldwell, who was born in Newberry District, South Carolina, in 1850 and moved with her family to Blue Springs, Mississippi, shortly afterward. She was turning out intricately pieced quilts of impeccable quality by the time she was fourteen years of age. She could not hear, and she worked by herself a lot of the time. She never married and was able to devote a great deal of time to her hobby. Her great-great-niece, Debbie Hall, writes that she always gave quilts as gifts to her nieces and neighbors on special occasions. Debbie Hall has four of her masterpieces and brought three in to be documented: a "Star" variation that has eight small stars circling a central "Star of Bethlehem" in each of nine blocks; a fine "Star of Bethlehem" in a red, green, and white color scheme; and a "New York Beauty" variation that the owner calls "Indian Rose." All three are nicely quilted, but the last two are masterfully done: they are covered with fine, close quilting at nine to ten stitches per inch (MQA#'s D-105, D-106, D-107).

Star quilts were popular. One very interesting example was a "King's Star," which has a segmented circle in the center, made by Martha Ann Gresham Denson, who was born in 1852 in Old Tishomingo County, Mississippi. The most outstanding feature of the quilt is that it is done in a strip set: the stars are arranged into seven vertical rows, some of which incorporate other blocks, and the vertical rows are stitched to one another with narrow blue sashing. The color scheme of the quilt stays in the yellow, blue, and tan range. A tan border finishes off the top and bottom edges.

Another star quilt is said by the family to have been inspired by the design of the floor in the Old Capitol Building. The maker, Louise Dickerson Fairchild, visited the Old Capitol Building around 1860 or 1861 and was moved to create this piece—certainly not the first time, nor the last, that a quilter's imagination has been sparked by the geometric designs of tile or parquet flooring. The colors of the quilt are very striking: red, black, and orange on a white background. It is one of many nine-motif quilts made in Mississippi during this period. Family history says that it was hidden away during the Civil War, when others of Mrs. Fairchild's quilts were burned.

pattern "Wild Goose," and it is indeed a bit wild—in the choice of color for the background, anyway. It is sort of a "poison" green, but it is a perfect foil for the dark green, brown, and white that are used to complete the perfectly pieced quilt.

A quilt of small "LeMoyne Stars" has been made uncommon by its setting pattern (fig. 3.6). The quilter first took two star squares and two printed fabric squares and sewed them together to make a four-patch block. She did this thirty times, then chose a colorful sashing; she placed a nine-patch square in a slightly different color scheme at the intersection of the sashing. The borders of the sides of the quilt are not the same as the ones at top and bottom. It's a very carefully put-together quilt, and one of the few that was signed: the maker quilted her name and the date in the sashing.

One example of the type of quilt generally called a "peddler's quilt" was brought to the documentation team from Corinth. It is reminiscent of paper-cutting, and, indeed, that is how such patterns are said to have come into being. They were given to women by the men who traveled the countryside, either in a wagon or with a pack on their back, selling household goods and notions. In the twentieth century, this type of merchant was known as "the rolling store man," but at the point in history with which we are presently concerned, he was probably still called a peddler. Some of them were skilled at folding and cutting designs which women would then interpret in cloth. They often resemble snowflakes. The documentation team found a name for this design, after much searching: "Washington Square." It is a block design, appliquéd and geometric. The color scheme was originally red, green, and white, but the green has turned to chartreuse in some areas and yellow in still others. The quilt is still a very handsome and original piece.[29]

Fig. 3.7. "Commemorative Quilt" made by members of the Eades family, Oxford, Mississippi. Quilt is dated May 26, 1865. It has silk fabrics for the top, cotton for backing, and a wool batting and is 68 inches wide by 80.5 inches long. MQA quilt no. O-25. Collection of the Mississippi State Historical Museum, Jackson.

Fig. 3.8. Blocks at the center of the quilt are inscribed "Jeff. Davis. President of C.S.A." and "Oxford. Miss. May 26th 1865."

A very fine four-pointed feathered star design known as "Pine Burr" or "Pine Cones" came from the needle of Rhoda Jane Hayes (1858–1925) of Jefferson County, Mississippi. The family calls the

The crazy quilt, which would reach the full-blown proportions of a fad before the end of the century, was beginning to make an appearance. A most interesting example was made between 1850 and 1870 by Emma Rebecca Trantham of Booneville. She made the quilt in strips, and she didn't use lots of different colors of fabrics—they are mostly tan, brown, and dark green, but she sprinkled tiny appliquéd triangles of color, like confetti, all over the piece. Then she added silk feather stitches, sort of wherever it suited her. Finally, she framed the quilt with a black-and-white randomly pieced border that completes the impression of a thoroughly modern piece of contemporary art. It makes you happy just to look at it, and her granddaughter, whose quilt this is, says simply, "We loved her very much."[30]

Distinctive Quilts and the Men behind Them

Two of the especially satisfying finds of the quilt documentation effort were the discoveries of a pair of quilts made by a Confederate soldier and of a commemorative quilt made to honor those who fought in the War between the States. Through the efforts of the Mississippi Quilt Association's Quilt Documentation Committee, the second quilt (figs. 3.7 and 3.8) has been given to the Mississippi State Historical (Old Capitol) Museum in Jackson, where it will be cared for as a valuable part of Mississippi's material culture. The gift of the quilt to the Old Capitol came about through the generosity of Mrs. W. R. Eades, whose husband is a direct descendent of the makers. Mrs. Eades wrote to the documentation committee to congratulate them on their efforts in mounting the quilt search and commented that she felt we were losing our heritage. Now at least a part of it will be preserved.

According to family tradition, the commemorative quilt was made by Eades family members at their home in Oxford, Mississippi, in honor of Jefferson Davis and the Confederate soldiers from the community. There has been some speculation that it could have been a fund-raiser. There are about forty-eight names or initials on the quilt, and Mrs. W. R. Eades was able to identify nearly all of them. The family Bible provided the key to determining that the makers were Laura Eades, Jane Rankin Eades, Mary Elizabeth Eades, Sarah Emiline Eades, Louisa Josaphine Eades, Ann Hannah Eades, Martha Florence Eades, and Laura Tom Levenia Eades. The current Mrs. Eades wrote, "These are my husband's aunts, and we visited and saw the quilt on the bed for over forty years. The Eades aunts are all now deceased."[31]

The quilt is made of pink silk squares and blue silk hexagons that link forty-two "Stars of Bethlehem," which are also of silk fabrics but in many different colors. The pink squares are the background for names and initials embroidered with black thread. Some of the names inscribed in the blocks are "Gen. Jackson," "Gen. Forrest," "Gen. Johnson," "Col. A. Wilson," and "Capt. A. Ward."

It is highly probable that Charles S. Crockett had no idea that he would one day be remembered for his wonderful quilts. Born on November 28, 1826, in Tennessee, he grew up to be a farmer and established a place called Crockett Farm in Neshoba County. (There is now a Crockett Avenue in Philadelphia, Mississippi, and some of his descendants make their home there.) Charles married Annie E. Pigg, and they had one son, Thomas Nathaniel Crockett.

When the Civil War broke out, Charles Crockett, like so many other men, had to leave his family to serve in the Confederate army. In the course of his tour of duty, he was severely wounded and

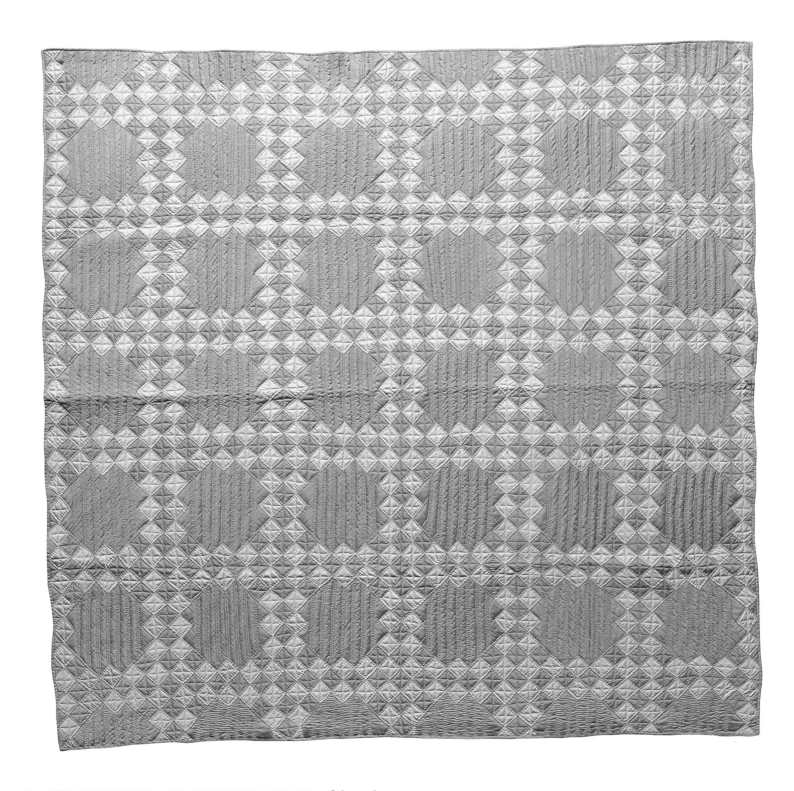

returned home to Crockett Farm. He was never able to return to the work of farming, so he took up quilting to pass the time. "Double Irish Chain" was apparently a favorite of his, because he made two of them between 1862, when he returned home, and December 4, 1867, when he died at the age of forty-one.

Comparison of the two quilts suggests that Charles Crockett entertained himself by exploring the different possibilities inherent in the design. One quilt is done in the conventional way, with colored "chains" (in gold) crossing the surface of the quilt (which is white) on the diagonal. In the second quilt (fig. 3.9), the chains run vertically and horizontally. Also, in this quilt, it is the background that is colored—a nice deep rose—and the chains are white. Mr. Crockett also chose a different approach for his quilting stitches in the second quilt; he placed seven double rows of quilting stitches straight across the solid blocks. In his gold-and-white piece, he also used double rows of quilting stitches, but he placed them on the diagonal, which is more common.

The "Irish Chain" was a great favorite of Mississippi quilters. The documentation teams recorded "Single Irish Chains," "Double Irish Chains," "Triple Irish Chains," and even a "Quadruple Irish Chain." This last quilt, a magnificent example of pieced work, was made by Martha Ellen Wade (1866–1934) of Lee County. She chose a "cheddar" and red color scheme for the chains and quilted the white solid blocks in double rows, as Charles Crockett had done, but she made diamonds in her quilting design by also stitching opposing diagonal rows.[32]

Summary

Without question, the supply of historic Mississippi quilts was greatly diminished during the War between the States and the years of deprivation which followed. Not only did the good women of Mississippi send their husbands, brothers, fathers, and sons off to war with the best the house had to offer, including quilts, but they used their quilts for many purposes, eventually using them up, as demand for bedding, bandages, and clothing grew ever more desperate. Nor was there much opportunity to replace those quilts when the war was over. Many who brought quilts to be documented recalled from family discussions that the years following the war, those known as Reconstruction, were often mentioned as being as hard to survive as those of the war itself. It took ten years for the state to struggle back to its feet, and it appears that quilt-making suffered during this time, although the practice did not completely vanish.

Fig. 3.9. "Double Irish Chain," called "Civil War Quilt" by the family, made by Charles S. Crockett of Crockett Farm, near Philadelphia, Mississippi, in 1862. It is made of all-cotton materials, with quilting at 5 to 7 stitches per inch, and is 74 inches wide by 80 inches long. The backing of the quilt is the same fabric as the background of the front, and a single-fold applied bias binding has been used to finish the edges. MQA quilt no. I-120. Collection of Bettye DeWeese and Tommie Kirkland, great-great-granddaughters.

CHAPTER FOUR

Postbellum Quiltmaking in Mississippi

1875 — 1900

The bed had been made up with a red-and-yellow pieced quilt that looked like a map or a picture, a little like his grandmother's girlhood painting of Rome burning.

—Eudora Welty, "Death of a Traveling Salesman"

GRADUALLY, THE STATE so physically ruined by war began to recover. An artist who worked on sketches of towns along the Mississippi River wrote a lovely description of Vicksburg in 1881:

> It is in the midst of some of the best scenery on the Lower Mississippi, being located on bluffs known as Walnut Hills, which extend for two miles along the river and rise gradually to a height of five hundred feet. It is about midway between Memphis and New Orleans, and is the largest city between them. As seen from the river it presents a highly picturesque appearance, and loses none of its attractiveness on a nearer approach. . . .
>
> Vicksburg is now a city of about fourteen thousand inhabitants, and is the chief commercial mart of that section of the Mississippi. It has rallied from the vicissitudes which it suffered during the war, and is now a prosperous, as well as a beautiful city.[1]

In 1870, only 4 percent of Mississippi's population of 827,922 persons lived in towns. Vicksburg was the largest city (12,443), followed by Natchez (9,057), Columbus (4,812), Jackson (4,234), and Meridian (2,706). Other cities of notable size were Holly Springs, Aberdeen, Canton, Pass Christian, and Grenada.[2]

Railroads throughout the state were repaired, rebuilt, extended, and reorganized. Railroad unions were formed, and the legendary Casey Jones belonged to two of them in Water Valley. Great strides were made in establishing schools and colleges: the state legislature had, in 1870, established a school system in each county headed by a super-

After the Civil War many farmers, both black and white, made their living by share-cropping cotton; entire families labored in the fields from dawn to dusk. Photograph by Eudora Welty, 1935–1940. Photograph courtesy of the Eudora Welty Collection, Mississippi Department of Archives and History.

Fig. 4.1. "Broken Dishes" made by Lou Vera Pierce Mott of Philadelphia, Neshoba County, Mississippi, from the 1875–1900 period. Quilt is made of cotton materials, backed with feed sacks and quilted in shells. MQA quilt no. E-84. Collection of Jennifer Sluis, granddaughter.

intendent appointed by a state board of education. Funding for state schools was set at $1 million, and an additional $2 million was spent by the counties for school buildings. By 1875, enrollment in public schools totaled 89,813 for blacks and 78,404 for whites. Ole Miss (the University of Mississippi) in Oxford was rebuilt and expanded; in 1882 it became the first college in the state to accept women and men—it was coeducational. In 1871, Alcorn University for blacks was established in Lorman, and Mississippi Agriculture and Mechanical College (later Mississippi State) was also founded for whites at Starkville. The Industrial Institute and College in Columbus, later the Mississippi State College for Women (now Mississippi University for Women), was chartered in Columbus in 1884, the first state-supported college for women

in the United States. There were already three other colleges for women in Mississippi, but they were church sponsored, private schools: Hilman College in Clinton, Grenada Collegiate Institute, and Whitworth College in Brookhaven. The first free public library, containing one hundred volumes, was instituted in Biloxi in 1898.[3]

Over 90 percent of Mississippi's population lived on farms, and the quilt documentation forms from this period show that the respondents were mostly farm families. There are, however, many different types of farmers, and we have no way of knowing what the term meant for each of the families represented in the quilt survey. There are sharecroppers, subsistence farmers, cattle farmers, produce farmers, small and large plantation owners. Many of the husbands farmed while practicing additional occupations. Eleven owned a general store in addition to farming; three were preachers who farmed; six were carpenter-farmers; six were educator-farmers; three owned a cotton gin in addition to farming, and two were contractors as well as farmers. One gold prospector, one justice of the peace, one blacksmith, one bricklayer, one trader, one section foreman, one laborer, and one cheese maker combined their vocation with farming.

Plantations, a term used here to mean a large enterprise with many laborers and hundreds of acres of land, didn't vanish completely after the War between the States, although the economic model on which they were based was greatly altered. Gradually, property that had lain idle or been barely cultivated since Reconstruction was returned to productivity, although many of the tracts were smaller than before the war. After the Civil War, many of the houses built in the countryside were of the popular architectural style of the day, and so came into being the Victorian plantation house. When the machine age came along and tractors replaced hand cultivation, many of these Victorian plantations flourished and became a good source of income for their owners.

Much of Mississippi's agricultural base was always the family farmer, the man who worked alone or with his wife and children, with additional help brought in on an as-needed basis. As in any profession, some farmers were more successful than others, and life was easier in some families than in those that had little money.

Sharecropping, a system of farming that developed in the postbellum years, came about in large measure because landowners had no money to pay wages, and destitute farmers had no money with which to buy land. Impoverished whites and freedmen turned to this scheme that allowed them to work the land and pay rent with a portion of the annual crop. In 1890, over 60 percent of Mississippi farm families were sharecroppers. In some counties, the number was closer to 90 percent.[4] It was a hard life; children rarely spent more than about six weeks in school because they were needed to work in the fields, both at planting and harvesting time. It was hard to make a profit: if everybody made a good crop of cotton in a year, the price would be low because supply was high; if there was a poor crop, the price would be high, but the yield might not be sufficient to cover the expenses incurred in making the crop. It was easy to slide into a condition of constant debt; people either learned to live with it or they left for greener pastures, mostly up North.

Many of the respondents in the quilt survey identified their ancestors from this time period as sharecroppers. From additional information written on the same forms, it seems that farm life produced women with a remarkably positive and cheerful outlook on life, despite their having to face circumstances that seem almost unbearable. Yel-

low fever epidemics regularly struck the state; the first one, in 1878, affected forty-six towns and killed over three thousand people. Another round of it in 1897 and 1898 caused the cancellation of the Ole Miss football season; twenty-eight locations were hit, and eighty-four people died. During the same period, there were 2,876 cases of smallpox.[5] People did not yet understand exactly how the viral diseases such as yellow fever and smallpox were spread, nor did they understand the correlation between their drinking water and bacteria-borne diseases such as typhoid and scarlet fever.

Many, many forms mention that the quiltmaker had numerous children, but raised only some of them to adulthood. Some women were widowed early in their lives and left with children to raise on their own, which they somehow did. There was often little material to work with, yet they made wonderful quilts. These women were resourceful and creative and continued to contribute to their families and communities, no matter what the fates doled out. The story of Helen Angelina Dollar McCraw (1858–1940) could be that of many of the quilters of the fourth quarter of the nineteenth century.

The daughter of Reuben Pinckney Dollar and Mary Frances Risenhoover, "Liney" grew up near Mehan Junction in Lauderdale County, Mississippi. In 1880 she married John Thaniel McCraw, whose family had come from Fayette County, Alabama. They made their home near Neshoba in Neshoba County, where he had a sawmill and general store. Between the time of their marriage and 1902, they had ten children, eight of whom survived to adulthood.

Both parents remembered the hard times following the Civil War and wanted to give their own children everything they needed, despite the scarcity of money. As with many rural southern folks, they grew or made almost everything their family needed, including beds, pillows, mattresses, cloth and clothing, shoes, and, of course, food. Having ten children meant making lots of quilts to keep everyone warm.

As the older sons grew up, they helped their father gather timber from their land, prepare the lumber, and build a new house, which was completed around 1904. Liney taught her daughters to quilt and do beautiful embroidery, crochet, knitting, and tatting. Though most of her quilts were long ago worn completely out, a few still survive to attest to her long hours of patient work and perseverance. She died in 1940 and is buried in the cemetery at Neshoba Baptist Church.[6]

The southernmost part of the state, which was not nearly so settled as the central section, began to sprout communities. One woman wrote with pride of her grandmother, Merinda Ellen Quarles, who made her home near the Gulf Coast:

> She and her husband moved to Long Beach in 1884 when the settlement consisted of thirteen families. She was a homemaker and ran a boarding house. Her husband was a farmer and a teacher and a postmaster. She had eleven children.
>
> My grandmother was an enterprising, wonderful lady. She gave the lot for our Presbyterian Church, also the pews when the building was completed. She was a charter member of the first Presbyterian Church as well as the other Long Beach Presbyterian Church."[7]

Mrs. Quarles also pieced about thirty-five quilts and gave one to each of her grandchildren.

Quilt Designs Become Very Inventive

The second half of the nineteenth century was a time of great creativity and inventiveness in quiltmaking across the country. Although the tough economic conditions of the third quarter had prevented them from keeping pace with the rest of the country in the making of new quilts and, consequently, the trying of new ideas, Mississippi's quiltmakers during the fourth quarter turned out pieces that are as intriguing, as colorful, as awe inspiring, and as remarkable as those made elsewhere in the United States. They also began to catch up in numbers of quilts: according to data collected in the quilt documentation effort, there were more than twice as many quilts made during the last twenty-five years of the nineteenth century than in all the years before 1875.

There were marvelous performances of piecing and intriguing applications of appliqué, and clever combinations of the two techniques. An especially cherished style, the crazy quilt, reached its zenith during this quarter-century. Another outstanding trend during this period in Mississippi was the use of a technique known as "feathering," which is the adding of a sawtooth border to a pattern. It gained such favor that it came to be almost a fad. (See separate discussions, "Mississippi Crazies," p. 87, and "Fancy Feathers," p. 78, for more information.)

This was also the time when great red, white, and green quilts were made in copious numbers. This color scheme was a great favorite of the late nineteenth century, and the quilts made during that time remain a favorite for collectors today. They were certainly greatly admired every time they appeared at a documentation day.

A distinctive single hue from this period of time is a bright orange, known as antimony orange or chrome orange, which had the ability to hold its color over the years without fading. Today the color is referred to as "cheddar," an apt description; it is also the color of those orange daylilies contained in nearly every southern garden.

Piecing Particular to Mississippi

There was such a proliferation of new patchwork quilts between 1875 and 1900 in Mississippi that one is drawn to the conclusion that quilters were trying to replace all those quilts lost during the Civil War and to create a stock for the future. An additional reason for the abundance of new designs could be that, for the first time, commercial patterns for quilts were available. They were expensive, costing as much as $1.25 per design, but they may have inspired some nascent quilters to take the plunge. At the same time, publications familiar to farmer's wives, such as *Good Housekeeping*, *The American Agriculturist*, and *The National Stockman and Farmer* began an exchange of pattern names and designs.[8] Although commercial patterns were available, some creative individuals made up their own patchwork designs.

Perhaps the pièce de résistance of Mississippi patchwork from this era, if one judges a quilt according to originality of pattern, is a design that none of the documentation team had seen before and could not find in any sources (fig. 4.2). One of the thrills of participating in a purely voluntary effort such as the quilt documentation project is the finding of a heretofore unknown pattern, and it appears that has been done with the discovery of this quilt.

When you first see a design this complicated, it is hard to believe that it originated with a farmer's wife in Mississippi more than one hundred years ago. (And, it may be that this one didn't—but no

printed record has been found as of this writing.) However, in our skepticism, we must remember that every one of the quilt designs so familiar to us, the ones we now take for granted, had to originate somewhere. One quilter had to sit down with scissors and paper or fabric and cut the pattern the first time. They all started somewhere, and some of them were published, and some weren't. Some were taken up with great enthusiasm and used in quilts by the hundreds; others were not repeated with such ardor. In the case of this quilt pattern with no name, the difficulty of its construction

Fig. 4.2. Unknown, possibly original, design made by Caroline E. Chapman Shepherd (1835–1915) in Newton County, Mississippi, in the 1875–1900 period. It is made of all-cotton materials, with fine, close quilting at 10 to 12 stitches per inch, and is 91.5 inches square. MQA quilt no. D-38. Collection of Joyce Walker Everett, great-granddaughter.

There were dozens of quilts produced from familiar patchwork patterns. Nine-patches, stars, positive-negative designs like "Drunkard's Path" and the "Irish Chain" (single, double, and triple), all were made in quantity. There were two new patchwork designs that Mississippi women took up with enthusiasm: the "Carolina Lily," a patchwork method for making flowers, and the "Log Cabin," a half-light, half-dark block that can be manipulated in setting together to form many different designs.

One example of "Drunkard's Path" is unusual because it is worked in three colors rather than the two for which the design was originally made—it is one of the oldest positive-negative quilt patterns in the American repertoire (fig. 4.3). (For another example also made in three colors, see figure 3.1, p. 42.) In this quilt, all the parts have not been used—the clamshell shape cut out of the red squares has not been used, nor has the one cut from the green squares. All the clamshell shapes have been cut from a third color, white. The result is a very complex design, with white circles in the centers of four motifs and green "reel" designs in the other seven blocks. The quilter must have had a flair for mathematics to have made such a precisely pieced quilt. She was a teacher and also worked at the post office; her husband owned a country store and was a bookkeeper for the railroad. They named their sons after heroes from the Civil War: Forrest and Butler.

The best-documented quilt in the survey was a "Cherry Basket" made by Addie Johnson for her hope chest (fig. 4.4). She kept a journal all throughout 1887, as she worked on the quilt and other items in her trousseau, but she did not even confide to her diary that her wedding date to Alex Morrow had been set for December 22 of that year. She hand-pieced the baskets of the quilt in solid fabrics of rusty red and green, set them into a white block,

Fig. 4.3. "Drunkard's Path" set into the "Love Ring" design, made by Florence Butler Jackson (1874–1952) of Amite County, Mississippi, before her marriage in November 1898. Quilt has cotton materials for top and backing, with wool batting; backing is of a red cotton print with horseshoes and a jockey; it is machine- and hand-pieced and quilted by the piece. MQA quilt no. E-66. Collection of Elizabeth Carr, granddaughter.

could have been a reason it never gained great and widespread popularity.

The quilt was made by Caroline E. Chapman Shepherd, born October 17, 1835, in Newton County, where she married and lived her entire life. Her husband was Joel Shepherd, a farmer; her children were named Willie Bragg and Maggie. Caroline Shepherd made at least one other quilt, which was given to her grandson, who never married. He gave the pair of quilts to his sister, and she gave them to her daughter, the great-granddaughter of Caroline Shepherd and current owner.[9]

then machine-appliquéd the floral printed handles for each basket. She put all the blocks on point when she set them together for the quilt top, so the baskets would sit up straight. Quilted flowers fill baskets and all surrounding areas, and Addie also quilted lots of overlapping circles, a sign thought by romantics to symbolize wedding rings. It is a splendid quilt, restrained and simple, with exquisite quilting.

When Addie's daughter, Mary, married Sam Coleman in 1906, Addie made a gift of the quilt to her daughter. She had signed and dated the quilt with her name and the year 1887 when she completed it, and she added the notation "Presented to Mary, 1906." She gave the quilt in a pillowcase upon which she had written, "When not in use, keep in this slip and it will not turn yellow, Mama. Every stitch quilted by Addie Johnson." She was justifiably proud of her creation.

Stars shone forth in great numbers from quilts made all over the state in the final quarter of the nineteenth century. A quilt by Birdie Ball, whose occupation was listed as "old maid," probably defines the Mississippi quilter's enthusiasm for stars better than any made during any period in the history of the state's quilting (fig. 4.5). She made a "Lone Star," then "Stars of Bethlehem" for the corner squares and side triangles; she put smaller "Stars of Bethlehem" in every blank corner of those corner squares and side triangles. She packed twenty-five whole stars and thirty-two half stars into a basic "Lone Star" design! It is a scrap quilt, and although there is no indication that Birdie followed any kind of color plan, the stars are all distinct. It looks like a great burst of fireworks—truly an original quilt!

Another quiltmaker, Priscilla Ann Jones of Neshoba, also made a "Lone Star" with supplemental stars in the 1890s. She worked with only two

fabrics, a red and a green, which created a very different look for this design that is often used to display a rainbow of color. The background of the quilt is green calico, printed with a tiny yellow dot design. The details, as well as half the diamonds for the "Lone Star," are done in a red fabric printed with a small-scale black figure. The two fabrics work together very nicely. Mrs. Jones (who, to the amusement of this writer, named one of her daughters Wealthy Ann) placed simple eight-diamond stars in the four corners of her quilt and framed

Fig. 4.4. "Cherry Basket" made by Addie Johnson Morrow of Eupora, Mississippi, signed and dated December 22, 1887. Quilt is of all-cotton materials, hand-pieced and machine-appliquéd, with fine, close hand quilting at 10 to 12 stitches per inch, and is 80 inches wide by 93 inches long. MQA quilt no. N-20. Collection of Elizabeth Morrow Cummings, granddaughter.

Fig. 4.5. "Lone Star" made by Birdie Ball of Pontotoc, Mississippi, in the 1875–1885 period. Quilt has all-cotton materials, quilted in shells (fans) at 6 stitches per inch, and is 72 inches wide by 78 inches long. MQA quilt no. P-04. Collection of Mildred Westmoreland.

Fig. 4.6. "Seven Sisters" made by Sarafi Margaret Wells Jones (1850–1891) of Philadelphia, Mississippi, around 1880. Quilt is of all-cotton materials, with fine close quilting, and is 68 inches wide by 82 inches long. MQA quilt no. J-25. Collection of Gwendolyn Jones Hammerman, granddaughter.

Fig. 4.7. Sarafi Margaret Wells Jones of Neshoba County, Mississippi, hand-carded the cotton that became the batting for her "Seven Sisters" quilt, 1880.

each of them with 1.5-inch wide strips of red fabric. She used half of this motif to fill in the side triangles.[10] This quilt is another example of the individuality in quiltmaking that defined the times.

There was a fondness for the star pattern known as "Seven Sisters," a name taken from the cluster of stars in the constellation of Taurus with the astronomical name of "the Pleiades." Some old-timers thought you could predict the weather according to the number of "sisters" you could see on any given night, and that may have contributed to its popularity among Mississippi quilters. The quilts shown in figures 4.6 and 4.8 are in a hexagonal set, but "Seven Sisters" quilts in a circular set were also documented. One was particularly memorable because the circular motif was bordered with a two-color diamond and triangle border. The maker, Ida Robinson Herrington (1873–1943) of Johnsonville (Neshoba County), made it a practice to stitch a quilt for each of her children as she waited for their birth. Her "Seven Sisters" quilt contains nine motifs, five with red stars, two with turquoise stars, and two with olive-green stars, and the motifs are put together in three rows of three with very

Fig. 4.8. "Seven Sisters" probably made by Kate Smith (b. 1868) of Florence, Rankin County, Mississippi, in the 1870–1890 period. Quilt is all-cotton materials, hand-quilted by the piece and in the border at 6 stitches per inch. MQA quilt no. G-16. Collection of David and Debbie Lancaster, grandson.

were "Chips and Whetstones," a design based on a five-pointed star; "World Without End," based on a four-point star; and numerous "Sunbursts" and "Rising Suns."[13]

Also stitched by the hundreds were many other traditional and nontraditional patchwork designs. A good example of a traditional pattern is the "Pinwheel" quilt made by Clementine Florence Taylor, who pieced 460 tiny little pinwheels, staying primarily with red or blue (with the occasional pink) scraps of fabric (fig. 4.9). She set the pinwheels together with sashing strips that were half the width of the pinwheel blocks (fig. 4.10). She used solid red setting blocks with white sashing and continued the red and white theme for her stripped borders. Unfortunately, the white of the quilt has discolored over time to a tan.

The overall impression the quilt gives is of an expanse of twinkling stars. Clementine was proud of her quilt; when she gave it to her daughter-in-law in 1920, she made the request that it never be used as a pallet. The request was honored, to the point that the present owner, Clementine's grandson, cannot remember the quilt ever being used even on a bed—it was always stored in the "quilt closet."

Pallets were mentioned several times—one intricately pieced "Roman Cross" was given to Emma Lee May of Decatur (Newton County) by her grandmother, Sarah Jane Ludlow, as her "pallet" quilt. Mrs. Ludlow gave the quilt to Emma Lee on the condition that "she not show it to anyone," although it is beautifully pieced and heavily quilted. It is a scrap quilt, and Mrs. Ludlow may have thought that kept it from being fine.[14]

A simple "Nine-Patch" can be a thing of beauty in the hands of a skilled quilter, such as Eliza Frances Turner, who turned it into a "Double Nine-Patch" and set it with a nice mossy print fabric in a

narrow strips for sashing. The quilting is excellent, and the quilt itself has been all over the world with Ida's great-grandson, who is a career navy man.[11]

Many other stars were stitched during this fertile time in Mississippi quiltmaking: there were "Rolling Stars," "Morning Stars," an eight-pointed star "made from the calico dresses worn by the quilter's daughter who died at age 18."[12] There

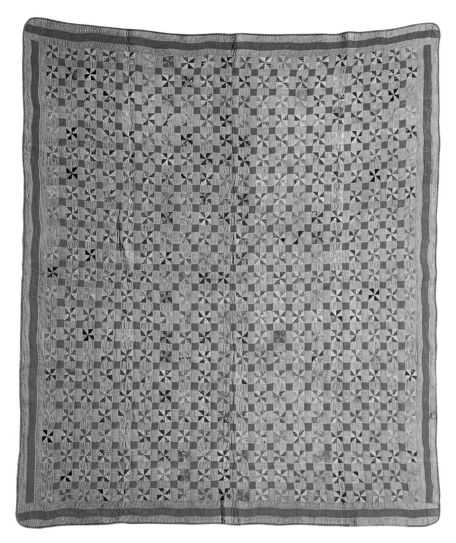

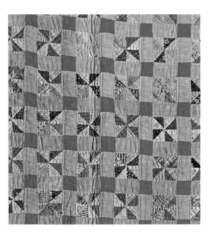

Fig. 4.9. "Pinwheel," or "Ma Taylor's Quilt," made by Clementine Florence Taylor (1859–1937) in Noxapater, Winston County, Mississippi, in the 1880–1890 period. It is of all-cotton materials, pieced and appliquéd, with hand quilting at 5 stitches per inch and some machine quilting for repairs, and is 67 inches wide by 77 inches long. MQA quilt no. D-89. Collection of Perry M. Taylor, grandson.

Fig. 4.10. The tiny blocks of this "Pinwheel" quilt are sashed with strips that are half the width of one block; the solid red squares of the sashing are one-fourth the size of a "Pinwheel." The smaller red squares are more dominant in the overall design than are the patterned blocks.

neutral brownish gray. Born in LaFayette County, Mississippi, "Liza" was an avid gardener who loved flowers, loved to read, and loved to sew. She never married, and after her mother's death she kept house for her father and her sister, who had been crippled with polio, at their farm at Toccopola in Pontotoc County. She kept up with the latest in quilt styles by swapping patterns with friends who had moved to Oklahoma. Her cousin, who has many of Liza's quilts, says, "Her hand sewing looks like our sewing machine stitches today."[15]

In later life, Liza Turner moved to Mount Moriah community in Calhoun County to live with relatives. When she died in 1931, she left a half dozen or so of her quilts to her niece in a handwritten will. Here are her words: "This is to say I mean when I am dead, Lora Cook is to have what few things I have, bed an[d] all. Mrs. Cook is to have what few pennies I leave for they have took care of me for near six years, took good care of me, one bed to sell or keep as they wish. I am writing this in her book journal. this is from my hand, Eliza Turner."[16]

Mrs. Cook, who is Miss Turner's fourth cousin, brought Miss Turner's quilts in for the Tupelo documentation day.

Hexagonal patchwork was used in Mississippi from as early as 1840 (see p. 22). In fact, a quilt very similar in style to the Millies Lake quilt was made by Victoria McLemore in 1887 for her trousseau. Many different colors of hexagons, mostly in solid fabrics, are set into a design known as "Diamond Field," or "Rainbow Tile." The multi-rowed "diamonds" are joined with solid green and brown rows of hexagons, and the quilt is then bordered in these two colors, with the side borders considerably wider than those at top and bottom. It was a very carefully made quilt (MQA# I-097).

Victoria, a pretty, blue-eyed brunette, was born on December 20, 1864, the niece of one of the earliest settlers of Meridian, Richard McLemore. She was one of nine children. Her father, Amos, had been taken prisoner during the Civil War but was paroled by Union captors so that he could continue his work as a nurse. When the war was over, Amos became a successful planter, eventually acquiring one thousand acres of land three miles northeast of Meridian. It was from this Victorian plantation that Victoria planned her wedding to Stephen B. Tucker, a farmer. The wedding took place on November 3, 1887, just before her twenty-third birthday. A formal photo of the couple shows both of them to be very handsome adults. Tragically, Victoria lived barely eight months beyond the wedding day, contracting typhoid fever and dying, while carrying her first child, on June 22, 1888, at Bonita, Mississippi.[17] Stephen Tucker kept the quilt and married a second time. The quilt and the story and photographs of its maker have descended to the present owner, a grandson.

Another hexagonal design shows the antecedents of the "Grandmother's Flower Garden" that would become almost too familiar during the 1930s and 1940s. In a design known as "Mosaic Flower Garden," a cluster of seven hexagonally patched "flower" motifs make a quilt block. These blocks are set in three rows of three, making a nine-block quilt; generous amounts of white space are included. Trapunto, or raised work, decorates those areas and also makes borders on all four sides of the quilt. The trapunto is cast as a vine, heavily laden with bunches of grapes; the date, 1883, is included in the stuffed and corded work. This lovely quilt was made by Fannie Cowan Stevens (1860–1936), in Guntown, Lee County, Mississippi.

One of the most original pieced designs recorded by the documentation team was called "Muscadine Hull" by the maker, Nancy Annie Nanney (1853–1920) of Itawamba County. She lived out in the country on a farm and perhaps used the things she saw in her everyday life as inspiration for the quilts she made for her seven children. Her granddaughter, who has the "Muscadine Hull," writes, "She loved her home and family—sacrificed for them."[18] The muscadine hull motif is composed of four segments, each of which is best described as a square with rounded sides. When these four segments are put together, the resulting shape sort of resembles the familiar French motif, the fleur-de-lis, except that there are four petals rather than three. Nancy Annie used blues, blacks, and a color that is now gray-brown for her twelve motifs (except for one, which is white), and she set them on a white background, then quilted the entire piece in the shell design. It is a very distinctive quilt, with a vaguely French feel, which was probably unintended.

In the winter of 1880, Margurette Carpenter was preparing for the annual making of her sons' suits on her farm in Itawamba County. She had spun the cotton fibers into yarn, then woven the yarn into a striped fabric on her loom. She had produced several yards of fabric because she wanted to have plenty for her sewing. As she laid out and cut the suits, she discovered that she had made more than the required amount—she had extra, enough for a quilt backing. She went out and purchased solid red and solid blue cotton and made herself a fine quilt of red and blue circles and "reels," in a variation of a "Turtle" design.[19] Her homespun backing has made the trip through the 120 years since then in much better shape than her purchased fabric—she would be proud.

Two quilts that emerged in the Heritage Quilt Search Project are almost identical to two (which are also exactly alike) in the Birmingham (Alabama) Museum of Art. The four quilts are all the same pattern and the same color scheme, red, white, and green (although some quilts have held their color better than others). Only the names of the quilts are different: the Mississippi quilts are called "Single Wedding Ring"; the Alabama quilts are called "Snail Trails." The oldest of the Alabama pair is shown in a photograph taken in 1898; it is thought to have been made around 1875 or 1880 by Mary Ann Rouse Thomas.[20] (In later years, her daughter, Mildred Thomas Cargo, pieced a duplicate of the original "Snail Trails," and her son, Robert Cargo, quilted it in 1981.)

The first Mississippi quilt, which comes from Scott County, was made by Nancy Louella Lang (1870–1961), who was "about 16" when she made it.[21] That would put it in the same general time frame as the original Cargo piece. This quilt has been repaired with a new backing, but the original fabric has never been washed. Very little information is available about the second Mississippi quilt, only that it was made by a Mrs. Regan and has been in the owner's family since "long before 1906."[22] The quilt documentation team estimated that it was made between 1850 and 1875.

The existence of these quilts in neighboring states supports the theory held by many quilt historians that, even one hundred years ago when communication was very primitive compared to what we know today, certain quilt patterns became popular at the same time in different parts of the country. Even though we may think so, our ancestresses did not live in an information vacuum; they had access to such publications as *Good Housekeeping, Godey's Ladies' Book*, newspapers, and, as mentioned earlier, various farm magazines that were carrying quilt patterns. In addition, there are many examples of women sending samples of fabric and quilt blocks to one another through the mail to illustrate just what a new quilt was going to look like. (Remember that the Natchez Trace was originally built to carry the United States mail. By this time, mail service was well established in all areas of the country, and letters were delivered fairly dependably.)

One of the designs that quilters traded during this period was "Log Cabin," a half-light, half-dark block which could be used to form any number of whole-top designs, depending on how the light and dark halves of the blocks were set together. Of the considerable number of these quilts that were made in Mississippi, one of the most interesting is a silk quilt in which the color is supplied exclusively through the plaid ribbons that make up the light half of the blocks (fig. 4.11). The quilt is set so that a colorful "Chinese Lantern" shape alternates with a black square. The elegance of its materials is the only thing that this "Log Cabin" has in common with the silk and velvet crazy quilts that were so very popular during the last quarter of the nineteenth century—the two patterns are as different as

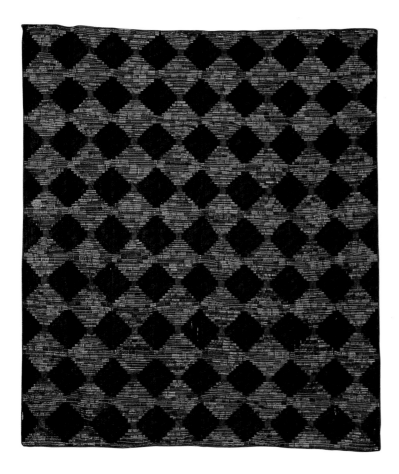

Fig. 4.11. "Log Cabin" made by Mrs. J. J. Hudspeth (1871–1964) of Ashland, Benton County, Mississippi, circa 1890. Quilt has silk top and homespun cotton plaid backing, no quilting, and binding is applied by sewing machine. MQA quilt no. O-28. Collection of Robert L. Lence, great-grandson.

Fig. 4.12. "Carolina Lily" made in Crawford County, Illinois, in the 1875–1900 period. With all-cotton materials and extremely fine hand quilting, at 12 to 14 stitches per inch, the quilt is 67 inches wide by 82 inches long. MQA quilt no. K-09. Collection of Mary Ann Norton.

can be. One is rigidly geometric, the other is completely free-form. But this era of quiltmaking was so full of invention that it welcomed both styles.

Most of the "Log Cabin" quilts of Mississippi were not of such exalted materials as silk. Most were cotton, some were wool, and many were scraps of these fabrics. Many were made with the traditional red square in the center, supposed to represent the hearth or chimney of the cabin. There are not so many of these quilts in Mississippi as in other parts of the country, perhaps because of the pattern's association with Abraham Lincoln, who was not popular in the South because he was president of the United States during the Civil War.

Lincoln was associated with a log cabin, having grown up in one; and somehow the quilt pattern of that name, by transference, became associated with him.

Another patchwork pattern that enjoyed great popularity in this final twenty-five year segment of the nineteenth century was the "Carolina Lily," which in some manifestations is known as "Mississippi Pink" (fig. 4.12). The only other pieced flower pattern to reach nearly the popularity of "Carolina Lily" was a tulip-like design, variations of which are known as "Turkey Tracks" or "Mississippi Oak Leaf."[23] Part of the reason quiltmakers love the lily and the tulip patterns so, in addition to the fact that they are so pretty, is that it enables them to make a floral design with patchwork rather than appliqué. Many quilters considered appliqué to be more difficult than patchwork, but most floral designs were intended to be appliquéd.

"Carolina Lily" can be made exactly like an eight-point star, with the two diamonds at the bottom of the design being colored to blend into the background of the block. (These two diamonds would be white if the background of the block is white, for example.) Other versions of the design call for two diamonds to be pieced to two trapezoids. Some utilize four diamonds for the petals and a triangle for the base. This last piecing method yields the design called "Dove in the Window," of which at least five examples were documented.[24] No matter what the exact pattern pieces are, it is the fact that the design is pieced that has been the attraction for many quilters. Some quilters pieced the flower, then appliquéd it onto a solid block, rather than piecing the entire block. Such a quilter was Cordelia Addy.

When Cordelia Addy's descendants gather every year, they always look forward to a visit with the wonderful "Carolina Lily" she made about 1880, at the age of fourteen (fig. 4.13). Her family had come to Newton County, Mississippi, from South Carolina in 1866, by way of a "private conveyance," according to a newspaper clipping kept in the family Bible. (The family guesses that a wagon was the means of travel.) Cordelia was born that year, but it is not known whether she made the trip with her family or arrived later.

Cordelia married Preston B. Shealy on March 27, 1884, when she was eighteen, in the home of her aunt and uncle, Mr. and Mrs. George D. Risinger; the Reverend Mr. T. H. Rivers performed the ceremony. The couple continued to live in Newton County, between Union and Conehatta,

Fig. 4.13. "Carolina Lily," called "Grandmother Shealy's Quilt" by the family, made by Cordelia Addy Shealy in Newton County, Mississippi, about 1880. It is of all-cotton materials, pieced and appliquéd with a blind stitch, and quilted by the piece around the design. The background is filled in with double straight lines of quilting, and there are single straight lines in the sashing; a fan pattern is in the borders. It is 71 inches wide by 87 inches long. MQA quilt no. C-112. Collection of Mr. and Mrs. "Bill" Underwood, grandson.

Fig. 4.14. *Seated*, Mr. and Mrs. Preston Brooks Shealy (*nee* Celia Cordelia Addy), with 6 of the 12 children they would have: *front row, left to right*, Della Estella (mother of current owner), May Jewell, and *(in Cordelia's lap)* Minnie Eunice; and *back row, left to right*, Virtie Elizabeth, Lewis Erastus, and Lilly Ava. Photograph is from 1896; Cordelia Addy Shealy is thirty years old.

and became parents of twelve children, eleven of whom lived to adulthood (fig. 4.14). One of the daughters, Della Estella, inherited the quilt; and her son, Bill Underwood, who now owns it, remembers visiting his grandparents as a child. He says the quilting frame was always up, with a quilt in progress, in the front room of the house.[25] This is the most treasured of all the quilts Cordelia Shealy made; many of the ones that came later were made for hard use that a family of thirteen would impose.

Several details in the Shealy quilt are worth notice. First is the way the motif is sewed to its background block. It is a toss-up as to which way of working is the most time-efficient: piecing the motif into the background or laying it on a solid piece of fabric and invisibly hand-stitching it down. Cordelia Addy chose the second method, and she also applied one red leaf and one green leaf on each motif. Second, she set ten blocks going in one direction and ten going in the other, so the quilt would have no definite top nor bottom. Third, she has used navy with red for the sashing and border strips, which provides a relief note to a red, green, and white color scheme; it punches up a familiar, although handsome, color plan.

The "Carolina Lily" has many variations, and they have been used by quiltmakers from this period of time to the present. It remained an adaptable, enjoyable, and versatile motif for quilters.[26]

Adventurous Appliqué

Just as experimentation with patchwork designs was without limits, so too were new forms of appliqué explored. No shape seemed beyond the reach of the intrepid Mississippi needlewomen of the 1875–1900 period. They happily scalloped edges of leaves and plumes, edges that could have been smooth; they cut

tiny circles out of colorful fabrics to make individual cherries and grapes; they made slender fabric stems for fantastic flowers that bloomed only in their imagination. Solid fabrics ruled for appliqué designs—most often red, combined with green and set on a white background. Occasionally, a dash of "cheddar" was included for spice.

Two excellent examples of the versatility of this technique come from one lucky woman, who inherited one quilt from her father's people and the other from her mother's people. She has already made arrangements in her will for the disposition of these two outstanding quilts to the next generation—each will stay with the quiltmaker's lineage. Both of the quiltmakers were born in Pike County, Mississippi, within seven years of one another, but it is not known whether or not they knew each other before their children married.

The quilt from the father's side of the family is a design that is not familiar to many, and the family did not have a name for it; but Martha Skelton, working on the documentation team, recognized it as "Meadow Daisy" (fig. 4.15). It was made by Cora Maybell Boyd White when she was about twenty-five years old. She and her mother, Dorothy Elizabeth, made many quilts together, something their children and grandchildren remember watching. Cora Maybell gave the "Meadow Daisy" quilt to her second son, Cleon Boyd White, as a wedding gift when he married Mary Alice Reeves in 1917. His grandson, Cleon Boyd White III, Cora Maybell's great-grandson, will be the recipient of the quilt in the next generation.[27]

The quilt from the mother's side of the family is a design called "Coxcomb and Currants," based, no doubt, on a familiar garden flower, coxcomb, and the berry of a shrub similar to a gooseberry (fig. 4.16). This design is a very old one from the eastern seaboard, and few quilts of this design are to be found in the Deep South. The quiltmaker's parents immigrated to Mississippi in 1811 from South Carolina, perhaps bringing an earlier quilt of this design with them, or the memory of such a quilt. This perfectly executed example was made by Salina Lucinda Felder (born in 1860) when she was about twenty-six years old. She made it a practice to pick her own cotton from first her father's, then her husband's fields; afterwards, she hand-picked the seeds out, then carded the cotton so it could be used as quilt batting or spun into yarn for weaving. She was an accomplished weaver, and at least one white counterpane she wove as a young woman still bears witness to her skill. The counterpane is finished with hand-tied fringe on three sides.[28]

Salina Lucinda married a minister, the Reverend J. R. G. Reeves, in Pike County. They had five children. This quilt was a gift to her youngest daughter, Mary Alice Reeves, when she married Cleon Boyd White in 1917. The quilt will go to Salina Lucinda's great-grandson, John Robert Walker, in the next generation.[29]

Another outstanding quilt was made by a mother as a gift for her son's marriage (fig. 4.17). The design she picked is called "Crown of Oaks," a wonderful choice for someone who loves appliqué work. The design is similar to one on a Scott County quilt from about thirty years earlier, around 1865; the design is known as "Hero's Crown" but was called "Oak Leaf and Acorn" by the family.[30] In the "Crown of Oaks" quilt, the leaves have been heavily quilted to indicate veining, but an interesting detail may be observed in the bottom row of leaves, across the entire width of the quilt: they are quilted in a different design.

Some very rare appliqué styles were greatly appreciated by all who saw them during the quilt documentation days, and it was the consensus that several very special quilts should be seen by as

Fig. 4.15. "Meadow Daisy," called "Red Flower" by the family, made by Cora Maybell Boyd White (1867–1946) of Pricedale Community, near McComb, in Pike County, Mississippi, about 1885. Quilt is of all-cotton materials, hand-appliquéd, with some machine work, and hand-quilted by the piece at 5 stitches per inch; it is 79 inches wide by 80 inches long. MQA quilt no. Q-89. Collection of Lena Lou White Kleinpeter, granddaughter.

Fig. 4.16. "Coxcomb and Currants" made by Salina Lucinda Felder Reeves (1860–1941) of McComb, Pike County, Mississippi, in 1886. Quilt is made of all-cotton materials, with a combination of machine-appliqué and piecing, some chain-stitch hand embroidery for stems of "currants," and fine, close quilting at 8 stitches per inch in a double fan design. It is 69 inches wide by 91 inches long. MQA quilt no. Q-90. Collection of Lena Lou White Kleinpeter, granddaughter.

Fig. 4.17. "Crown of Oaks" made by Ellen Proctor Landrum in Stewart, Webster County, Mississippi, in 1896. Quilt is made of all-cotton materials, including hand-carded cotton for the batting; it is machine-appliquéd and hand-pieced, with hand quilting at 5 stitches per inch, and is 73.75 inches wide by 78.5 inches long. MQA quilt no. C-42. Collection of Doris Landrum Daughety, great-granddaughter.

many people as possible. The first is a design called "Cockscomb and Tulips" (fig. 4.18), which may lead the reader to look for similarities between this quilt and the "Coxcomb and Currants"; none will be found. This design is based on a circle, with the fern-like shapes that are the "cock's combs" making the outer perimeter. These shapes are copied in the quilting designs that enhance the seams with which the four blocks of the quilt are joined. There are actually several types of flowers in the motif, among them, two different kinds of tulips and a rose. Some of the tulips are also included in the quilting designs. The family calls this the "Peden Family Quilt," in part because Mattie Peden married John Thomas Peden (making her full name Mattie Peden Peden). Mattie's family, of Irish heritage, came into Mississippi from the Carolinas. Mattie made this quilt before her son was born in 1895; he joined his only sibling, a sister. Mattie died two years after his birth, in 1897.[31]

The second special appliqué quilt was made by Laura Larkey Beard, whose father was killed at Vicksburg during the war. She never married and lived with a family in Raleigh (Smith County), Mississippi, for board and keep, piecing quilts in her spare time. When her brother's wife died in childbirth in 1900, she moved in with him, to care for him, the infant, and six other children below the age of twelve. She made as many as twenty-five quilts, of which only four remain, including the "Mongolian Flower" (fig. 4.19).[32] (One of the other three is a remarkable "Magnolia" or "Dahlia" variation: a twelve-block quilt worked in a planned color scheme that now appears as deep blue, yellow, and tan, with accents of white: the variety the maker was able to achieve in the placement of these three main colors is still clear enough to impress the viewer.)

Fig. 4.18. "Cockscomb and Tulips" made by Mattie Peden of Kemper County, Mississippi, in the 1890s. Quilt is made of cotton materials, with a wool batting; appliqué is blind-stitched; quilting is by the piece and in intricate designs in green and off-white thread. It is 70.5 inches wide by 78 inches long. MQA quilt no. D-81. Collection of Doris Gray, granddaughter.

Fig. 4.19. "Mongolian Flower" made by Laura Larkey Beard (1860–1948) of Raleigh, Smith County, Mississippi, in 1890. Quilt is made of cotton materials with a wool batting; motifs are hand-appliquéd with a whip-stitch, and some machine work was used in setting the blocks together. Hand-quilted by the piece and with heart designs at 7 stitches per inch, it is 67.5 inches wide by 86.5 inches long. MQA quilt no. I-53. Collection of Myerl Langford, great-niece.

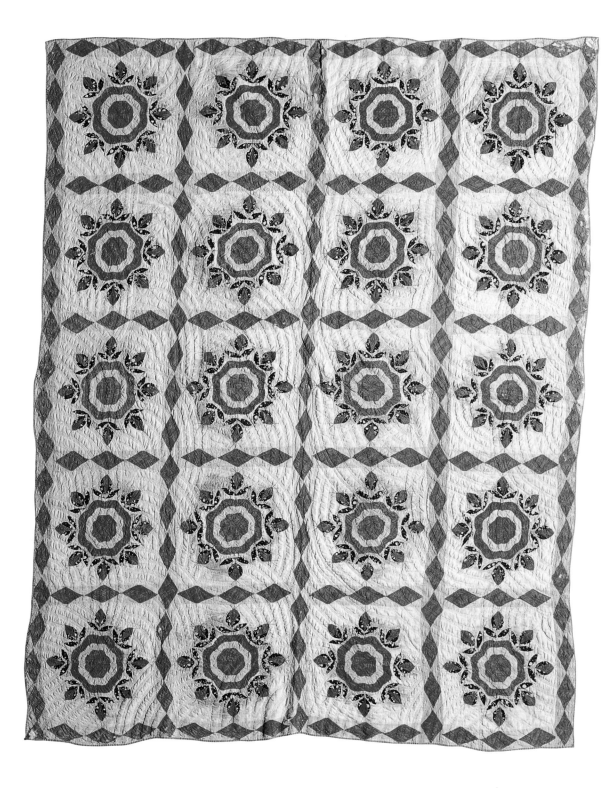

Fig. 4.20. "Whig Rose," known as "Rose Appliqué Quilt" by the family, made by Ann Shorter Alexander (1850?–1923?) in Simpson County, Mississippi, about 1890. Of cotton materials, it has hand-appliquéd and embroidered flower motifs, pieced sashing and border, and fine hand quilting at 7 stitches per inch in a fan design. It is 61 inches wide by 78 inches long. MQA quilt no. B-15. Collection of Betty N. Byrd and Dorothy A. Nunnery, granddaughters.

Fig. 4.21. Ann Shorter, maker of the "Whig Rose," was born in Brackston, Mississippi, the daughter of a family that moved into the state from the Carolinas in 1833. She married Thomas Jefferson Alexander, a farmer in Simpson County; they had eight children. She was very active in church-related activities. Although she probably made other quilts, this is the only one that has been saved. Photograph courtesy of Betty N. Byrd and Dorothy A. Nunnery.

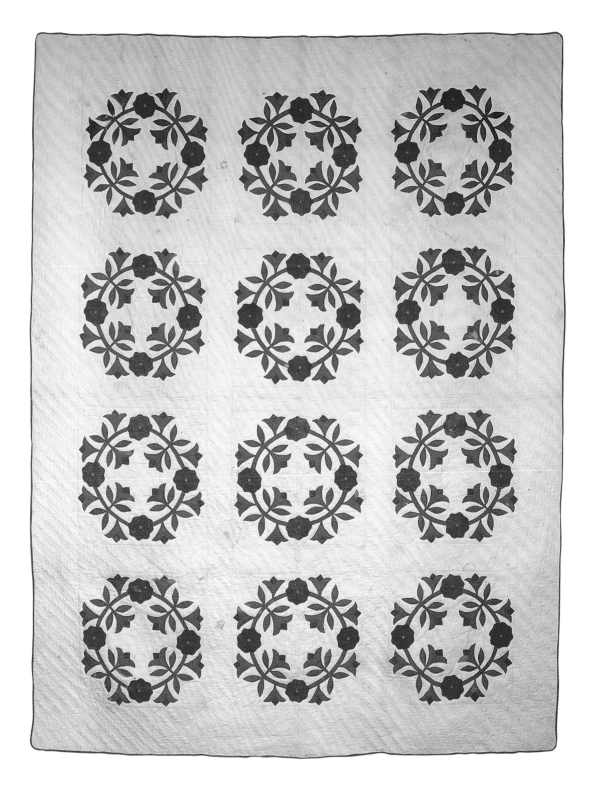

Fig. 4.22. "Rose Wreath," or "Centennial Wreath," by Maggie Jane McIlwain Oakley of Starkville, Oktibbeha County, Mississippi, in the 1890–1920 period. Of cotton materials, with possibly a wool batting, the quilt is appliquéd with a blind stitch by hand and has fine, close hand quilting at 9 stitches per inch, with a "sand dollar" motif quilted in the corners of each block. It is 77.5 inches wide by 100.25 inches long. MQA quilt no. N-12. Collection of Warren and Mary Oakley, grandson.

Margaret Watson McGahey, who was born January 28, 1824, in Scotland (fig. 4.23). When she was twelve years old, her family immigrated to America; the passage by sailing ship took nine weeks. She later married Alexander Frank McGahey of Pickens County, Alabama. It was there they settled and raised a family of ten children, and there that she made this quilt, for the birth of a grandson, Oscar McGahey.

The family recounts the story of Frank McGahey's service in the Confederate army: he was discharged in 1865 after serving at Vicksburg, and he and two companions were returning on foot to Alabama when Frank was taken ill near Bolton, Mississippi, west of Jackson. He was taken in and cared for by a "widow woman," and when he died at her home, she buried him on the grounds.[33] Margaret Watson McGahey lived until January 25, 1901.

The quilt came into Mississippi with Oscar McGahey in 1888. The McGahey's house caught on fire sometime around 1924, and Mrs. Oscar McGahey shouted to her daughter, the present owner of the quilt, "Get the trunk out of the house because the deeds and Daddy's quilt are in it." The mother and daughter wrestled the trunk and two other pieces of furniture from the burning house, the only things they were able to save.[34]

Favorite Fruits

Flowers were not the only subjects for appliqué. Two fruits were especially popular, the pomegranate and the pineapple (see figs. 4.24, 4.28, 4.29, and 4.30). Each design is frequently called by the other's name, and designs that do not appear to have anything to do with either fruit, such as tulips or cotton bolls, are often called by one of the two names.

Fig. 4.23. "Appliquéd Flower" made by Margaret Watson McGahey in Pickens County, Alabama, in 1879. Quilt is made of all-cotton materials; hand-appliquéd with a blind stitch; hand-quilted, by the piece in the sashing, and echo-quilted in the blocks, at 6 to 7 stitches per inch; and is 62 inches wide by 85 inches long. MQA quilt no. I-24. Collection of Louise McGahey Doolittle Edmondson, great-granddaughter.

The first thing a quilt lover notices about "Mongolian Flower" is that this is not a commonplace design; the second thing is that, unlike most appliqué quilts, this one consists of twenty identical blocks. Repeat blocks such as this are most often seen in patchwork quilts. A sharp-eyed observer will pick out the third interesting detail—the hearts quilted in the green and red appliquéd shapes. One wonders if Laura had a secret beau and if this quilt was intended for her trousseau.

The third quilt is a design identified only as "Floral Appliqué," and it was made around 1879 by

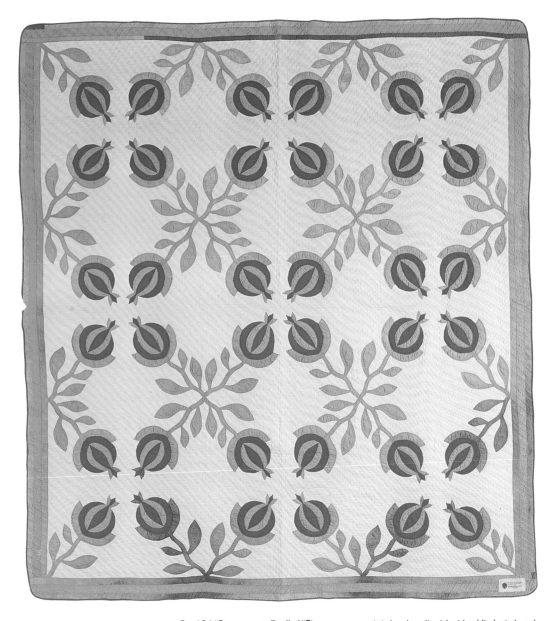

Fig. 4.25. Byrdie Haggard Hurst
(1878–1965)

Fig. 4.26. Eugenia Haggard
Dempsey (1883–1973)

Fig. 4.27. Alice Haggard Ferguson (1885–1954)

Fig. 4.24. "Pomegranate," called "Pineapple" by the family, made by Byrdie Haggard Hurst (1878–1965), probably with help from her sisters Alice Haggard Ferguson and Eugenia Haggard Dempsey, in Fern Springs (earlier called Skillet, not far from Lid and Handle), Winston County, Mississippi, around 1900. Of all-cotton materials, it is hand-appliquéd with a blind stitch and hand-quilted by the piece and in diagonal rows, to fill the background, at 10 to 11 stitches per inch. Quilt is 81.5 inches wide by 90 inches long. MQA quilt no. I-63. Collection of Myrtice H. Fulton.

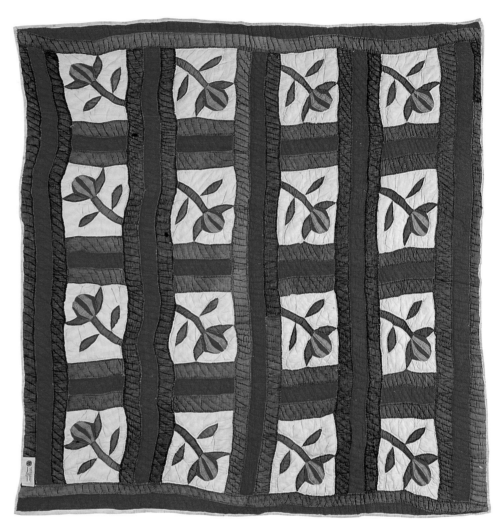

Fig. 4.28. "Pomegranate" thought to have been made by Rebecca Martin Stokes of Mississippi, circa 1890. Of all-cotton materials, the quilt is hand-appliquéd with a blind stitch; it has some machine work, and the borders were possibly attached later. Design is echo-quilted, and the background is filled in with parallel rows of hand quilting. It is 72.5 inches wide by 83 inches long. MQA quilt no. N-50. Collection of Sally Wasson, great-niece.

Fig. 4.29. "Pomegranate," called "Tulip" by the family, made by Crossie B. Leonard (1865–1957) in Newton County, Mississippi, circa 1885. Quilt is made of all-cotton materials, with a backing called "yellow muslin" by the family. It is hand-pieced and hand-quilted by the piece, and the background is filled in with diagonal lines at 5 stitches per inch. The quilt is 72.5 inches wide by 76 inches long. MQA quilt no. Q-19. Collection of Ponjola Andrews, granddaughter.

Fig. 4.30. "Pineapple" with plume accents made by Mary Jane Germany Hatcher of Nanih Waiya community (location of the Birth Mound of the Choctaw Tribe), Winston County, Mississippi, about 1890. Of all-cotton materials (originally red and green, faded to orange and tan), it is hand-appliquéd with a blind stitch, has some machine work, is hand-quilted all over in echo-quilting at 6 stitches per inch, and is 67 inches wide by 67.25 inches long. MQA quilt no. N-43. Collection of Kathleen Upshaw, granddaughter.

The pineapple as a motif in American design has a well-documented history. It was first a symbol of purity, then of hospitality, which continues to be its meaning today. It is not always easy to recognize a pineapple quilt; for example, one made in 1888 in Atlanta, Arkansas, is named "Prickly Pear," but it is basically the same design as the "Pineapple" shown in figure 4.30; the only differences are that it has one leaf instead of three, and the supplemental motifs are more discreet. It is in the red, green, and white color plan and features exquisite quilting at eight to nine stitches per inch, with feathered cables along the joining seams of the blocks.[35]

The pomegranate is a semitropical fruit (its name means "seedy apple"), and although its history as a decorative motif in America has not been as rich as the pineapple's, it is a familiar motif on fabrics influenced by East Indian art. Pomegranate trees grew well and bore fruit in gardens across the South. It may have been because it was a familiar, yet still somewhat exotic, fruit that it found such favor with quilters. It could also be that it was a fairly simple design to execute—five segments go together to make the colored fruit part of the design, then green leaves are added. This basic design is appliquéd onto a background, repeated as many times as required, and embellished with additional greenery as desired. The portion of it where quilters used their discretion was at the distinctive little tuft at the blossom end of the fruit. In most versions, it appears as a tiny tulip shape, although some quilters left it off altogether.

Fancy Feathers

There are all kinds of "feathers" in quilting: one type is appliquéd as the plume of the "Princess Feather" design; another is pieced with triangles to make a border that can be added to all kinds of designs as extra adornment; the third is quilted, as in the "feathered" wreaths and cables that add immeasurable elegance to a quilt and signal a sure hand at work. Here is a closer look at the two methods of manipulating fabric to form feathers—beginning with the appliquéd plume design known as "Princess Feather."

The name may first bring to mind an old-time garden plant, but the quilt pattern named for it barely resembles the flower. The name actually started out as "Prince's Feather," after the plume on the Prince of Wales's dress uniform. Mississippi quilters started making it during the third quarter of the nineteenth century, and they stitched it in many different ways. They also named it different names: "Princess Bloom" and even "Cucumber." The standard pattern is that of eight plumes rotating clockwise around a tiny eight-pointed star, but Mississippi quilters made variations on the center motif and the number of blades. In the two examples shown here (figs. 4.31 and 4.32), the individual makers stayed pretty well within the standard format for the design, but each maker applied very fine needlecraft skills to her quilt and chose the red, white, and green color scheme in solid fabrics that signify a "best" quilt.

The quilts are both from around 1890, and each is basically a four-block quilt. The more formal piece, with the four whole blocks (fig. 4.31), incorporates the technique of stuffed work (frequently called trapunto), in which a section of the design is raised above the surface of the quilt. This is accomplished by stuffing cotton from the back side of the design into the area to be raised. In this example, it is the appliquéd plumes that have been stuffed, which is rather unusual. The most common application for stuffed work is the emphasizing of cer-

tain areas of a design that has been executed with nothing but quilting stitches, as in all-white or whole-cloth quilts. (In rare and ornate designs, such as those of Baltimore Album quilts, sometimes appliquéd details such as grapes or cherries are stuffed, but those are the exceptions.) This is one of the few examples of stuffed work to emerge in the documentation project.

One can only wonder why the maker of the second quilt decided to make four half-blocks to go with the two full blocks of her design (fig. 4.32). Perhaps she preferred a rectangular rather than a square quilt. She used the technique of reverse appliqué to make the white center of each plume, and she created the sharp points that make such a nice feathery edge with a hand blind-stitch.

There were several variations on the "Princess Feather." One variation reduced the number of plumes to four. In one such design, the main plumes were red, but there were four green plumes arching out from each corner of the nine blocks; they would have created an interesting secondary design of whirling blades if the quilt had not been sashed with stripped sashing and corner blocks of four triangles. Although the needlework is without fault, and the quilting is very fine and close, the design is not completely successful because of the sashing, which interrupts those secondary motifs. It was made around 1875 by three Savell sisters in Philadelphia, Mississippi.[36]

All "Princess Feather" quilts were not red, green, and white. A very pretty example from Blue Springs in Union County, from this 1850–1875 period, displayed peach-colored plumes with deep

Fig. 4.31. "Princess Feather," provenance unknown, in the 1880–1890 period. Quilt is of all-cotton materials, with appliqué, patchwork, and trapunto in the plumes and very fine, close quilting at 11 stitches per inch. It is 79 inches square. MQA quilt no. O-07. Collection of Dot Main.

Fig. 4.32. "Princess Feather," maker's name unknown (possibly Mrs. McCully, as family calls it the "McCully Quilt"), from Winston County, Mississippi, in the 1875–1890 period. Quilt is of all-cotton materials; appliqué, reverse appliqué, and piecing; and hand quilting at 9 stitches per inch in varied designs, including stars, leaves, and hearts. It is 90 inches wide by 95 inches long. MQA quilt no. N-02. Collection of Bruce and Sue Mitchell, great-great-grandson.

green bases. It had hearts hidden in the quilting.[37] Another, from Blue Mountain in Tippah County, was made by Susan Turner, circa 1880, and is very striking in that the plumes are either black or blue-black, centered with brown or yellow circles. The plumes are a different shape from most other "Princess Feathers": the pattern is called "California Plume."[38] (To see an example of Susan Turner's quiltmaking, see figures 3.2 and 3.3.)

A most colorful "Princess Feather" was made in the 1930s with four different-colored plumes on each of four motifs. The red, gold, olive, and pale-blue feathers were each centered with a pink-and-white pieced circle.[39]

Feathered Edges

A "sawtooth" edge, pieced of light and dark triangles, that adds interest to many designs is also known as a "feathered" edge. Piecing the triangles together to exactly fit a specific length is a tedious procedure, especially when the feathering must be shaped around a curve. Close inspection of many old quilts has revealed that the triangles can be made of two different sizes. For example, a strip might be made with light triangles that are larger than the colored ones. Also, different parts of a design might require different-sized triangles—this has certainly been the case with feathered stars, such as the one shown in figure 4.33, in which the longer straight edges will require larger triangles than will the inside corner of the points.

Quilters in the nineteenth century cut each triangle by hand and carefully hand-stitched the triangles together as demanded by the pattern they were making. This could mean tapering a seamline by a thread's width to make pieces fit together per-fectly. Current quilters have devised a few speedy techniques for making the feathers, but even so, there is no truly easy way to make a complicated feathered design.

Many designs are taken from the ordinary to the sublime with the addition of feathered edges. Star designs are especially adaptable to feathering. The four-point star of "World Without End" can be feathered, then set a little differently, and it becomes the "Mayflower Quilt."[40] A plain wheel quilt becomes "Rocky Mountain Road" or "New York Beauty" with the addition of feathering to the four quarter-circles in the corners of each block and with lavish feathering of the sashing strips (figs. 4.34 and 4.35). A "Double Wedding Ring" design becomes "Indian Wedding Ring," or "Pickle Dish," when the arcs are feathered (fig. 4.36). Feathered edging is what makes a "Sunflower" design—without it, the poor flower would have no petals (fig. 4.37).

"Suspension Bridge" (fig. 4.38) is a "feathered wheel" design, similar to "Rocky Mountain Road," or "New York Beauty," except that no feathering is used in the sashing. The dramatic difference that sashing makes can be imagined by thinking of two "Suspension Bridges," one set with stripped sashing, as in figure 4.38, and the other set block to block.

One of the most fascinating of all feathered designs is one called "Rattlesnake" by the family. Listed as "Chinese Fan" in standard quilt references, it is a complex design involving pinwheels and fans with wide feathered borders. It could be interpreted to represent a snake coiled onto itself; there was certainly opportunity aplenty in early Mississippi for a quilter to observe the real thing. The quilt is in a faded orange and green, but wisps of its fiery youth remain.[41]

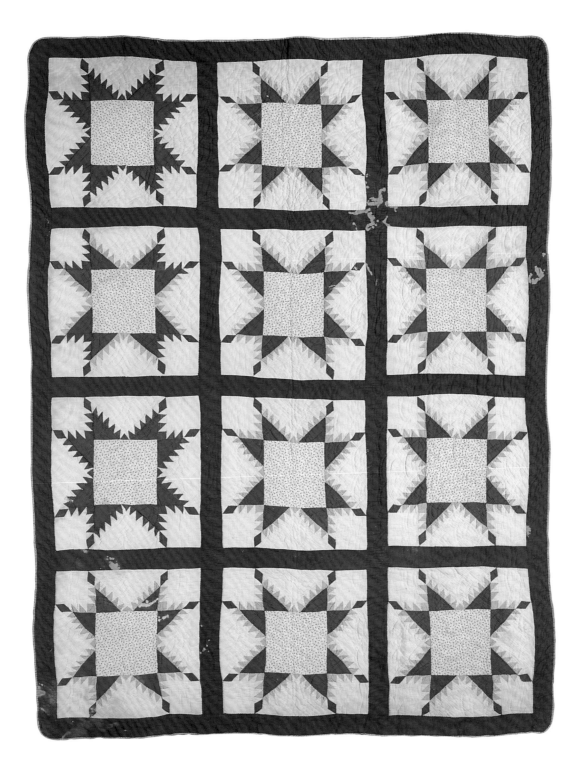

Fig. 4.33. "Feathered Star" made by Evaline McKay Forman (1854–1914) in Mize, Smith County, Mississippi, circa 1899. Evaline had preceded her husband in death by 33 years; John Robert Forman died in 1947. During the division of the Forman estate, Desmond Holmes Ward, the youngest son of Lora Forman Ward (who was the oldest child of Evaline and John Robert Forman), pulled this quilt from the trash and asked his mother if he could have it. She took the quilt and washed it for him. Desmond Holmes Ward married Loney Milner in 1940. At the death of Desmond Holmes Ward, his wife, Loney Ward, became the owner. Of all-cotton materials, the quilt is beautifully pieced, hand-quilted in an overall pattern of clamshells, and is 61 inches wide by 80 inches long. MQA quilt no. A-25. Collection of Loney Ward.

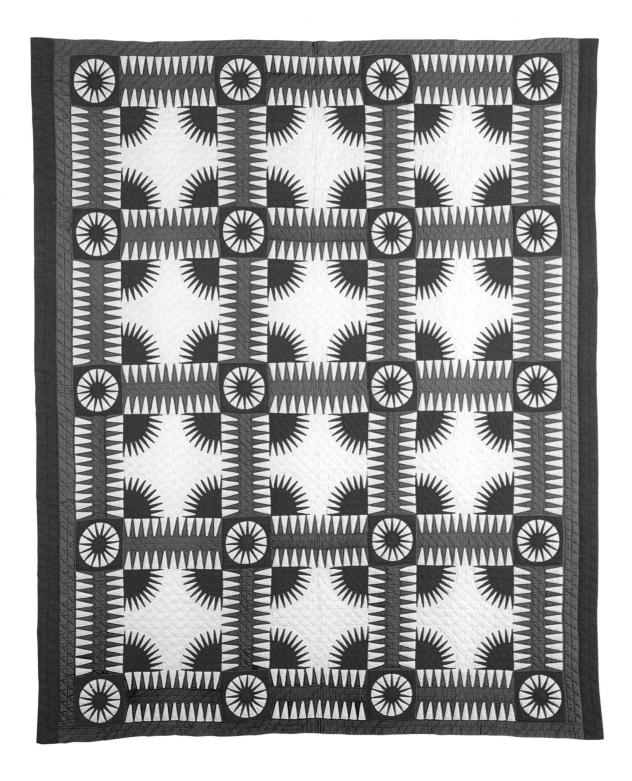

Fig. 4.34. "Rocky Mountain Road," called "The Rocky Mountain" by the family, made by Margaret Jane House Warren of House, Neshoba County, Mississippi, in the 1880–1890 period. (She may have been helped by her sister-in-law, Sara Ann Warren, who taught her great-niece, the current owner, to piece the "Nine-Patch" block.) Quilt is of all-cotton materials and is hand-pieced. It is hand-quilted by the piece and in hanging diamonds in the background at 9 stitches per inch. One edge has the knife-edge finish; it is 72.75 inches wide by 87.75 inches long. MQA quilt no. D-11. Collection of Nell B. Harrison, great-grand-daughter.

Fig. 4.35. "New York Beauty" variation made by Meg Ferguson of Enterprise, Union County, Mississippi, around 1890 as a gift for her niece, Lee Jones (Todd), born on April 24, 1891. Of all-cotton materials, the quilt was hand-quilted in 1941 by the piece and with decorative designs, including initials, at 7 stitches per inch. It is 66.25 inches wide by 74 inches long. MQA quilt no. R-03. Collection of Suzanne Abernethy Parker, great-great niece.

Fig. 4.36. "Pickle Dish," or "Indian Wedding Ring," made by Mrs. Strum in Neshoba County, Mississippi, in 1890. Quilt top is of solid-color cotton fabrics, backing is a brown-and-tan cotton plaid, and batting is of wool. Hand quilting is done at 6 stitches per inch. It is 73 inches wide and 88 inches long. MQA quilt no. I-07. Collection of Sheila Watson, great-granddaughter-in-law.

Fig. 4.37. "Russian Sunflower," called "Mariner's Compass" by the family, pieced by Annie M. Tucker (1870–1944) at age 16 and quilted with help from her mother, Margaret Baker Tucker, and her grandmother, Carolyn Ross Tucker. This was Annie's bridal quilt for her marriage to Thomas Dunkley; it was made in the Martin community of Lauderdale County, Mississippi, in 1886. Of all-cotton materials, it is hand-pieced and hand-quilted at 6 stitches per inch and is 65.75 inches wide by 80 inches long. MQA quilt no. L-71. Collection of Marilyn Logan, granddaughter.

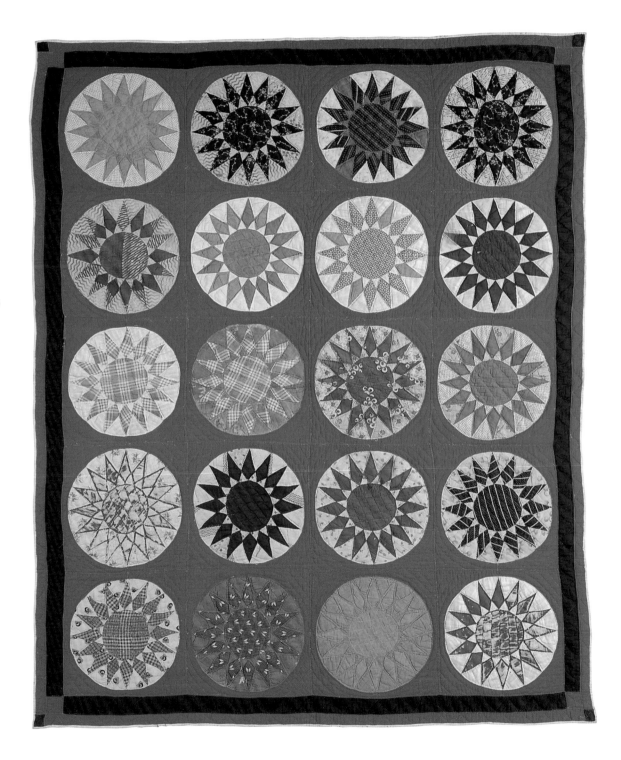

Fig. 4.38. "Suspension Bridge" made by
Helen Angeline Dollar McGraw of Neshoba
County, Mississippi, in the 1890–1900 period. Quilt is of all-cotton materials, hand-
quilted at 6 stitches per inch, and is 68
inches wide and 77 inches long. MQA quilt
no. C-95. Collection of Joy Rushing, granddaughter.

Mississippi Crazies

One of the things that makes life in the South special is that we love our crazies—they are so very interesting. And when it is made clear that we're talking about quilts, the discussion often turns to show-and-tell. There is no quilt style that has more potential for linking the present to the past, and everybody who has an old one wants to share its stories. As the documentation teams began their work, they knew they would probably see lots of crazy quilts, but they were not expecting the huge numbers that actually showed up at the quilt search days.

As might be expected when there are so many examples, there were different interpretations of the central theme. There emerged two basic types of crazy quilts: the dearly treasured antiques of silk, velvet, and heavy embroidery; and those made from the block pattern known as crazy patch, made of cotton and/or wool scraps. The second undoubtedly derived from the first, but as time has passed, the choice of materials and style of execution has changed until the crazy-patch block has entered the quilt repertoire as a versatile pattern for using up odd bits of fabric. Truth be told, many of the crazy quilts made after the Victorian era were not constructed with the same romantic motives that informed the earlier ones. (Officially, the era ended with Queen Victoria's death in 1901; the Victorian style of decorating, and in quilts, lasted longer in the southern United States than elsewhere, until about 1920.)

We might think of the antique velvet and silk quilts as the grande dames of the genre, the ones to be treated with respect and from whom we can learn a great deal of history. These old quilts were often sentimental tributes to family or friends, and they could, in some instances, be read almost like a journal. In the earlier pieces, deliberate effort was taken to include scraps of clothing that had been worn for weddings, christenings, graduations, even funerals and mourning—any and all of those ceremonies and occasions that mark life's great passages. One example from Amite County, made in 1896, is said to have incorporated family clothing, particularly from the grandfather (Maurice Henry Jackson) and a great-aunt (Louise). The family thinks that friends may have contributed either fabrics or work to the quilt, because the maker, Florence Butler Jackson, called it a friendship quilt. She was a schoolteacher who also worked at the post office, and her husband was a bookkeeper with the railroad.[42] Mrs. Jackson made thirty full blocks, each containing a fabric swatch on which has been embroidered a particular flower: lily, daisy, rose, black-eyed Susan. This fragment is usually placed toward the center of the block, then surrounded with numerous other pieces. The pieces are heavily embellished with a wide variety of embroidery stitches.

We have all marveled at quilts that contain silk ribbons won as prizes in horse shows, fairs, or other events or worn as part of a uniform of some kind. Such ribbons personify the motivation originally behind the crazy quilt, which was basically the making of a fabric diary. The individual fabric patches were touchstones to particular memories and a way of immortalizing the individual from whom it was taken. As this notion came into full flower, women began to create elaborate embroidered motifs or scenes to illustrate particularly meaningful moments or incidents. The treasured thought might be represented by the rendering of, say, a robin or a bluebird, but that simple motif represented, perhaps, a memorable afternoon with the needlewoman's sweetheart who later became her husband and the father of her twelve children.

Fig. 4.39. "Crazy Quilt" made by Caroline ("Callie") Ann Berry Brooks (1829–1893) at Sunnyside plantation, near Wakefield in Tate County, Mississippi. Many dates are embroidered on the quilt, with the most recent being 1893. It is made of cotton and wool materials in solids and checks and is backed with a cotton print. The quilt has no batting and is tacked to the backing. It is 66 inches wide by 76 inches long. MQA quilt no. O-72. Collection of Ida Fitzpatrick Wallace, great-granddaughter-in-law.

A really spectacular quilt of this genre, made about 1880, was brought to the documentation effort by Annabelle and Bob Meacham; he is the great-grandson of the maker, Mildred Meriwether (1854–1935). She married James Tate Gabbert, a merchant and farmer; they lived in Senatobia, Tate County, Mississippi, where the Meachams live today. The quilt is centered with a skillfully drawn thread portrait of a couple in a phaeton being drawn by a pair of trotting horses, one white and one

black. This portrait is worked on a background of fuchsia-colored silk. It is surrounded by a completely random placement of crazy patches, almost every single one of which is embroidered with a motif. All are different, even though there may be two different versions of the same flower. For example, a fuchsia blossom is rendered twice, once in color and again in white outline.

"Each of the pictures depicted some event or thing of importance in her [Mrs. Gabbert's] life. The central picture shows her and her husband riding in their carriage. He took her for a ride when he got home from work each day, so they could have a few minutes, without the children, to talk and discuss the events of the day. They had eleven children," said Annabelle Meacham.[43]

One of the blocks of the quilt portrays the Jersey cow that was tethered in the lane beside their house, which was across the street from the courthouse. Another shows a pair of bluebirds tending a nest; Mrs. Gabbert, in her quest for accurate representation, stitched actual seeds in place around the edge of the nest.

A quilt from the family of a circuit rider is, like the Gabbert quilt, a fabric diary (fig. 4.39). The Reverend Joseph Howard Brooks was born on March 24, 1815, and one of the squares toward the center of the quilt has his initials and the year of his birth embroidered in red thread. In the square next to his are the initials of his wife, Caroline Ann Berry, but her birth year is not given. In different squares across the surface of the quilt are the initials of their nine children, all of whose two first names began with the same letter: William Watson Brooks, Joseph Joyner Brooks, Thomas Tate Brooks, Sallie Sykes Brooks, Lula Lenora Brooks, Berry Boswell Brooks, Caroline Cottrell Brooks, Henry Howard Brooks, and Keener Kavanaugh Brooks. (The last child was named for two Methodist bishops.) There are many other initials as well, and random dates are scattered about on the quilt, some of which are not the birth dates of the children.

The Brooks descendants are fortunate to have many references in which their family is mentioned. The patriarch, Joseph Howard Brooks, was an itinerant preacher of the Methodist-Episcopal Church, South, and a founding member of the Methodist Organizing Conference in north Mississippi in 1870 (fig. 4.40). He also kept a plantation, Sunnyside, in the vicinity of Holly Springs, as his congregations were not able to provide housing or much of anything else for him. One of his sons and a grandson would also become members of the Methodist clergy. Even with all the documentation of the family, it is not possible to completely decipher all the initials on the quilt. The family supposes it to be a quilt made for a wedding as a family keepsake.[44]

There are many breathtaking examples of the skill of Victorian needlewomen in the crazy quilts of the last quarter of the nineteenth century. Such is one made by Catherine Lotterhos in Copiah County (fig. 4.41). The focal point of this quilt is a large center block of black velvet that is heavily embroidered with a spray of flowers and a date, "Dec. 25, 1888" (fig. 4.42). It is framed by many crazy-patch blocks, each of which appears to contain a patch with an embroidered flower. The colors of the patches vary from black to pale blue and royal blue; the flowers on each are different. Embroidery stitches highlight the seamlines that join the patches. Some of the silks have deteriorated, but it is still possible to enjoy the great variety that were used to make the quilt.

"The Lotterhos, Huber, Lieb and Mangold families, tied together through marriage, immigrated to the United States from Germany in the early 1800s, settling in Copiah County. They prospered as mer-

Fig. 4.40. The Reverend and Mrs. Joseph Howard Brooks, married Tuesday, July 14, 1846. They had 11 children, 9 of whom survived. The Reverend Brooks was a circuit rider and served several Methodist congregations in north Mississippi and southwest Tennessee, many of which met in homes or schools before churches were built.

Fig. 4.41. Miss Catherine Lotterhos was not yet a year old when her mother died, on February 8, 1854, and she was 6 when she moved to America from Germany with her family. A schoolteacher in Copiah County, she never married and lived most of her life in Crystal Springs, Mississippi. She was 78 years old when she died there on December 28, 1931.

chants in cotton and produce, eventually becoming the biggest produce shipper in the state, with clients all over the United States. I am a descendant of the families and am proud to have the quilt in my possession," writes Mary Esther Huber Walker.[45]

Many Mississippi crazies follow the basic plan of the Lotterhos quilt, in which the center square is the showiest of the quilt, the one with the most outstanding embroidery. Often the background of this block is black velvet or silk, and many times the date appears here. In some examples, the most important block is placed a bit off-center, for reasons that are not entirely clear.

The other plan used for Mississippi crazies is one that produces a result not unlike an aerial view of farmland (see figs. 4.43 and 4.44). This effect is particularly noticeable when plain, solid fabrics,

Fig. 4.42. "Crazy Quilt" made by Catherine Lotterhos (1853–1931) of Copiah County, Mississippi, and dated December 25, 1888. Made with velvets, silks, and wool batting, it is heavily embroidered and is 85.5 inches wide by 93.5 inches long. MQA quilt no. C-136. Collection of Mary Ester Huber Walker.

Fig. 4.43. "Crazy Quilt" made by Mary Elizabeth Castleman (1852–1936) and her daughter, Laura Castleman Marron (1878–1964), in Adams County, Mississippi, circa 1900. Friends and family contributed to the quilt; two monograms, "SBW" and "MV," are for persons unknown. Each block is worked in a general pattern of placing a large central shape first, then surrounding it with smaller pieces. Of silks, velvets, and brocades, it has been repaired using some synthetics; it is 66 inches wide by 67 inches long. MQA quilt no. F-77. Collection of Miriam Marron Montgomery, great-grand-daughter and granddaughter.

Fig. 4.44. "Crazy Quilt" made by Mary Ann Davis Grady (1854–1913) in Natchez, Mississippi, in 1892. Initials are those of her children, and the dates are of their birth. (One son was born after the quilt was made, so his initials and birthday are missing. Also, the initials of twin daughters are in the same block.) Made of velvets, sateen, ribbons, taffeta, and rayon, with lavish use of embroidery, it is 51 inches wide by 71 inches long. MQA quilt no. CC-07. Collection of Margaret Burns Humble, great-niece.

such as wool or cotton broadcloth, are used. Squares are defined by embroidered boundary lines, but the shapes within can be completely random. Sometimes the fancy embroidery along seamlines can resemble a line of trees on a fence row.

A crazy quilt of the type that looks like a topographical map was made by Frances King and her sister, Ruth Ringold Franklin, both of Greenwood, Mississippi. They made this quilt in 1942, rather late for a crazy, but it just shows that quilt patterns stay in the public consciousness for a long time. Ruth was in a wheelchair for many years, and quilting was something she could enjoy with no restrictions. She and Frances called their work "Help You Get Well" quilts—they were made to help them feel better.[46]

In addition to the lavish display of fancy embroidery stitches that has come to be expected on crazy quilts, Mississippi needlewomen were fond of embroidering sentimental motifs on scraps of fabric and then stitching them into their crazies. Again and again the documentation team found silhouettes of hands, traced with embroidery, sometimes accompanied by the name of a child and his or her age. But the handprints didn't always belong to children, sometimes they were of adult friends and relatives.

Of course, most crazy quilts were not quilted. Tying, also known as tacking or tufting, is the practice of securing the backing in place at regular intervals across the piece. Many quilters made the tacks as unobtrusive as possible. However, one quilter, Molly Fancher of Union in Neshoba County, used colorful yarn to make the ties, in a deliberate effort to add to the decorative aspect of the quilt. For example, in one corner block of navy the entire design is worked with multicolored knots with long yarn tails. The quilt is bordered on three sides, and the borders are tied also. The quilt has a very festive feel—the colorful yarn looks like confetti sprinkled across the surface.

Summary

The creativity demonstrated in the quiltmaking during the last quarter of the nineteenth century was astonishing, and Mississippi quiltmakers kept up with the rest of the country in production of awe-inspiring quilts. Indeed, the quilts from this period are the ones that stimulated and sustained the interest in quilt history, an interest enjoyed by many people today. Even one hundred years later, we are not so far removed from these quiltmakers that we can't learn something about them. Historians and collectors, who may never intend to make a quilt themselves, can appreciate and enjoy the fabulously inventive and beautifully stitched pieces from this time. It is the delight of ownership of these quilts that has inspired many great private and public quilt collections around the country. And, in many cases, these older quilts have taught collectors so much about creativity and inventiveness that they have expanded the scope of their collections to include highly experimental work being made today. The legacy of these quilts is far-reaching.

Fig. 4.45. Mary Ann and Anthony Grady of Natchez, Mississippi, on their wedding day, June 6, 1883. Photo courtesy of Peter Burns, grandson.

CHAPTER FIVE

Early Twentieth-Century Quiltmaking

1900–1930

"She'll be buried under that," said Aunt Beck softly.

"I'm going to be buried under 'Seek No Further,'" said Granny. "I've got more than one quilt to my name that'll bear close inspection."

—Eudora Welty, *Losing Battles*

AT THE BEGINNING of the twentieth century, many parts of Mississippi were still frontier areas. In areas covered by virgin stands of white pine, the land would not grow cotton, and many of the settlers in those regions supported themselves by herding cows and sheep and by growing sweet potatoes, still an excellent crop for many farmers.[1] This pastoral lifestyle changed dramatically as timber companies and the railroads discovered the state, particularly the southern area.

Hattiesburg (named for Hattie Lott Hardy, the wife of the town's founder, Captain William H. Hardy) grew to be the largest city in the section of Mississippi known as the Piney Woods, which begins at the northern tip of the DeSoto National Forest and stretches south to the Gulf Coast. Hattiesburg's prosperity has, from its beginning, been based on a forest-products industry that got its start in the 1880s. In 1900, the value of timber shipped to market exceeded that of cotton by $5 million. As timber companies began exploiting the abundant stands of forests, Mississippi became a leading supplier of lumber to the nation, exporting over 1 billion board feet from its thousand-plus sawmills in 1925 alone.[2] By 1930, the virgin timber that originally covered much of the state was gone, completely clear-cut.

At one time in the first half of the twentieth century, more than half of all workers in the state were employed in some aspect of the timber business. After a lag time during mid-century, timber and forest products have once again become important. Woodlands of fast-growing yellow pine have replaced the original white pine, and they now supply thriving businesses in timber and lumber; 80 percent of the southeastern counties of Perry,

The flood of the Mississippi River in 1927 was one of the most devastating natural disasters of the twentieth century. In Cary, Mississippi, people and their possessions were displaced as waters rose to rooftop level. Photo courtesy of the Mississippi Department of Archives and History.

95

Fig. 5.1. "Pine Tree," thought to be an original design, made by Ola Williams of Neshoba County, Mississippi, in the 1880–1900 period. Quilt is made of all-cotton red and faded green fabrics, with two borders on two sides, one border on two sides, and a woven plaid backing. It is hand-pieced and hand-quilted in an all-over fan design and measures 76 inches wide by 77 inches long. MQA quilt no. I-25. Collection of Mary Fox, daughter.

known as a needleworker, quilting and supplying beautifully made christening outfits to several states.[3]

It might seem that the pine tree would have been a popular motif with quilters, living as they did among huge first-growth forests of unimaginable size, and with their families often employed in work associated with timber. This supposition has proved to have little basis; only a handful of pine tree quilts surfaced for documentation. Among them, though, was a quilt with a most original setting for a pine tree design (fig. 5.1). It comprises four big trees, pieced of half-square triangles, whose tips are at each of the four corners of the quilt. The bases of their trunks meet in the center of the quilt, and an octagon is formed by the last row of "branches" on each tree. This octagon is of solid red fabric, as is the remainder of the background, and of such a dominant shape that it takes a few moments to pick out the pine trees in the quilt. It is such a unique piece that the documentation team thought it must be an original design.

Other examples of tree quilts most often utilized a block pattern, set in multiple rows of numerous trees. One quilt in a "Tree of Paradise" pattern repeated a green-and-white pine tree block twelve times in an unusual diagonal set that was emphasized with red-and-green stripped sashing.[4] "Cedars of Lebanon" was the name used for a colorful scrap quilt in which twenty trees were set with white setting blocks, giving the overall effect of a lovely grove. The maker was said to be prouder of this quilt than any she made.[5] Leaf shapes provided design inspiration a bit more often than trees, but there were not many "Maple Leaves," "Tea Leaves," or "Autumn Leaves." There were probably not ten quilts of the nearly two thousand documented that were of a tree or leaf theme.

Greene, Stone, Wayne, Jasper, and Clarke are covered with forests.

Many quilters' families were involved in the timber and lumber business, mostly as loggers, but some as saw men at lumber mills. In fact, one quilter, Carrie Butler Brown, who traveled on horseback all the way from Tennessee to southern Mississippi (Amite County) to settle and establish a new home, suffered the death of her husband in a logging accident. Forced to support herself and her children, Mrs. Brown went on to become well

Slow but Significant Change toward Urbanization

Although most quilters, like the population at large, lived on farms, a few urban centers were gaining strength, and their growth would continue throughout the twentieth century. By 1910, the urban population had grown from 4 percent to 11.5 percent, with Meridian replacing Vicksburg as the most populous city. The five largest cities were Meridian (population 23, 285), Jackson (21, 262), Vicksburg (20,184), Natchez (11, 791), and Hattiesburg (11,733).[6]

The last county to be organized in the state was Humphreys, established on March 28, 1918. A new capitol was dedicated in Jackson on June 4, 1903, with a crowd estimated at 25,000 gathering to see, among other wonders, the eagle on the top of the dome. The eagle measures fifteen feet at wingspread, is eight feet tall, gold-leafed, and cost fifteen hundred dollars. The old capitol would become the Mississippi State Historical Museum, a division of the Mississippi Department of Archives and History and the repository for many significant Mississippi quilts and textiles, as well as other artifacts pertaining to the history of the state.

Transportation systems improved at a great rate. Paved highways were built to serve the increasing numbers of people who owned automobiles. Jackson set a speed limit of fifteen miles per hour for straight-away driving and seven and a half miles per hour for turning corners.[7] In 1920 there were only 667 tractors in the state, one for every four hundred farms; mules were still the major power source for plowing and hauling.[8] Mississippi Power and Light was formed in 1925 and eventually provided electricity and gas, as well as trolley service, in Jackson. Delta Airlines put Jackson on as a regular stop between Atlanta and Dallas in 1929;

the next year a municipal airport at Hattiesburg was opened.

Those who would shape the famous literary heritage of Mississippi were beginning to be heard. William Faulkner, who had been born thirty-two years earlier, published his critically acclaimed book *The Sound and the Fury* in 1929. Two writers who would become as celebrated as Faulkner were born shortly after the century turned: Eudora Welty in Jackson on April 13, 1909, and Tennessee Williams in Columbus on February 26, 1911.

The United States entered World War I in 1917, occasioning the building of Camp Shelby near Hattiesburg as a principal training center for the army, with some 30,000 recruits getting their basic introduction to military life there. A smaller facility was built at West Point for the air force. In all, 66,000 Mississippi men and women served in the armed forces in this mercifully brief involvement;[9] peace was declared in 1918. An unexpected consequence of World War I for Mississippi was that it was indirectly the cause of great migrations of African Americans from the state. The war had caused a labor shortage in northern cities such as Chicago, and thousands of black people began moving away to the promise of a better life, where one could earn fair wages and get ahead. Between 1910 and 1920, almost 150,000 blacks left Mississippi; there was a brief reduction in departees in the 1920s, but the pace picked up again between 1930 and 1940, with another 150,000 leaving. In the 1940s, more than 300,000 blacks migrated out of the state.[10] Surely these migrations depleted the state of many African American–made quilts from the first half of the twentieth century and earlier, because it stands to reason that family quilts traveled north with their owners.

In 1919, one of the first supermarket chains in the United States was started with the opening of the first Jitney Jungle store in Jackson.[11] Although it is quite possible that no one fully recognized its significance at the time, the opening of a supermarket signaled a new freedom for the housewife; no longer would she have to provide, with her own labor, such items as milk and fresh produce. With this new and convenient availability of basic goods, she would be unfettered from hours of backbreaking work. What would she do with the time? Could she spend more time quilting?

Weather without Warning

One of the most devastating natural disasters of the century occurred with the 1927 flood of the Mississippi River. This perhaps provides the reason why so few quilts from the Mississippi Delta were found in the quilt documentation effort. There had been floods before—in fact, a terrible one had hit the state in 1897—but there had never been one like this. At 12:30 P.M. on April 21, 1927, after months of rain, a levee at Mounds Landing near Greenville gave way and flooded nearly three million acres of Delta land; the flood from this one break—and there would be additional ones downriver—put water over the tops of houses seventy-five miles away in Yazoo City. The water moved quickly through the break, "making a sound like a storm coming through the woods" as it rolled inland in a wave more than five feet high. Within thirty-six hours, the entire Delta was under from two to eighteen feet of water.[12] Incredibly, the river was more than one hundred miles wide in some places.

More than 185,000 people were forced out of their homes to crowd together on the tops of Indian mounds and levees. Five months later, nearly half of them would still be living in refugee camps. Thirty thousand people fled the Delta, never to

return.[13] The river lay over the land until September, forestalling a cotton crop and depriving the area of its major source of income for the year. The destruction was as bad or worse as that wrought by the Civil War.

In the entire flooded region, fifty per cent of all animals—half of all the mules, horses, cattle, hogs, and chickens—had drowned. Thousands of tenant-farmer shacks had simply disappeared. Hundreds of sturdy barns, cotton gins, warehouses, and farmhouses had been swept away. Buildings by the tens of thousands had been damaged, and in towns whole blocks had become heaps of splintered lumber, like the leavings of a tornado. In some places great mounds of sand covered fields and streets. On the fields, in the forests, in streets and yards and homes and businesses and barns, the water left a reeking muck. It filled the air with stench, and in the sun it lay baking and cracking like broken pottery, dung-colored and unvarying to the horizon.[14]

Can there be any doubt that hundreds, perhaps thousands, of quilts were destroyed in this great devastation? And if there were quilts to be found when the waters finally receded, were they salvageable? It is highly doubtful that the terrible mud could have been removed sufficiently to return any quilts to a usable condition.

The job of rebuilding was almost impossibly difficult, but there was a surge of determination, energy, and activity, and people began to clean up and rebuild. The Red Cross distributed hundreds of thousands of packets of vegetable seeds so that people could plant vegetable gardens: beans, squash, tomatoes. The refugee camps "swarmed with home economists and agricultural extension agents who taught captive audiences how to sew, make soap, can vegetables, raise poultry, protect cistern water from mosquitoes."[15] Surprisingly, many sharecroppers in the Delta at the time of the flood had no experience with raising gardens; vegetables were thought to be a waste of good farmland, so they usually bought what they ate on credit from the company store. Also, there was little understanding of the role that good nutrition played in health; the home economists and agricultural extension agents provided valuable educational services, and the changes they helped to bring about were of great benefit, not only directly to the impoverished flood refugees, but to their children and succeeding generations.

Natural disasters were not limited to floods. The state was frequently visited by tornadoes; in 1908, a series of tornadoes killed 155 people and injured 970, with most of the damage sustained in Wayne and Lamar Counties. In 1920 a tornado in east central Mississippi killed 130 people and injured 659. Hurricanes were a factor; on September 21, 1906, a single hurricane killed 350 people in Mississippi and Louisiana.[16] Fires also took their toll; one of the disadvantages of urban life was that a fire could quickly sweep through and destroy the entire commercial section of a town. In 1900, for example, a fire in Biloxi wiped out not only ninety buildings in the business district, but a large part of an exclusive residential district; in 1906, twenty-three commercial buildings, including the newspaper office, burned in Fayette; in 1921, a fire destroyed fifty buildings in Pascagoula.

It is a miracle that so many quilts survive from this period of time, and it is a tribute to Mississippi's quilters that they got to work and replaced all those quilts that were taken from them in the battles they had to fight against nature. One group of five quilts not only were reported to have been saved from a house fire, but survived the 1927

flood. They were made over the years from 1900 to 1925 by Sallie Brown Wilson, wife of a planter and mother of two children. She was the daughter of Irish immigrants; her father came to this country when he was fourteen years old and settled eventually in Camden, Mississippi, where Sallie was born.

Sallie reportedly made "dozens of quilts," all of which were "labors of love and special to her." That is probably the reason she made sure they survived both disasters that visited her family. "She tried to make a quilt for each grandchild as a keep-

Fig. 5.2. "String Star," set in the "Rocky Road to Kansas" pattern, made by Sallie Brown Wilson (1873–1948) of Caile, Sunflower County, Mississippi, circa 1900. This quilt survived the 1927 flood of the Mississippi Delta. Of all-cotton materials, with a brown-and-white checked backing, it is hand-pieced and hand-quilted in an all-over design of fans at 5 stitches per inch; one edge has knife-edge finish. It is 67 inches wide by 76 inches long. MQA quilt no. H-51. Collection of Nancy Sykes, great-granddaughter.

Fig. 5.3. Essie Emaline Epting Myers, October 1904

Fig. 5.4. Essie Emaline Epting Myers with her husband and four sons in 1946

Fig. 5.5. Essie Emaline Epting Myers in 1950

sake," reports one of her granddaughters, who has not only her own special quilt, "Floyce's Butterfly," which is named for her, but a second quilt with eighty different butterflies, and a third one in a segmented "Wheel" design. A "Rocky Road to Kansas" (fig. 5.2) is now owned by a great-grand-daughter. One quilt, made for a grandchild who died at the age of fifteen, is now owned by a great-granddaughter; the family calls it "Dot's Snow-ball," but it is also known as the "Hummingbird" or "Periwinkle."[17]

Mississippi Quilting Continues to Thrive

Quilting, at the beginning of the twentieth century, had generally fallen into disfavor across the United States. There was beginning to be a great population shift from the farm to the city, and women were being attracted to other pursuits. The crazy-quilt fad had passed and was being roundly criticized in publications of the day.

None of this national attitude affected Mississippi quiltmakers in the least. They continued making quilts as they always had. Indeed, it is southern women, particularly the ones who lived in the country, who must be given the credit for keeping the art of quilting alive during this time of great change in the nation at large. A writer in *Scribner's Magazine* saw the trend and defined it as early as 1894: "But it is to the more remote districts of the Southern states that one must go to find this domestic industry carried on most zealously. A . . . correspondent . . . writes thus: 'The quiltmaking is in general confined to the farmer's wives and daughters.'"[18]

This is confirmed by the research done into the making of textiles in Mississippi by Mary Lorenz and Anita Stamper:

The one type of needlework to which virtually . . . every woman referred . . . is quilting. Quilts were valued for their beauty and utility. Martha Jane Mixon . . . made over 360 references to quilting during [her] diary years 1873–1909. Among the identifying terms she used were "Texas Star," "Morning Star," "Mosiac," "Sugar Loaf," "Economy," "Old Maid's Ramble," "Cradle," "Log Cabin," the shell quilting stitch, home-spun quilts, domestic quilts, worsted quilts, and carding cotton to pad the quilt. There were many references to carding cotton for quilts, and apparently the majority of the . . . quilts were filled with cotton. She made many references to cutting scraps or quilt scraps and to sewing on quilt pieces, and to quilting, which would have been stitching the layers together. On one occasion she mentioned putting another quilt in frames.[19]

The documentation effort was fortunate to learn a great deal about one outstanding Mississippi quilter of the first quarter of the twentieth century from a grandson and great-grandson who brought in a stack of about sixteen of her quilts for documenting at the Vicksburg documentation day. The men were not sure of the names of the quilt designs, so they referred to the quilts as "Miss Essie's Quilt #3," or "Miss Essie's Quilt #8." They did, however, know a great deal about "Miss Essie."

Essie Emaline Epting Myers (1885–1963) (figs. 5.3, 5.4, and 5.5) was descended from one of a group of German Lutherans who migrated to Mississippi from South Carolina in the 1830s or 1840s. She had maybe a little better than an eighth grade education, gained from rural and community schools in Smith County, Mississippi, where her husband, John Milton Myers, taught. She and her husband also farmed, and she made her own cheese and butter.

She raised four sons, and it was for her menfolk that she made her twenty or so quilts, which are still in the possession of the family (fig. 5.6). She got her quilt patterns from her mother, her imagination, and farm magazines. Her quilting designs came mostly from her mother and other family members. The tops she pieced were usually of fabric scraps she saved from sewing for family members, and she gladly took sewing scraps from other sources. She inspired others of her family to learn how to quilt by providing them with a pieced top.

Miss Essie encouraged family members to save printed chicken-feed sacks for use in quilting. She dyed unprinted chicken- or cattle-feed sacks for use as quilt backings; red was a favorite color, and she used it often. (Some of the backings are now pink, the result of many washings.)

"She continued to piece quilts, well into the late 1950s [when she would have been in her seventies]. She may have been assisted in some quilting by others in neighborhood, especially her mother, Mrs. Mary Ida Elizabeth (Roberts) Epting (1860–1926); her mother-in-law, Mrs. Rebecca (Boykin) Myers (1846–1921), or her sister-in-law, Mrs. Levic Bell (Shots) Myers."[20]

Miss Essie's quilting frame, sewing machine, and some sewing tools are still held in the Myers family. Two of the great-grandson's favorite quilts made by Miss Essie were special single-bed-sized quilts made for his father in the late 1950s. Some of her quilts brought in for documentation were a "Bird of Paradise" variation, circa 1920; "Necktie," 1920s; "Pinwheel," 1920s; "Dove in the Window," 1930s; a nine-patch variation known as "Proof thru the Night," circa 1910; another "Nine-Patch," circa 1920; and "Flock of Birds," from the 1900–1910 period.

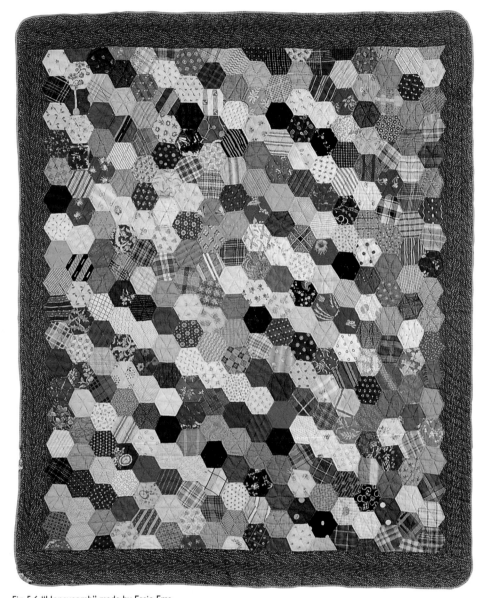

Fig. 5.6. "Honeycomb" made by Essie Emaline Epting Myers in Raleigh, Smith County, Mississippi, circa 1900. Of all-cotton materials, with woven shirting for backing, it is hand-pieced and hand-quilted in an overall design of hanging diamonds. It is 83 inches long by 67.5 inches wide. MQA quilt no. E-17. Collection of William M. Myers, grandson.

Not for Women Only

Many other men brought quilts in to be documented, and those quilts were clearly as dear to them as anything they owned. Quilts provide a tactile link to the past and to a particular person in a way unequaled by other artifacts. It is comforting to hold a quilt and know that a loved one touched it years ago. There are very few things in our lives that come to us charged with as much emotion as quilts, and men can be just as sentimental about them as women.

One man brought in a wonderful "New York Beauty" from his great-grandmother, Elizabeth Anderson Thoms. She was born in 1841, perhaps in Alabama, and was sent to school in Edinburgh, Scotland. On her return voyage to America, she met her future husband, who took her to Vaiden, Mississippi, where she lived the rest of her life. She had two children, one of whom was the present owner's grandfather. Her quilting legacy lives on, through her great-grandson and one superlative piece.[21]

But, men didn't just collect quilts. "Their mother taught all of them, boys included, to quilt," states the daughter of one of sixteen brothers and sisters in Covington County, south Mississippi.[22] This writer's father-in-law, who is from Sunrise, in Forest County, Mississippi, regularly quilted with his mother throughout the late 1920s and early 1930s. He recalls, "She had so much work to do, I just wanted to help her out."[23] (He also plowed with a mule and made two bales of cotton on two acres of farmland his father let him have in 1930.)

Men's participation in quilting may have been, for the most part, as helpers. One of the things they did was to help cut out the pieces. A story from 1900 tells about five-year-old twin girls, Mary Carpenter and Martha Russell, who undertook to make a one-patch quilt. Their grandfather, W. J. Lang, cut out the squares for them. Their mother, Louella Russell, and both their grandmothers, Martha Russell and Fanny Lang, also helped. It turned out really well with all that expert help.[24]

Women reported that their husbands, brothers, uncles, or some man in their life had made them a set of quilting frames. Sometimes the man would help her install the frames in the room she specified. And sometimes, the two of them quilted together (as recalled by Estabelle Reid on p. 126).

There were some instances of men making entire quilts, as in the examples of the Civil War veterans who could not work after the war because of their injuries. A similar experience caused the making of "Rock Garden," a four-point star quilt done in red and green, set on a yellow background, and bordered in red. Family history says that this quilt was made in 1930 by a six-year-old boy who was unable, because of an illness, to attend school for about six weeks. He had a little help from his mother.[25] One man, Jess Williams, had an artificial leg which restricted his activity, so he and his wife, Mable, worked on quilts and other crafts together. They made a spectacular appliquéd "Butterfly" quilt in the late 1920s or early 1930s of twenty-one black cotton velvet butterflies set onto a yellow cotton satin background. The butterfly blocks alternate with black cotton velvet blocks, and the outer edges of the quilt are scalloped and bound in the black fabric. The quilting, all by hand, is some of the best the documentation team saw and includes feathered wreaths quilted in the plain black blocks at nine stitches per inch.[26]

Another man made four quilts, and it appears that he did it just because he liked to piece on the treadle sewing machine, although he did suffer from tuberculosis and may not have been able to be active. The quilt that was brought in for documenting is in navy and white solid fabrics in a very intricate feathered square design know as "Danger Signal." He machine-quilted this piece, which he made about 1900, even signing it in machine stitching with his full name, William Carpenter. He lived in Dry Creek in Prentiss County, Mississippi, and was a "fine Christian man."[27]

The Popularity of Piecing

But quilting was generally a woman's passion, and they were passionate about patchwork; the overwhelming majority of quilts from this time period were pieced. Many of the designs from the preceding years were refined and made smaller, almost miniaturized (see fig. 5.7). It looks in some instances as though the quilter was being a bit competitive—trying to see how many pieces she could put in a quilt. A tiny "Nine-Patch" from Amite County, made about 1900, contains 324 little blocks in a quilt that is only seventy inches wide and seventy-one inches long. It was made by Edith Haag Ashley of Gloster for her hope chest, and she set her little blocks on point, spacing them with pink setting squares, then finishing with pink-and-white stripped borders.[28] Another tiny "Nine-Patch" was also made about 1900 by Carrie Stroud in Meridian, but she set her 210 four-inch blocks into straight rows, spacing them with plain blocks from a brown "chicken-wire" print.[29]

Feathered edges of the type that was so popular at the end of the nineteenth century continued to be used to embellish and enhance otherwise plain designs. The redoubtable Essie Myers used a double feathered edge around a plain square to make a design known as "Flock of Birds" around 1910.[30] But new uses were also found for feathering. One clever quilter turned a "Pickle Dish," the design made with feathered strips shaped into an oval, into

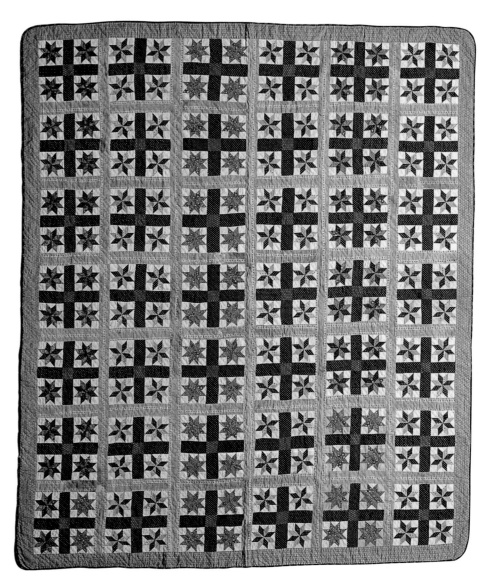

Fig. 5.7. "Tiny LeMoyne Star" made by Mary Louise Duke Pace, probably in Lee County, Mississippi, in the 1900–1910 period. Initialed "LM" on the back, the quilt has cotton materials for top and backing and a wool batting. Hand-pieced and quilted at 6 stitches per inch in an all-over diagonal design, it is 74 inches wide by 87 inches long. MQA quilt no. P-101. Collection of Jo Ann Wolf, cousin.

Fig. 5.8. "Lone Star," called "Texas Star" by the family, made by Virginia Chadwick Barnett, mother of former Mississippi governor Ross Barnett, in Standing Pine, Leake County, Mississippi, in the 1910–1920 period. Quilt has all-cotton materials, and the cotton batting still contains some seeds; it is hand-pieced and quilted with two colors of quilting thread (black and white) by the piece and in the background. The quilt measures 73.5 inches wide by 80 inches long. MQA quilt no. D-123. Collection of Virginia McMullen, granddaughter.

Fig. 5.9. "Star of Bethlehem," maker unknown, from the Ollhoff estate in Meridian, Mississippi, circa 1920s. Of all-cotton materials, backed with natural-colored cheesecloth and hand-pieced and quilted by the piece, it is 65 inches wide by 74 inches long. MQA quilt no. D-01. Collection of Nannie Beall.

Fig. 5.10. "New York Beauty," called "Sunset" by the family, made by Alma and Ella Gookin, nieces of President Jefferson Davis, in Corinth, Alcorn County, Mississippi, circa 1925. Quilt of all-cotton materials is hand-pieced, with some machine work, and hand-quilted by the piece at 6 stitches per inch. A knife-edged finish is on one side of quilt, the front is brought to the back on one side, and a single-fold applied binding is on the other two sides. MQA quilt no. P-35. Collection of Jeff Perrigo.

an "Airplane" by adding outriggers to the widest part of the oval, which was then visually transformed into the body of the plane.[31] A "Birds in the Air" was made into a "Diamondback" snake by planning the feathered strips to zigzag horizontally across the quilt.[32] (The maker inserted feathered strips into the center of rectangles, which she set side by side to make this very interesting quilt.)

A beautiful design pieced of red and green diamonds and triangles, called "Sugar Loaf," was discovered in a quilt made in Pike County in 1910.[33] It is a good example of a "best" quilt from this time period. The precise geometry of the pieced pattern is complemented by the clean white triangles against which it is set. It contains double borders on all four sides, with a planned change of color from the sides to the top and bottom—green and white on one, red and white on the other.

Stars, especially those pieced of myriad diamonds, were a widespread choice as a quilt motif. The "Lone Star," also called "Star of Bethlehem" or "Texas Star," was made more often during this time than in years before (see figs. 5.8 and 5.9). A variation, the "Broken Star," in which the central star is surrounded by twenty-four diamond-pieced segments, also began showing up in significant numbers. "Star of Bethlehem" was sized down and used as a repeat-block motif, sometimes called "Harvest Sun," "Blazing Star," or "Civil War Star."[34] One star quilt shows the trend toward miniaturization that seems to have been a bit of a trend during this time: four-inch "LeMoyne Stars" are packed onto a medium-sized quilt so that 168 of them twinkle and twirl across the surface (fig. 5.7).

The first thirty years of the twentieth century also saw the enthusiastic use of many one-patch designs. Examples of this type of quilt are the "Honeycomb" made by Essie Myers, shown in figure 5.6, and other such quilts made of one shape

repeated until the desired size of the quilt is reached. As devotion to this type of quilt grew, curved and interlocking designs such as "Clamshell" and "Double Ax" would begin to be seen in the state's quilts, but at this stage, shapes were limited primarily to squares, rectangles, octagons, and hexagons.

Rectangles were set into one of two styles: "Brick Wall" and "Hit or Miss." Twenty of the first

Fig. 5.11. "Brick Wall," called "Brick Quilt" by the family, possibly made by Maude Englehardt in Gulfport, Mississippi, in the 1920s. Made from worn men's woolen suits, with a woven gingham backing and a worn woolen World War I army blanket for batting, it is machine-pieced, hand-embroidered in red, and hand-quilted at 4 stitches per inch. It is 70 inches wide by 81 inches long. MQA quilt no. J-59. Collection of Ursula Ruth Jones, great niece.

and sixteen of the second were documented. "Brick Wall" (fig. 5.11) has staggered rows of rectangles, so the seamlines do not align; in "Hit or Miss," the seams are all lined up. (Or, the attempt is made to line them up, which perhaps provides the origin of the name!) Both designs appear to have been used mainly as a way of utilizing wool scraps, particularly men's suiting material. A few of these quilts were made from excess fabric cut off the ends of pants legs during the hemming of men's trousers. In many of the quilts, the seams were embellished with hand embroidery, often in colors such as red or pink, providing a bright accent to the blacks, grays, dark blues, browns, and tans of the woolen fabrics. The same general repertoire of stitches used on crazy quilts is found on these one-patch woolen quilts.

The only double-sided quilt to be found in the documentation effort was a variation of "Brick Wall" with the intriguing name of "Hairpin Catcher." It is made with squares, with every alternating one colored black. All the fabrics except three are solids, in pale green, pale blue, and pink; there is a medium-toned violet, a blue, orange, and white print, and two different red-and-white prints. The quilt is the same on both sides. Although it is probably a utility quilt, the piecing is very precise, with all the corners matching perfectly. It was made in the 1920s in Cockrum, DeSoto County, Mississippi, by Betty Bowen Eason (1864–1960), a homemaker and farmer. This mother of seven children had only a fourth grade education, yet she wrote her autobiography over a period of thirty years, with mention of it being made in the Memphis *Commercial Appeal*, in Eldon Roark's column, "Strolling."[35]

There were some "Hit or Miss" and "Brick Wall" quilts done in cottons. One, made of squares,

has the colors arranged so that it looks to be made of long strips that are woven over and under one another.[36] In another, each row of rectangles is pieced of two fabrics, a light and a dark, which adds to the visual energy of the quilt.[37] A similar piece was done with tobacco sacks dyed black and yellow; the documentation form said, "Used to lay out my son on when he died. It was the only time it was used."[38] This "Brick Wall," or "Zigzag," quilt is one of two (of those found in the documentation effort) that were used in funerals; the other is a "Double Wedding Ring," which was draped over its maker's casket (p. 129).

That well-loved motif, the pineapple, was the subject of one of the very few appliquéd quilts from the first thirty years of the new century. It was made by Geneva B. Redus in Hattiesburg and quilted by a lady in Corsicana, Texas, with very fine, close quilting at nine stitches per inch.[39] This "Pineapple" is different from earlier examples in that it is much more realistic. It is rendered in red, with lots of green leaves and stems; there are twelve of them set on a white background.

One of the most distinctive quilts in the survey could not be obtained for photography. Called the "Adkins Quilt" by the family, it is made of alphabet blocks that are arranged so that the names of the mother, Sudie Adkins, the father, D. A. ("Davie") Adkins, and the son, Joseph Dillard Adkins, are spelled out. Sudie died when her only son was very young, but her husband stored the quilt away and gave it to Dillard Adkins upon the occasion of his marriage.[40] It was made about 1924 or 1925 and is illustrative of the type of independent thinking and creativity that were typical of Mississippi quiltmaking in the first quarter of the twentieth century.

String Quilts

Surely this Bible verse, Mark 2:21, was familiar to many a Mississippi quilter and inspired her not only in her daily mending of worn garments, but in her quilting as well.

No one sews a patch of unshrunk cloth
onto an old garment; if he does, the patch
tears away from it, the new from the old,
and leaves a bigger hole.

There is no better endorsement for the technique of string quilting, which is basically a way of using any little scrap of fabric one might have, no matter how small, how worn, or how many uses it has been put to before. In fact, the term "string" is said to come from "apron string," because some housewives were so thrifty they recycled even the ties from their worn-out aprons for quilts. A more accurate definition of "string" is that it is a scrap that is longer than it is wide.

String quilts have always been popular in the South, but the Amish of Pennsylvania, Ohio, and Indiana, who were also farmers, like most southerners of this time, made them too. The string method is a good one for the type of loosely woven fabrics found in some of the feed and flour sacks that were commonplace on a farm. The piecing of these quilts does not require precision, which is not really possible with coarse fabrics.[41] String quilts are made in a random patchwork style, usually on a foundation fabric or paper. (Although they employ the same techniques as crazy quilts, string quilts were made for a completely different reason. They were made to be used, and crazy quilts were for show.) String quilts may be made by hand, by machine, or with a combination of the two methods.

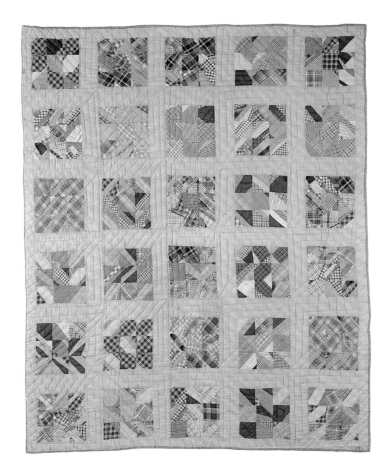

Fig. 5.12. "Nine Patch String Quilt" made by Ora Richardson of Little Rock (Newton County), Mississippi, in 1924. Of all-cotton materials, it is hand-quilted all over in "ells." It is 71 inches wide and 84 inches long. MQA quilt no. D-87. Collection of Shirley Hutcherson, great-niece.

Many of these quilts are ingenious in their use of pattern. The basic building block for a string quilt is most often a square, onto which the strings are laid diagonally. It appears, from examining Mississippi string quilts, that it is instinctive on the part of string piecers to place the wider strings across the center of the square and the narrower ones toward the outer edges; again and again this sort of placement was repeated. In some instances, the center strings in the square would be made from the same fabric, so that when four squares were put together, an X of color would appear. With the addition of sashing around each group of four,

Fig. 5.13. "String Quilt" made by Julia Pitts Shannon (1890–1982) of Pontotoc, Mississippi, in the 1930s. Of all-cotton materials, it is hand-pieced and hand-quilted in an all-over square grid at 5 stitches per inch and is 75 inches wide by 83 inches long. MQA quilt no. K-53. Collection of Irene T. Guthrie, granddaughter.

such quilts would take on an appearance resembling that of a regular pieced quilt.

Once the basic string squares were made, they could be set together any number of ways: placed cheek-by-jowl, with no alternate setting blocks or sashing; gathered into four-patch or nine-patch blocks, then set with sashing; or spaced with setting blocks with or without sashing. And sometimes, the sashing itself was string-pieced, and used with string-pieced squares, to make a real puzzle of a quilt.

Shapes other than squares were used, with the second most popular one being a triangle. String triangles can be fitted together to make a square, with seamlines making an X across the center. If the fabrics are planned so that the same diamond of fabric is in the center of each triangle, a star will emerge (fig. 5.19). Another kind of string star is made when the background of the quilt is string-pieced, utilizing a diamond shape, and fitted around solid-fabric diamonds, which emerge as four-point stars (figs. 5.2 and 5.20). Yet a third type of "String Star" is one in which the eight diamonds that compose a "Star of LeMoyne" are string-pieced. Such a quilt was made by Lois Cagle Clingan of Tishomingo County; she used fertilizer sacks for the backing and, since she had no money to buy thread, saved the thread from the sacks and "divided it like embroidery thread and used it to piece and quilt with."[42]

Some quilters laid their strings straight across the squares and set the squares together alternating the direction of the strings, so that their finished quilts resemble woven ribbons. Or, they elected to make long strips of strings and set them together with sashing, in a design called "Roman Stripe," like the one made by Lizzie Berryhill Miles in Winston County, Mississippi, about 1915; she made her sashing with a pink and a blue strip and finished the sides with the same.[43] Mrs. Miles's quilt is a

Fig. 5.14. "Michigan," a string quilt made by Della Ahrend Pahnka of Lorman, Jefferson County, Mississippi, in the 1920s. Of all-cotton materials, it is hand-pieced and hand-quilted in an all-over fan pattern at 3 stitches per inch and is 64 inches wide by 79 inches long. MQA quilt no. K-02. Collection of Linda R. Stuart, granddaughter.

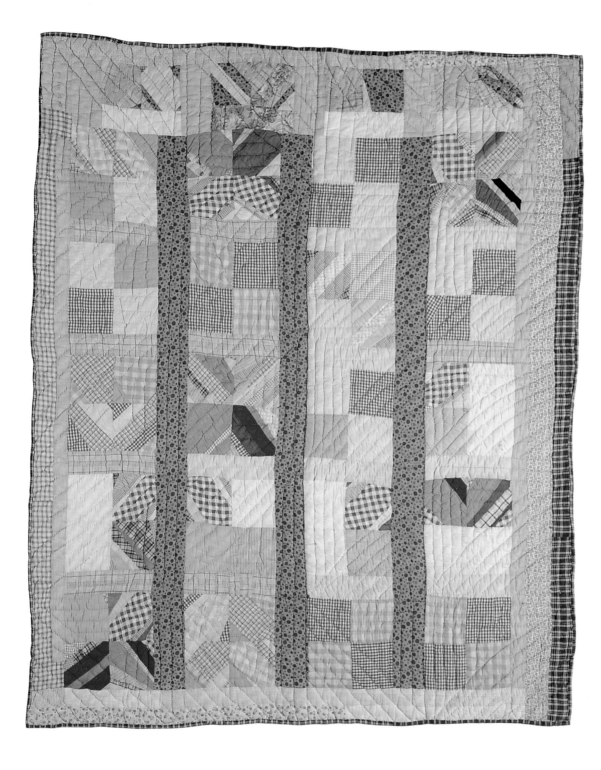

Fig. 5.15. "Four-Patch" string quilt made by Ora Richardson (1902–1989) of Little Rock, Newton County, Mississippi, in 1928. Of all-cotton materials, it is hand-pieced and hand-quilted in an all-over design of right angles and diagonals and is 65 inches wide by 80.5 inches long. MQA quilt no. D-88. Collection of Shirley Hutcherson, great-niece.

Fig. 5.16. Ora Richardson (1902–1989), maker of the "Four-Patch" string quilt, circa 1928

Fig. 5.17. "Nine-Patch" string quilt made by Tchula Walker Webb of Sturgis, Oktibbeha County, Mississippi, in the 1930s. Made of all-cotton materials, mostly old clothes, and backed with a cowboy print, it is hand-pieced, with some machine work, and hand-quilted in an all-over design of right angles with green thread at 4 stitches per inch. It is 66 inches wide by 77 inches long. MQA quilt no. H-75. Collection of Dina Ellis, niece.

Fig. 5.18. "Mother's Choice" string quilt, called "Christmas Gift Quilt" by the family, made by Arvie Dale (Smith) Pinnex (Mrs. Joseph) Clemons (1885–1965) of Hamilton, Mississippi. Signed in embroidery by the maker, it was made for her grandson, George Clemons Pittman, for Christmas 1941; George was 4 years old at the time, and one of 16 grandchildren for whom Mrs. Clemons made gift quilts. Quilt is all-cotton materials, string blocks are hand-pieced, and red circles are appliquéd by hand with a blind stitch. Hand-quilted by hand in a design of repeated sets of concentric circles at 5 stitches per inch, it is 64.5 inches wide by 83 inches long. MQA quilt no. C-69. Collection of Alicia Pittman.

Fig. 5.19. "Spiderweb," maker unknown, found in mother-in-law's closet after her death, circa 1930. Of all-cotton materials, with a black-and-white checked star in the center of each block, surrounded by scraps of all colors, it is machine-pieced, with tan feed sacks for backing, and hand-quilted by the piece. It is 64 inches wide by 76 inches long. MQA quilt no. C-68. Collection of Ann Lee, daughter-in-law.

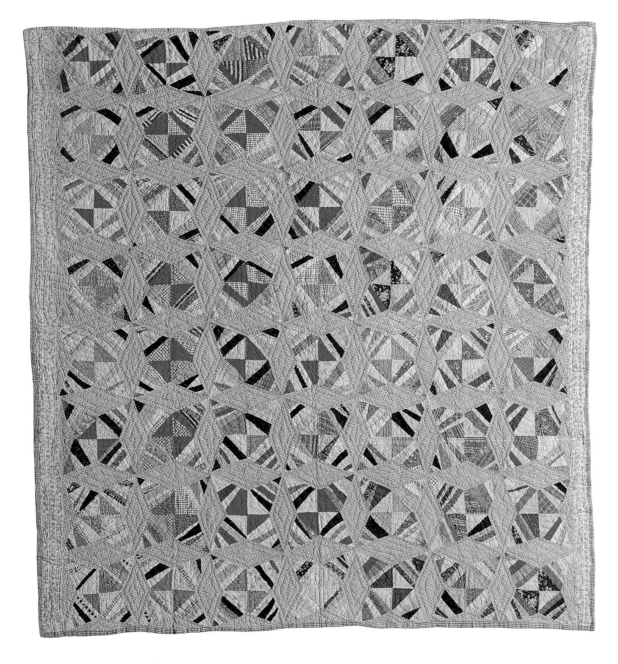

Fig. 5.20. "Rocky Road to Kansas," called "Newspaper Quilt" by the family, made by Nancy Ellis Self (1832–1903) of the Oktoc community, Oktibbeha County, Mississippi, in the 1890s. A granddaughter, Nancy Rawls Graver Oakley (1894–1972), remembered cutting newspaper templates for it as a child. The quilt has always been stored in a special pine quilt-box, which is still in the family. Of all-cotton materials, it is hand-pieced and hand-quilted at 5 stitches per inch and is 67 inches wide by 71 inches long. MQA quilt no. N-09. Collection of Warren (grandson) and Mary Oakley.

veritable catalog of fabrics from the early 1900s, and she arranged her strips so that she had the darks in one strip, the yellows in another, and so on. She was a very careful quiltmaker, as indicated by her seven-stitches-to-the-inch quilting, pretty fine for a string quilt.

African American Quilts of the Twentieth Century

One hope of the Heritage Quilt Search Project was that quilts made by women (or men) of color would play a large part, but there were relatively few quilts whose provenance could be determined as African American. Consequently, the few that were discovered were regarded as rare clues to a past that has yet to be fully revealed. The dozen or so African American quilts documented tend to support the theory that quilts made by women of color look just the same as quilts made by white women—the same patterns were used, the same materials, and the same way of working. There was no distinct and different aesthetic that identified a quilt as African American. This is contrary to a popular notion, circulated in the early 1990s, that quilt-makers of African heritage worked with some sort of subconscious design imperative retained from their ancestors in Africa—such as working in strips, haphazard settings, and so on. The findings in Mississippi concur with those of Cuesta Benberry (an outstanding quilt historian whose scholarship is impeccable), who holds the premise that African American quilts differ in no discernible way from Anglo quilts; and, although perhaps not credited, they were always there, blending quietly into the material culture, as do so many anonymous quilts.

Of special interest to the study of Mississippi

quilts was Benberry's discovery of a quilt made in Natchez around 1900 by Sarah Miller, who came from a family of "black Creoles, or as they were historically termed, Creoles of color. In Louisiana and the Gulf States, interracial descendants of French and African parentage formed a large and distinct ethnic group. . . . Although Creoles of color were partially African, they identified more with the French than with the blacks. They spoke the French language, practiced the Catholic religion, and were oriented toward the French culture. Many of the wealthy colored Creoles sent their children to France to be educated."[44]

The French influence is quite pronounced in Sarah Miller's quilt: thirty-two fleur-de-lis motifs are appliquéd in two rows surrounding a central medallion. The central design is unique; it is derived from the fleur-de-lis motif and incorporates heart shapes. Only navy and white fabrics are used, and fine quilting complements the precise appliqué of the motifs. The quilt has descended through several generations to the present owner.

Mother-daughter quilting was documented in a group of quilts made by an African American woman and her daughter from Newton County, Mississippi (figs. 5.21, 5.22, and 5.23). The mother was Crossie Barks Billingsley Leonard (1865–1957), born on July 5 to Minerva Aldridge Barks and Louis Barks, their first free-born child. Della Billingsley Posey, a teacher, was the daughter of Crossie Barks and Henry "Tab" Billingsley and learned her quilting skills from her mother. Mrs. Leonard made a "Pomegranate" quilt (see p. 76) from fabrics she special ordered from either the almanac, the Sears catalog, or *Progressive Farmer* magazine. She also bought the fabric for a "Monkey Wrench" quilt through the same source.[45]

Mrs. Leonard's quilts were her hobby, but her daughter, Mrs. Posey (1893–1997), quilted more out

Fig. 5.21. "Spider's Den" made by Crossie Barks Billingsley Leonard (1865–1957) of Newton County, Mississippi, in the 1900–1920 period. Of all-cotton materials, with solid fabrics for top and "yellow domestic" (family name) for backing, it is hand-pieced and hand-quilted by the piece at 5 stitches per inch. It is 64.5 inches wide by 85 inches long. MQA quilt no. Q-20. Collection of Ponjola Posey Andrews, granddaughter.

of necessity than for pleasure, according to her daughter, Ponjola Posey Andrews. It was not that Mrs. Posey didn't enjoy making her quilts—"She was still thinking about quilting at 97 years of age, when she died"—but she made them as cover during hard times, when there was little with which to work. Some of the fabrics in her "Bow Tie" quilt (fig. 5.23) are from old clothing, but Mrs. Posey also shared Mrs. Leonard's mail-order scraps; this was definitely the case with a quilt that was not documented named "Sunburst," which Mrs. Andrews described as "primarily blue and white in the center, then filled in with scraps." The backing on the "Bow Tie" quilt is made from fertilizer sacks dyed with red clay and set with copperas. Ponjola Andrews remembers that her mother also used elderberries to dye some of the fabrics she used in her quilts.[46]

The cotton for the quilt batting was scrapped from the field at the end of the season. Often the Leonards and the Poseys would have these "end scrappings" ginned at the local gin; if not, they would pick the seeds out by hand. In either case, they hand-carded the batts. In sum, this family obtained the materials for their quilts from a variety of sources, buying new materials through mail-order, taking their batting and dyestuffs from the land, and recycling fertilizer sacks. Although the methods of obtaining materials may be better documented in this family than in others, they are by no means unique. Other families, white as well as black, were intimately familiar with the same procedures.

An African American family quilt in the design known as "Spool" or "Bow Tie" was brought in to the Meridian quilt documentation day by Mattie Davis, whose great-aunt, Julie Moore, had been an exceptional person. "She could neither read nor write, and worked in the field much of her life, but

Fig. 5.22. "Broken Dishes," called "Pin-wheel" by the family, made by Crossie Barks Billingsley Leonard (1865–1957) of Newton County, Mississippi, in the 1900–1920 period. Of all-cotton materials, with another quilt used as batting, it is hand-pieced and hand-quilted in an over-all pattern of right angles and is 65 inches wide by 74 inches long. MQA quilt no. Q-21. Collection of Ponjola Posey Andrews, granddaughter.

she and her husband worked together to build their own house after they were in their eightieth year," said Mrs. Davis. Mr. and Mrs. Moore were sharecroppers and, later, cemetery attendants. Mrs. Davis recalls helping to pick the seeds out of the cotton that had been scrapped from the field to use as batting for the more than one dozen quilts made by Mrs. Moore. Neighbors often came to quilt, and they would help with each others' quilts. Sometimes they set the quilt frames up in the yard.[47]

The Smith-Robertson Museum in Jackson is devoted to African American artifacts, and within its collections is a grouping of eighteen quilts, most of which are anonymous and were made after 1945, past the cutoff time for this particular documentation project. The Smith-Robertson Museum also now holds some of the African American quilts that were previously housed at the Center for Southern Culture in Oxford; most of these are also late twentieth century. (A great gathering of Mississippi quilts and quilters is presented in Roland Freeman's excellent book, *A Communion of the Spirits*, but these are also post-1945, beyond the time span for this search.)

Among those quilts in the Smith-Robertson collection which are worthy of note is an interesting flag quilt. It is the oldest quilt in the collection and dates to the period of 1860–1880. The quilt is a flag quilt but is clearly not meant to be a duplication of the American flag, but a representation of it (fig. 5.24). It contains forty-two stars and twenty-four stripes and is tied, not quilted.

At least three quilts were made by African American nurses for their white charges, and are still held dear by the white families who own them. Edna Lee Williams, who raised two children for a white family in the Delta, gave them a quilt she made for the children to nap on. It is pieced in browns and blues, with a few pinks thrown in, and

the pieced blocks are set on point against solid red setting blocks. The red really speaks out; it would have been a rather pedestrian quilt, with its big pieces and dull colors, but the red made it quite striking. It is backed with solid white domestic and quilted in a random utility pattern. The family just called it "Edna's Quilt."[48]

A quilt was made by Sharah Ann ("Patience") Shepperdson (Mrs. Edmund) in Sunflower County for her charge, Robbie Martin, in 1932. Mrs. Martin wrote an extensive and fascinating documentation of all the materials in the quilt, beginning with the

Fig. 5.23. "Bow Tie," called "Gentleman's Neck Tie" by the family, made by Della Billingsley Posey (1893–1997) of Newton County, Mississippi, in 1930. Of all-cotton materials, with a backing of fertilizer sacks dyed with red clay and copperas, it is hand-pieced and hand-quilted and is 77 inches wide by 78.5 inches long. MQA quilt no. Q-22. Collection of Ponjola Posey Andrews, granddaughter.

Fig. 5.24. "Flag," provenance unknown, believed to be African American, in the 1860–1880 period. Of all-cotton materials, it is hand-pieced, hand-appliquéd, and tied or tacked with blue thread in a random pattern. It is 78 inches wide by 57.5 inches long (wider than it is long). Collection of the Smith-Robertson Museum, first documented by the Center for Southern Culture at the University of Mississippi.

Fig. 5.25. Sashed "Drunkard's Path," provenance unknown, believed to be African American, circa 1930. All cotton materials, hand-pieced and hand-quilted in irregular sweeps. It is 71 inches by 84 inches long. MQA quilt no. SR-10. Collection of the Smith-Robertson Museum.

batting, which was made of the samples that the men who graded cotton extracted from each bale. The sample would have been ginned, meaning the seeds would have been removed, but it had yet to be carded. Patience did the carding with her set of cards, "two flat little wooden paddles with little metal pins sticking up," that were ordered from Sears. Mrs. Martin wrote that the fabrics of the top of the quilt were made from the "best pieces of worn-out garments. At the store, my mother sold bolt material for fifteen cents a yard. This was the Depression and no money—all new cloth was used in clothes. This quilt has my brother's shirts and sister's dresses along with my own." She even specified that the quilting was done with "Number 8

Mercerized Heavy Duty Coats Cotton Thread, [which was first manufactured] in 1850." The back of the quilt was made from sugar and salt sacks which were "ripped open and boiled in the wash pot. . . . This quilt had a whole year of sacks including sugar for jams and jellies. The salt was used for curing hog meat."[49]

Mrs. Martin gave a very detailed description of the making of a set of quilting frames:

Made by J. R. Martin were poles three inches wide by one inch thick by seventy-two inches long. With a brace and bit he bored about five holes four inches apart from the ends of each pole. The quilt was wrapped around the poles on all four sides. The ends overlapped and a ten-penny nail dropped in each hole to hold it together. You took out the nails to let out or roll up the quilt, and re-placed them in different holes. Heavy cord string was attached to all four corners and run through pulleys in the ceiling. These cords were pulled even to lower or raise the quilt. When [the quilt] was lowered to three feet off the floor, the quilters could sit in cane-bottomed chairs on all four sides and work.[50]

The quilt about which all this technical information is furnished is a very interesting "Checkerboard Geometric." At first glance, it looks like a regular twenty-five-patch block, but closer inspection reveals several unusual details: first, the block is constructed with rectangles, not squares; and second, the rectangles are set in diagonal rows within each block. There are fourteen rectangles in each block, set in rows, from outside to the center, of one, two, and four, then back to outside again with four, two, and one. Triangles are inserted at the corners and sides of the block to make it square. Each block is worked in a light-dark set to make the "Checkerboard" effect. Although it was obviously made as a utility quilt, it is clear that Patience loved to piece and that this was not her first quilt.

A remarkable textile, now in the New England Quilt Museum, was made in Mississippi a decade before the century turned, in 1890. Former slaves of Dixie Plantation, which was said to be near Garden City (Franklin County), Mississippi, joined with northern whites and friends of the plantation owner to make a quilt (fig. 5.27) for A. V. and Cynthia Ball, who were returning to New England after a thirty-year stay in this southwestern Mississippi county. They were related to John Whitehead, the owner of Dixie Plantation, because both his children (a son and a daughter) married Balls—a sister

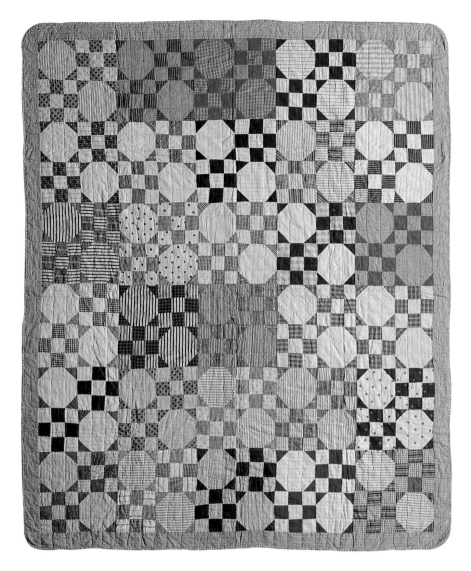

and a brother. It is not clear what drew the two families together in the beginning, but that they were very close is certain. Any number of visitors came down to Franklin and Lincoln Counties (the Whitehead daughter and her husband, Fred Ball, lived in Brookhaven), spending protracted stays at a hotel named the St. James, which was a sort of colony for northerners.

The plan for making the quilt was that each

Fig. 5.26. "Snowball and Nine-Patch," called "Mammie's Quilt" by the family, made by Mattie Smith of Thomaston, Georgia, circa 1900, and brought to Mississippi in 1967. Of all-cotton materials, it is hand-pieced and hand-quilted in an all-over grid pattern and is 65 inches wide by 79 inches long. MQA quilt no. C-147. Collection of Rose Wilson.

person would contribute a block, and their name would be inscribed on the white sashing strips next to the block. One person, a Ball relation, wrote all the names in pencil; it was not until fifty years later, in 1940, that another Ball descendent began embroidering over the penciled names. Occasionally, the signee (or the scribe) would include a personal notation: "Mrs. James Mitchell, Post Master's wife," or, "Nellie Ball, Fred's sister, married Shep Whitehead. So you can see the old plantation are our folks." The first four rows of names appear to be those of the northerners who came to visit at the St. James Hotel; the next four rows were the names of southern white people; the final five rows are freed slaves and other African Americans. Their inscriptions say things like "Aunt Elizabeth Dean, Slave," "Aunt Jane Holmes, Slave," and "Fannie Voyse 'Old Aunt E-'dee Slave of another plantation owner." The top was put together, but the piece was never quilted, and few of the names were embroidered in thread.[51]

Summary

Scrappy folks make scrappy quilts. The Merriam-Webster dictionary defines scrappy as "having an aggressive and determined spirit." Could there be a better description of the typical Mississippi quiltmaker? Those who can survive on whatever God gives them, no matter how little, can make quilts out of whatever is at hand. Even if there were only scraps, defined in the dictionary as "pieces, fragments, discarded material, or refuse," those scraps were worked into quilts that also have an aggressive and determined spirit, just like their makers.

To the twenty-first-century quiltmaker, the term "scrappy" means a quilt that is full of life and many different fabrics—a quilt so desirable that today's quiltmaker often deliberately makes scraps just to sew into a scrappy quilt!

Without question, the quilts of the first quarter of the twentieth century reflect a different design ethic from those of the final quarter of the nineteenth, almost as though a subtle change had come over quiltmaking as the century turned. Although the number of quilts that were made increased, there appears to have been a different attitude toward them—they were not so lavish in design, color use, or technique. The quilts are more straightforward in their presentation, much less fanciful. The emphasis is on technique and layout of the motifs on the quilt, not on invention nor experimentation. There are far fewer quilts that look to have been made with fabric purchased especially for the quilt—nearly all the quilts from this period appear to have been made from the scrap bag. Indeed, the overriding characteristic of the quilts of this time is that they are made of scraps.

The ultimate scrap quilt is the string quilt. The technique began to show up in a few quilts from the 1875–1900 period, and since that time literally thousands of string quilts have been made in Mississippi, and they continue to be made to this day. Although quite a few, about thirty-five, string quilts were documented, we can be sure that many more were made and have been used up over the years. They are the ultimate utility quilt, and, as such, they generally get the roughest treatment. And, because of their lack of status, they were probably left behind by their owners, who took other quilts to be documented.

Fig. 5.27. "Mississippi Friendship Quilt" made by former slaves of Dixie Plantation, guests at St. James Hotel, and residents of Franklin and Lincoln Counties in Garden City, Mississippi, circa 1890. It is a cotton quilt top, hand-pieced and hand-embroidered, and is 83.5 inches wide by 90.5 inches long. Collection of the New England Quilt Museum.

CHAPTER SIX

The Golden Age of Mississippi Quiltmaking
1930–1945

There were snow-white curtains of wiry lace at the window, and a lace bedspread belonged on the bed. But what old Solomon slept so sound under was a big feather-stitched piece-quilt in the pattern "Trip around the World," which had twenty-one different colors, four hundred and forty pieces, and a thousand yards of thread, and that was what Solomon's mother made in her life and old age.

—Eudora Welty, "Livvie"

EVEN AS THE NATION SUFFERED through the greatest economic disaster known to modern history, quiltmaking in Mississippi flourished. It has been said that most people in the state were already so poor that they didn't notice there was a depression going on. That may not be entirely true, because, as one relief worker wrote to Governor Martin S. Conner in 1933, "Families lack sheets, pillow cases, and towels. Their quilts, which served for every purpose, have been reduced to shreds. Most people own no underwear and many times have only one outer garment."[1]

The Great Depression began not, as is commonly thought, with the stock market crash of 1929—that was merely the most distinctly observable event—but with the overproduction of consumer goods in the 1920s. The national economy

that drove the Roaring Twenties was one based on making household goods such as washing machines, linoleum, and vacuum cleaners as well as developing the new technology of telephones, radios, and movies. Also, great building programs were underway for highways, airports, and other public facilities. People were captivated by all the new products available to make their lives easier, and many took advantage of payment plans when they didn't have cash, in order to live with unaccustomed time- and labor-saving luxuries. By the late twenties, everyone who could manage to somehow pay for these new products had them; however, manufacturers did not scale back, and factories continued production based on sales projections that had steadily risen for several years. "With the leveling of consumption from 1925 to

Small town, Mississippi, in the early 1940s. Photograph by Eudora Welty. Photograph courtesy of the Eudora Welty Collection, Mississippi Department of Archives and History.

125

1929, these industries soon found themselves over-producing. A recession began, with the resultant layoffs and further drops in consumption. Some 5000 banks failed before 1929."[2]

Over nine million savings accounts were wiped out, hundreds of thousands of people lost their jobs, and businesses went bankrupt overnight. In 1930, fifty-nine banks failed in Mississippi, and another fifty-six went in 1931; cotton fell in 1931 to 5.66 cents a pound, down from a high of 22.88 cents in 1922; in 1932, another twelve banks failed, and the annual average income was only $126 per year. Thousands of Mississippians lost their homes because they didn't have the money to pay their taxes.[3] The state's forests had been clear-cut, and the lumber industry was gone. (A fast-growing vine was imported from Japan in 1930 to help prevent the erosion of soil in former timberlands; today it is hard to imagine a Mississippi landscape in summer without kudzu.)

Many Americans were on the road, traveling about from place to place to look for work. One of the documented quilters, Estebelle Reid, sent along her life story in her own handwriting to be included with her quilts. Not only does it give a firsthand account of how "plain people" fared during the Great Depression, it shows her complete and lasting love for her husband. Her story, as she wrote it, follows:

I was an 18-year-old Missouri girl [in 1929]. And in our part of Mo. ever[y] Saturday night a dance was given in eather a barn or a home—and over the state line in Kansas. A company was putting down a 24-inch pipeline and a bunch of young men were working for the company and attending our dances. [That is] where I met my husband. After marriage in 1930, we moved in [to] a home of old people. She was quilting, and got

me started to piecing a "Lone Star" quilt. I was 3/4 of the way of having it finished when some-one shot my husband's brother [as they were] bird-hunting and killed him. So, we packed up to come to his furnel [funeral]. Not realizing the company he was working for was due to close because the Depression hit. No work to go back to.

I needed 1/2 yard of what I was making the quilt out of. So I sent some money to the lady where we were staying to send it to me, and she did. When [I] finished [it], we were living with the dead brother's wife and children. No work. My husband and I quilted the quilt, and this is the finished product. When finished, my second was started. The brother's wife lived in Columbia, Mississippi.

Quilt No. 2 The Irish Chain: My sister-in-law's neighbor had a bunch of small scraps, and I told her if she would let me have them to piece myself a quilt, I would piece her one also when finished. My husband and myself quilted it, [in] 1931.

When a man [whose] home had been [in] Philadelphia, Miss. needed to have someone to drive a pair of mules and wagon back to his home, we took off, with a load of plow tools, a pig, and a real small dog. We were the last people to come to Neshoba County in a covered wagon. By that time, the Depression was really bad. So we was close to the river and a neighbor taut my husband to catch fish. He made a cotton and corn crop.

He rolled his own cigarett[e]s out of Country Gentleman tobacco. I had been saving all the lit-tle sacks and desided to make a quilt out of them. In 1934, I had it finished, and I and my husband quilted it. By our coal oil lamp. We owned no radio—and t.v. had not been invented. We laughed, talked, and quilted.[4]

It is clear from reading this letter that the Reids could have used some help in finding work. Help came in the form of the New Deal programs, instituted shortly after President Franklin D. Roosevelt's inauguration in 1933. These programs, of which there were several, more or less invented projects and jobs in order to provide income for the nation's unemployed; this is not to say that the projects were not serious endeavors. They were indeed, and the nation still benefits from many depression-era federal projects. Several were very familiar to Mississippians: the CCC, or Civilian Conservation Corps, worked on reforestation, highways, and anti-erosion projects, among other things. It came to Mississippi in 1933, and by 1941 a total of thirty-three camps had been established. In 1935, about 20 percent of Mississippi's workforce was employed in Civil Works Administration projects.[5] The AAA, the Agricultural Adjustment Act, paid farmers to reduce the acreage they planted, in order to reduce overproduction so that prices would rise.

Perhaps the best-known program of the thirties was the WPA, or Works Progress Administration, which promoted handcrafts, among them quilt-making.[6] A presentation quilt (fig. 6.1) was made by a group of ladies in a WPA project for their supervisor, Caro Weston. "They really appreciated my aunt and all that she did for them as individuals, and as a group," said the current owner, Mrs. Weston's niece.[7]

There is a school of thought that holds that Americans in general didn't spend the entire ten years of the depression moping about in the gloom, telling one another stories of suicides and disasters. Because everyone was pretty much in the same boat, everyone pulled together and shared what little they had. Some people remember the depression years as times of great neighborliness, when people shared inexpensive pleasures like playing cards and

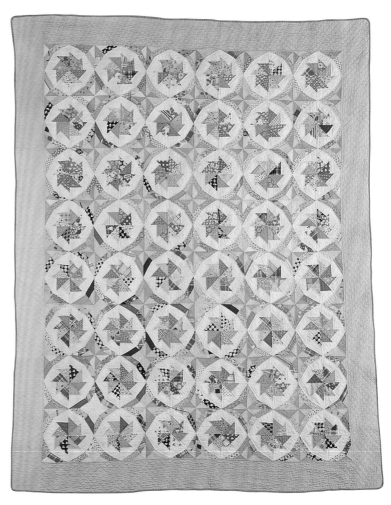

board games, such as Monopoly and bingo, and putting together jigsaw puzzles, all while they listened to the radio.

It could be that this "we're all in this together, so we'd just as well make the best of it" attitude was particularly strong in Mississippi, and perhaps that is the underlying reason why so many quilts were made during the 1930s. What better way to pass the time with your neighbors than by piecing and quilting? There is a marvelous vitality to the quilts of this decade, almost as though the quilts could speak of the determination of their makers to find better times ahead.

Fig. 6.1. "Pinwheel" variation made by a group of ladies in a WPA project in Bay St. Louis, Hancock County, Mississippi, in the 1930s. Of all-cotton materials, the quilt is hand-pieced, with some machine work, and hand-quilted by the piece, with cross-hatching in the borders, in green thread. It is 71 inches wide by 89 inches long. MQA quilt no. Q-01. Collection of Mildred Fountain, niece.

A sign that the times were getting better appeared in 1938 with the opening of a major industry, Ingalls Shipyard in Pascagoula; three years later, the world's first all-welded passenger ship, the *African Comet,* was launched from the shipyard. During the World War II years, Ingalls produced sixty-one ships in fifty-five months, with the sixty-first launching, a transport ship named the USS *Sea Tarpon,* in January of 1945, five months before victory in Europe was declared on May 5.[8]

The United States entered World War II on December 10, 1941, after the bombing of Pearl Harbor; eleven Mississippians, ten navy men and one marine, died in the Japanese attack.[9] Despite the personal tragedies suffered by many, the war improved business in the state and brought it out of the economic hard times of the depression. In 1945, the average annual income had risen to $605.

The cotton crop of 1945 was just under ten million bales, the smallest since 1934, a result, no doubt, of so many farmers being away at war. In the absence of men on the farm, women did what had to be done, just as "Rosie the Riveter" took over in the factories. Cathryn Edwards, writing about her grandmother, Kate Lott, of Columbia in Marion County confirms the ability of women to cope, during wartime or anytime: "'Miz' Kate could plow a field; pick cotton; send field hands out to work; cook dinner for ten to fifteen field hands on a wood stove; teach an adult education class; write poetry; sing ballads; rock grandchildren; and still find time to quilt!"[10]

Although more farmers had tractors, there were still 328,687 mules in the state. The demonstration, in September of 1944, of International Harvester's mechanical cotton-picker at the Hopson Plantation near Clarksdale signaled the future. The machine could pick cotton sixty times faster than a man; the age of mechanization was coming to Mississippi. Truly, at the end of 1945, the state was poised for positive change—economically, culturally, and socially—and, although the changes sometimes crept in very slowly, Mississippi would eventually live up to the promises of the future that seemed so possible in 1945.

The Golden Age of Quiltmaking: the 1930s and 1940s

The thirties were the time of the Great Depression, the time during which Eudora Welty made her moving, wonderful photographs that reveal to the present generation, who live today in such abundance, how so many lived then, in such deprivation. And even though those tough times lasted at least ten, maybe more, years for most families, those same years easily could be named the "Golden Age of Quiltmaking in Mississippi." More quilts were made in the state during 1930 to 1945, during the Great Depression and World War II, than at any other time, according to the figures gathered by the documentation effort.

Quiltmakers drew on familiar patterns, such as stars and log cabins, but they also had plenty of access to the new commercial patterns that were being produced by dozens of manufacturers and sold through accessible retail outlets such as the Sears Roebuck mail-order catalog and many, if not most, newspapers. Magazines such as *Progressive Farmer,* standard reading material for most Mississippi families, also carried quilt patterns, and most of them eventually added a woman's editor to whom farm wives addressed a lively correspondence. Women's magazines of the time, among them *Good Housekeeping, Woman's Day,* and

Ladies' Home Journal, often worked with well-known quilt designers to offer their readers exclusive new projects. Even those patterns that were copies of well-known quilt designs proved irresistible, if they were said to be available only through one particular source.

Quiltmakers generally embraced the new quilt patterns as the way to achieve modern, up-to-date designs, a way to bring a contemporary feeling to an old and familiar form of handwork. Kits and patterns provided a means for quilters to enjoy the sensation of a new craft, although one that employed techniques with which they were already familiar. There was none of the aversion to kits that is part of the quilter's mentality today; it is surprising to learn that some of the winners of prestigious quilt contests in the 1930s were made from kits. Recognition was given to the effort required to beautifully stitch a quilt, whether from a kit, a commercial pattern, or a traditional design: the emphasis was on skill more than on originality.

Not only did quilters warmly welcome the general concept of commercial patterns, they were greatly enthusiastic about certain designs. Everyone who has ever heard the word "quilt" can identify a "Double Wedding Ring" (figs. 6.2 and 6.3) and a "Grandmother's Flower Garden" (fig. 6.4), both of which became popular after being produced as commercial patterns, although they were not new and original designs. Quilters looked forward to trying out the popular new patterns, and they learned through the grapevine about which skill levels were needed for the various patterns, which ones were easier for a beginner, which ones should be postponed until one felt very confident. There was sort of a graduated tier of competence tacitly understood for the popular patterns.

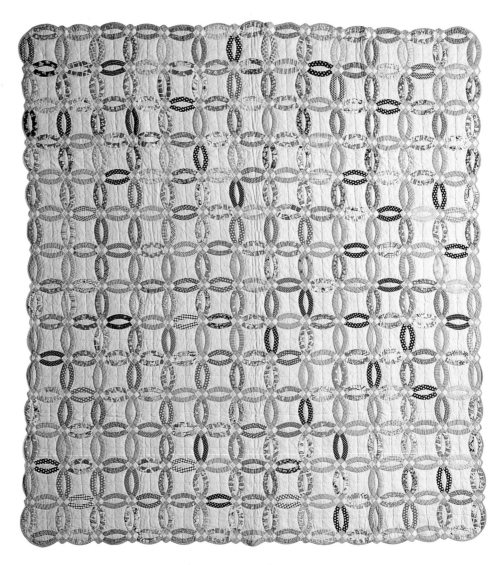

By the 1940s, there was a bit more spending money available for quilters to buy the specific fabrics they wanted for their quilts. There are many more solid-fabric, planned color schemes in quilts than in previous years (excepting the red, white, and green scheme of the mid to late nineteenth and early twentieth century). There are some rather daring blends of color, as evidenced by the quilts presented on these pages.

Fig. 6.2. "Double Wedding Ring" made by Cynthia Ludlow (1899–1995) of Decatur, Newton County, Mississippi, in the 1940s. This quilt was draped over the quiltmaker's casket at her funeral on November 9, 1995. Of all-cotton materials, it is hand-pieced and hand-quilted at 6 stitches per inch and is 69 inches wide by 75.5 inches long. MQA quilt no. D-29. Collection of Emma Lee May, daughter.

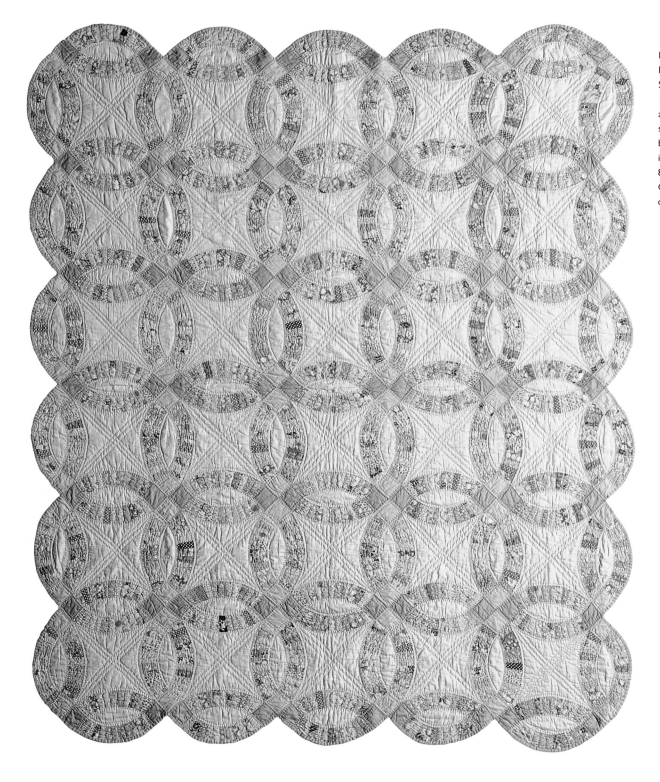

Fig. 6.3. "Double Wedding Ring" made by Effie Downey Trussell (b. 1885) of Pine Springs, Lauderdale County, Mississippi, in 1932. Of all-cotton materials, it is pieced and has a solid-color orchid backing; the scalloped edge is bound with single-layer binding. It is hand-quilted at 6 stitches per inch and measures 73.5 inches wide by 85.5 inches long. MQA quilt no. D-137. Collection of Willa Smith, granddaughter of maker.

Fig. 6.4. "Grandmother's Flower Garden" made by Laura Percy Shaifer of Port Gibson, Claiborne County, Mississippi, circa 1940. The quilt is made of all-cotton materials, pieced, with a shaped edge. Collection of Libby Hollingsworth, niece.

Fig. 6.5. "Stars of Alabama" made by Gladys Wingo (b. 1904) of Booneville, Prentiss County, Mississippi, in the 1930s. Of all-cotton materials, it has multi-scrap stars, and the striped fabric of the backing was brought to the front as binding. Utilitarian quilting was probably done by a group. It is 67 inches wide, 83 inches long. MQA quilt no. J-04. Collection of Mary Abbott, daughter.

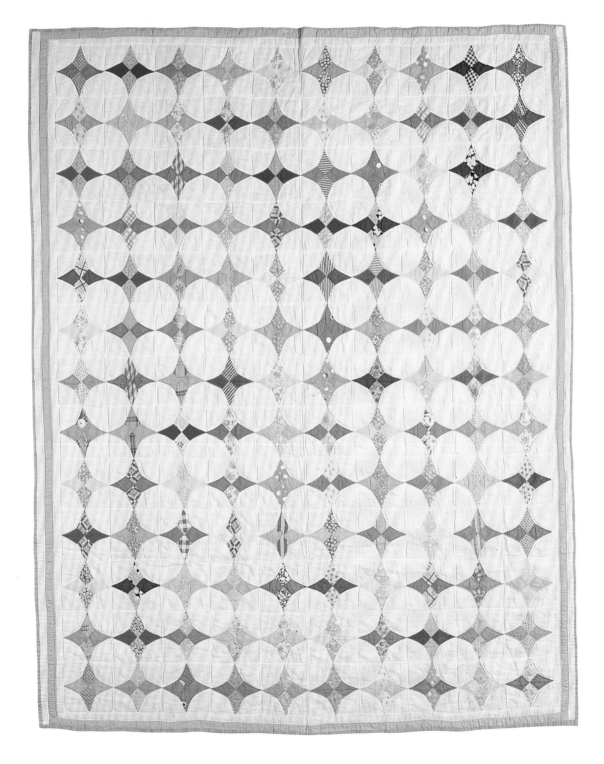

Fig. 6.6. "Danish Star," also known as "Periwinkle" and "Hummingbird," called "Cotton Boll" by the family, made by Bessie Ratcliff Moorman in Lauderdale County, Mississippi, in the 1930–1940 period. Of all-cotton materials, it is machine-pieced, hand-quilted by the piece at four stitches per inch, and is 67 inches wide by 85.5 inches long. MQA quilt no. D-100. Collection of Muriel Prather.

Fig. 6.7. Bessie Ratcliff Moorman, maker of the "Danish Star" quilt. Photograph courtesy of Muriel Prather.

Fig. 6.8. "Brunswick Star" made by Polly Trantham (b. 1905) in Hills Chapel, Prentiss County, Mississippi, in 1939. Of all-cotton materials, with a combination of hand and machine piecing, it is hand-quilted by the piece at 4 stitches per inch and is 66 inches wide by 82 inches long. MQA quilt no. P-86. Collection of Shirley H. Johnson, daughter.

Fig. 6.9. "Star of Bethlehem," also known as "Star of the Magi," called "Prairie Points" by the family, made by Viola Varnado Blades in Kentwood, Louisiana, circa 1940, and brought to Mississippi in 1945. Of all-cotton materials, with a combination of hand and machine piecing, it is hand-quilted in an all-over fan design and is 66 inches wide by 87.5 inches long. MQA quilt no. E-19. Collection of Jo Ann Green, grand-daughter.

Fig. 6.10. "Pineapple Log Cabin," called "String Quilt" by the family, made by Salina Lucinda Felder Reeves (1860–1941) outside McComb, Mississippi, circa 1930. Of all-cotton materials, with a combination of hand and machine piecing, it is hand-quilted by the piece at 4 stitches per inch and is 74.5 inches wide by 81.5 inches long. MQA quilt no. Q-91. Collection of Lena Lou White Kleinpeter, granddaughter.

Fig. 6.11. "Butterfly" made by May Bell Thompson of Natchez, Adams County, Mississippi, in 1940. Of all-cotton materials, with a combination of hand and machine piecing and appliqué, it is hand-quilted at 5 stitches per inch and is 71 inches long by 92 inches wide. (Some restoration has begun of the shattered black fabric of the butterfly bodies.) MQA quilt no. F-41. Collection of Marjorie Marlow Binns, granddaughter.

Fig. 6.12. "Lotus Blossom," or "Richmond Beauty," called "The Lotus" by the family, made by Mrs. W. B. Donavan (1873–1964) of Hattiesburg, Forest County, Mississippi, in the 1930–1940s period. Of all-cotton materials, hand-pieced and appliquéd, the quilt is hand-quilted in an all-over diagonal pattern, with butterflies in the center of the blocks. It has borders on three sides and is 80 inches wide by 92.5 inches long. MQA quilt no. C-114. Collection of Sarah Martin.

Fig. 6.13. "Touching Stars of Bethlehem" made by Catherine Rebecca Cox (1856–1944) in Newton County, Mississippi, in 1934. Of all-cotton materials, with possibly a flannel sheet used for batting, it is hand-pieced and hand-quilted by the piece and has feathered wreaths in setting blocks with fine, close quilting at 8 stitches per inch. Measurements were not recorded. MQA quilt no. R-38. Collection of Catherine F. Baker, granddaughter.

Sacks in Quiltmaking

Fig. 6.14. "Joseph's Coat," also known as "Rainbow," called "Tobacco Sack Quilt" by the family, made by Lettie Daniels (b. 1913) in Booneville, Prentiss County, Mississippi, in 1932. Made of all-cotton tobacco sacks dyed with natural dyes, with cotton batting and fertilizer sacks for backing, it is hand- and machine-pieced and hand-quilted at 4 stitches per inch. It is 70 inches wide by 85.75 inches long. MQA quilt no. P-10. Collection of Lettie Daniels, maker.

al; this was during the last quarter of the nineteenth century. In 1899, a quilter wrote to *Progressive Farmer* to say that six flour sacks were sufficient for a backing for a medium-sized quilt.[11]

Up until the last quarter of the nineteenth century, prepackaged goods were a rarity. One took one's market basket along when shopping, purchased the desired quantity of a product, and simply placed the purchase in the market basket for transport home. Even for large quantities, the buyer provided the container. Wrapping of any type of purchase was minimal—perhaps a sheet of newsprint would be folded around a fish, for example. The availability of prepackaged goods was very limited, nationwide, until the beginning of the twentieth century; and when prepackaging became the way to ship and distribute goods, inexpensive fabric was often the container—not paper, to which we are accustomed today. No sooner were products delivered to the consumer in fabric than quilters started using such fabric in their quilts.

By the mid-thirties, clever manufacturers of feed and flour sacks had begun printing designs especially meant to attract the quilter's eye, hoping to increase sales of the product and to stifle competition from paper manufacturers, who were eyeing a lucrative market. Quilters happily took the printed sacks up as lagniappe, but they did not limit their use to these special sacks; they also utilized sugar, salt, fertilizer, and tobacco sacks.

Here is another account of tobacco sacks being used for quiltmaking, confirming Estabelle Reid's mention of such a practice. Lettie Daniels wrote,

When I was seventeen years old I made this quilt [fig. 6.14]. These were the days before ready-rolled cigarettes. Smoking tobacco was sold in cloth sacks together with papers to roll the cigarettes. My husband used this smoking tobacco, there-

Even before the Great Depression took hold of the state, there was a well-honed tradition of learning how to make do with what was available and how to re-recycle the smallest bit of fabric into a quilt. The Mississippi Quilt Association survey showed that by the time of the depression, the tradition of string and scrap quilts was already firmly embedded in the state's quilting traditions. The use of sacks in quiltmaking corresponds with the time that fabric began being used as a packaging materi-

fore, I had many sacks. To make the top of this quilt, I took the tobacco sacks apart, washed and bleached them. I then sewed the clean sacks together to make long strips. The strips were dyed different colors using different kinds of bark, etc. and then were sewn together on an old treadle sewing machine and hemmed. The lining for the quilt was made of fertilizer sacks which had been washed and dyed with some scrap dye my mother had. The color turned out blue.[12]

Mrs. Daniels went on to relate how she obtained her quilt batting, a tale that was told to the documentation team hundreds of times.

> The cotton used as batting for the quilt was picked in the cotton fields after the main harvest was finished. This was called "scrap cotton." My father carried the scrap cotton to the gin the day after the last bale was harvested and got the seeds removed. Every night after supper I would use bats to pull the cotton apart. I would stack the cotton in a chair until I had plenty to put inside the quilt. We lived in a two-room log house that had a front porch, and we were glad to have this quilt to sleep under because it was really warm.[13]

Many of the sacks that back utility quilts from this time retain the stenciling that identifies the original use. Caddie Hudson Butts (1903–1989) of Union, in Newton County, made quilts throughout her life to provide bedcovering for her husband and six stepchildren. One of her quilts is backed with sacks that contained cottonseed meal from a mill in the town of Newton—the lettering is still perfectly visible. (Cottonseed meal was fed to livestock as a good source of nutrients.) Other pieces in Mrs. Butts's quilts contain fabrics that were described by the documentation team as "dyed yel-

low" or "dyed brown," undoubtedly the result of home-dyeing feed or fertilizer sacks. Mrs. Butts, in another frugal measure, worked one of her quilts over an old one.[14]

"Rubbed off '6-8-8' till hands were sore," begins Nancy Myatt Stephens, as she tells about preparing fertilizer sacks to be used for quilt batting. (Note to those readers unfamiliar with commercial fertilizers: Each number refers to the percentage of a specific nutrient, such as nitrogen, contained in the fertilizer. Different fertilizers were needed for different crops, and the combination of numbers is different; a fertilizer could be labeled 8-10-10, for example, depending on what type of crop and what time of the year it was to be used.) "Used lye, poured first soaking around flowers. Needed many soakings," Mrs. Stephens wrote (MQA# D-154). Again, the "waste not, want not" code of living dictated that the nutrients leached out of the fabric should be used. And even though lye is caustic, it is an organic material obtained from wood ashes and is not harmful to plants.

The most intriguing use of tobacco sacks was for a summer spread; the sacks were undyed, so the spread is simply a broad expanse of white rectangles that have been carefully pieced together.[15] Another example of sacks alone being used as the design was found in a piece in which the top was made with four chicken-feed sacks printed in an attractive design of bouquets of blue daisies with yellow centers; the sacks were opened up and sewed together to make a type of whole-cloth feed-sack quilt. The top was put together in 1943 in DeQueen (Sevier County), Arkansas, by Floretta Listenbee (1871–1962) and quilted in the summer of 1945 in Lafayette County, Mississippi, by Lillie Hellums (1895–1984).[16]

Along with the use of sacks came, in many instances, a familiarity with natural dyestuffs. Even

Fig. 6.15. "One-Patch," called "Feed-Sack Quilt" by the family, maker unknown, from Louisiana, circa 1930s. It is of all-cotton feed sacks, pieced, and is backed with feed sacks on which the lettering "Money Maker Mix" is still visible. Hand-quilted in an all-over design of fans, it is 66 inches wide by 89 inches long. (The large scale of the triangles in this piece makes the quilt appear small, perhaps the size of a crib quilt, although it is actually a regular double-bed-sized quilt.) MQA quilt no. E-89. Collection of Judy Williams.

Fig. 6.16. "Fluttering Butterfly" made by Effie Lou Morgan Kuykendall (1862–1947) of Coahoma, Coahoma County, Mississippi, in the 1930s. Of all-cotton materials, the quilt is hand-pieced, with striped feed sacks for backing, and hand-quilted by the piece at 4 stitches per inch. It is 75 inches wide, 90.5 inches long. MQA quilt no. H-37. Collection of Jane Eason Weathersby, granddaughter.

Fig. 6.17. "Basket of Flowers," called "Tulip Basket" by the family, made by Rachel Ann Scott (1885–1974) of Swampers community in Franklin Parish, Louisiana, in the 1930s, and brought to Mississippi in 1940. Of all-cotton materials, with feed sacks for the quilt top, it is hand-pieced and embroidered, and hand-quilted "in the ditch" at 5 stitches per inch. It is 64.5 inches wide by 92.5 inches long. MQA quilt no. M-03. Collection of Nellie Scott Pharr, daughter.

Fig. 6.18. Rachel Ann Scott, the maker of "Basket of Flowers," was born Rachel Ann Chapman in 1885 in Rankin County, Mississippi. She moved to Louisiana when she was 19 years old and married John Douglas Scott 2 years later. She raised 5 children and made each of them 12 quilts.

as late as 1943, Mississippi quilters were using native materials to dye their quiltmaking fabrics. A quilt set like a checkerboard in red and blue squares was called "Mamma's Hand-Dyed Quilt" by her children and grandchildren. The accompanying note relates that "Grandpa picked poke-salad berries and wild cherry berries and bark and made the dye. Mamma sewed them [a reference apparently to tobacco sacks] and quilted in a "Log Cabin" [right-angle] design."[17]

Printed sacks did not appear until the early 1930s and, in the beginning, packaged flour and sugar. Soon, though, chicken feed, dog food, horse feed, potatoes, cornmeal, rice, and salt were delivered to the general store in printed feed sacks. Many garments were made of these materials, and the garments later were cut apart and used for quilts. Sometimes, though, the sacks went directly to quilts. In the example shown in figure 6.15, in which feed sacks are used exclusively as the fabric for the top, a good overview of the variety of colors and prints available may be seen.

Appliqué Artist

There is only one quilter to have had three of her quilts selected for inclusion in this book of outstanding Mississippi quiltmakers; although she continues to make quilts, the ones included here were made in the 1940s (figs. 6.19, 6.20, and 6.21). Her name is Lavada Rushing Brewer, and she was taught how to quilt by her mother, Bessie Rushing, who was taught by her mother. Lavada Brewer began her lifelong passion for quilting in Tylertown at the age of seventeen. A seamstress by profession, Mrs. Brewer is, quite simply, gifted with the needle. In addition to making wearing apparel for clients and working as an alterations expert for various

department stores, she has, in the past, quilted for other people. In one four-year span, she quilted forty-eight pieces: thirty-eight for one client and ten for another.

Mrs. Brewer works with an old-fashioned quilt frame, which she pulls up to the ceiling when she is not using it. It hangs over her bed, so she has a quilt as a canopy when she is resting. Although the quilts shown on these pages are appliquéd, she also

Fig. 6.19. "Iris Appliqué" made by Lavada Rushing Brewer from a Herrschner kit in Natchez, Mississippi, in 1945. Made of all-cotton materials and hand-appliquéd with blind stitch and buttonhole stitch, the quilt has hand-embroidery and is hand-quilted with fine, close quilting at 6 stitches per inch. It is 73.5 inches wide by 88.5 inches long. MQA quilt no. F-94. Collection of the maker.

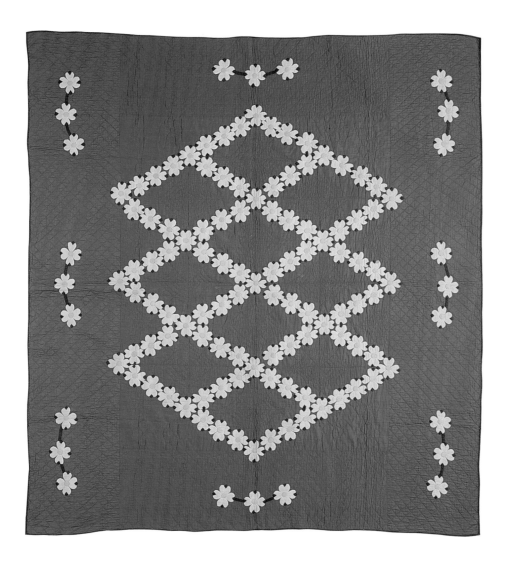

says, she can just look at a picture and copy the quilt.[18] Eighty-eight years old at the time she brought her quilts in for photography, Mrs. Brewer is still quilting and still planning her future quilts.

Summary

This era of Mississippi's history ended quite differently from the way it began. In 1930, the Great Depression was affecting every family in the state; fortunately, most people still lived on farms, and as long as they could earn enough money to pay property taxes each year, they could stay on their land, raise a garden, and feed themselves. Jobs were very hard to come by, from any source, and federal programs such as the CCC helped many people make it through the tough times by providing employment and wages. By the end of the era, Mississippi had helped to win a great war in Europe, and its economy was back on its feet.

Quiltmaking may have slowed somewhat during the depression, but even so, more quilts were made during the years between 1930 and 1945 than any other fifteen-year span in the state's history. World War II brought the rest of the world into the state, broadening its perspective in many ways, and the quilts began to reflect this new "world view." Mississippi's quilts started to look like those made in the rest of the country more than at any other time in its quiltmaking history. Indeed, quilts all across the country began to be more alike in appearance, a trend which has been lamented by quilt writers because it is thought to signal an end to innovation. The production and wide distribution of commercial patterns did result in a certain sameness of appearance in many quilts, but Mississippi quilters nearly always add their own touch of

Fig. 6.20. "Dogwood" made by Lavada Rushing Brewer in Natchez, Mississippi, in the 1940s. Of all-cotton materials and hand-appliquéd with a blind stitch with some machine work, it is hand-quilted with designs of dogwood blossoms, spiderwebs, and a diamond grid with fine, close hand-stitching at 9 stitches per inch. It is 79 inches wide by 84 inches long. MQA quilt no. F-92. Collection of Lavada Rushing Brewer.

makes pieced quilts, and she has even made a pair of "cheater-cloth" quilts that were printed in a "Double Wedding Ring" design. She loves to reel off the names of her quilts, just like a proud grandmother would talk about her grandchildren, and she prides herself on being able to exactly copy kit quilts and pattern quilts, without having to purchase either. One of the quilts (fig. 6.19) is made from a kit she actually bought, but generally, she

individuality, a little something to make their quilt special. They are like quilters everywhere in that regard—they want each quilt they make to reflect their own point of view.

A special aspect of the quilts from this period of time was the connection of owner to maker, something that wasn't always possible with older quilts. Many of the quilts in this last block of time were made within the memory of folks who consider themselves middle-aged now: we saw our mothers and grandmothers make the quilts we now sleep under or display in our homes. Consequently, the documentation team heard many more personal, charming, heartwarming recollections of the quiltmakers from the current owners of the quilts than in any other previous period. Particularly enchanting were the pet names the quilt owners had for their grandmothers. Mrs. Kukendall, the maker of the "Fluttering Butterflies" quilt (see fig. 6.16), was called "Mama Doll" by her grandchildren. Another quilter was called "Good Mama" by hers. One person wrote on the documentation form about her "Grandmother's Flower Garden": "When my grandmother covered me with this quilt, she told me the sun in the flower garden would keep me warm all night long."[19] Herein lies the true reason that the people of Mississippi love their quilts and have managed to somehow keep the old ones and make new ones through flood, fire, war, tornadoes, economic depressions, and other terrible tribulations. They are a beautiful, comforting link to the past, a way to keep our dear departed always with us, and they will keep us warm all night long.

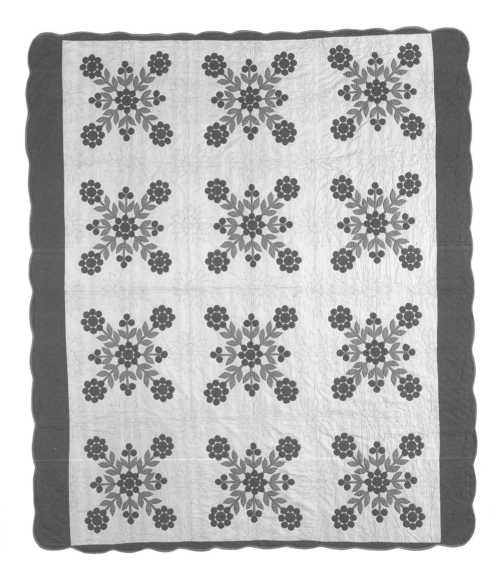

Fig. 6.21. "Cherries" made by Lavada Rushing Brewer in McComb, Mississippi, in 1943. Of all-cotton materials and hand-appliquéd with a blind stitch, it is hand-quilted with red thread in fine, close quilting at 7 stitches per inch. It is 74.5 inches wide by 84.5 inches long. MQA quilt no. F-55. Collection of Janet Sturdivant, grand-daughter.

CHAPTER SEVEN

Special Quilts

It showed a pattern as faint as one laid by wind over a field of broomsedge. It was the quilt that had baked on the line all day.

—Eudora Welty, *Losing Battles*

THIS CHAPTER CONTAINS SEVERAL groupings of quilts that defy easy categorization, for any number of different reasons. Some types of quilts do not easily fit into a particular time span, as they were made throughout the entire period covered by the quilt documentation effort. Examples include children's quilts and quilts made specifically to be entered in contests. Not only were certain *types* of quilts made throughout all the years covered in this study, but so were certain *designs.* Variations of the "Wheel" design were made from the antebellum period forward and are still being made today; the documentation committee chose several of the "swirled ball" or "peppermint" type of wheel designs to be photographed.

Also not easily categorized are quilts that incorporate specialized or unusual methods of applying the design, such as painting or embroidery, or those that employ fabric techniques other than the standard patchwork, appliqué, and quilting and are made without the traditional three layers of quilt top, batting, and backing. (There is argument among quilters about whether or not the textiles that fall outside the traditional parameters actually qualify as quilts, but the quilt documentation teams included them because their owners consider them to be quilts.) Examples of this second category are the "yo-yo" and "biscuit" quilts, as well as those that utilize folded fabric methods, and they will be explained in greater detail below, in the section called "Unique Techniques."

The most awe-inspiring private collection of quilts in the state is the Shaifer collection, located in Port Gibson. Consisting of thirty or more pieces, the collection spans four generations of quilters, all of whom were related to one another. Although the

Whether used in a plantation mansion, a simple farmhouse, or on a houseboat, quilts have kept Mississippi families warm for as long as the state has existed. Houseboat life, Mississippi, 1939, by Eudora Welty. Photograph courtesy of the Eudora Welty Collection, Mississippi Department of Archives and History.

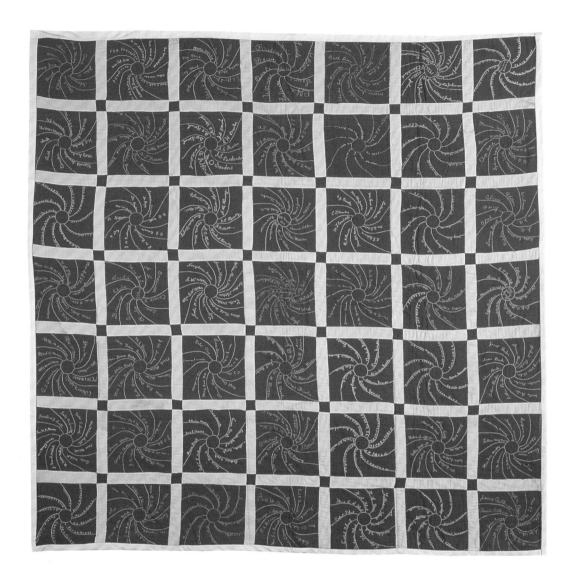

Fig. 7.1. "Embroidered Fund-Raiser Quilt" made by a group of women to raise money for a piano for the Shady Grove School in Attala County, Mississippi, 1926. Mrs. Z.A. Wasson was chairman and also bought the finished quilt for $35.00. A fee of 10 cents was charged for each signature. Of all-cotton materials, it is hand-embroidered and hand-pieced and is hand-quilted at 4 stitches per inch. MQA quilt no. N-52. Collection of Billie Wasson, son.

entire group has been photographed by the Mississippi Quilt Association, space permits the inclusion of just a portion in this chapter of special quilts.

Quilts that contained writing were found from the antebellum years forward. Most of such quilts appear to have been made either as fund-raisers or as friendship pieces. Let us start our look at special quilts with these fascinating artifacts.

Written in Fabric and Thread: Fund-Raiser, Friendship, and Single-Letter Quilts

A significant and surprising number of inscription quilts—those with writing or letters of the alphabet on them—appeared for documentation. There were about fifty such quilts, close to 7 percent of the total number documented, which is a relatively high percentage for a special-interest genre. That

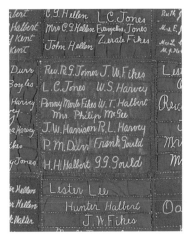

Fig. 7.2. "Signature Fund-Raiser Quilt," called "Red and Blue Church Quilt" by the family, made by women of Oak Grove Baptist Church of Lake, Scott County, Mississippi, in 1914. Embroidery was done by Ruth Fikes Jones, Susanna Roland Davis, Laura Harvey Jones, Martha Hallert, and others. Of all-cotton materials, pieced in a combination of hand and machine work, it is hand-quilted in straight lines underneath each signature at 5 stitches per inch. It is 79 inches wide by 85 inches long. MQA quilt no. C-11. Collection of Carl Jones.

Fig. 7.3. The purpose of this quilt was to raise money to paint the church, and 10 cents per name for each of the 10 to 12 names embroidered in each block raised the needed amount. A quilting bee was held to finish the quilt, and it was then sold for $3.00 to Mrs. J. W. Fikes.

there were so many of these quilts is particularly interesting in view of the fact that so few individuals signed their own quilts. A conclusion one could draw is that it was considered all right to sign the quilt if it was for a good cause, for some reason other than signing one's own work: signing one's own work would be vanity, but if you did it to be remembered to a friend or if you paid to have your name on a fund-raiser quilt, then you were just going along with the crowd.

Another possible reason for so many of these quilts could be that they were considered too precious to use. When there are hundreds of names carefully embroidered on a quilt, a certain amount of respect seems appropriate. The piece is clearly a record of some particular point in time or of a special event, and the quilt becomes more of a historical document than a bedcover. As one gentleman said, "Reading this quilt is a 'Who's Who' of the Shady Grove community in 1926" (fig. 7.1).

On the other hand, one Methodist minister's family from Randolph, Pontotoc County, brought in two signature quilts that appeared to have been used a great deal. The quilts were gifts from one or more congregations the minister had served, and surely the women who made them would be gratified to know they had given something that the minister's family needed and used.[1] The red-and-blue embroidered signature quilt (figs. 7.2 and 7.3) has also been used; sleeping under such a piece brings home what most people consider the real purpose of a quilt: to provide warmth. (Plus, sleeping under such a piece surely gave a feeling of connection to all the people named on the quilt, making for sweet dreams!)

Fund-Raiser Quilts

Quilts with many signatures, which were usually embroidered in thread, were made for many reasons. One reason was for remembrance, examples of which are the silk quilt made to honor soldiers of the Confederacy (fig. 3.7, p. 48) and the "Mississippi Friendship Quilt" from New England (fig. 5.27, p. 122). Mostly, though, quilts with many embroidered signatures were conceived as fund-raisers for some worthy cause, usually associated with a church. One quilt with a particularly intriguing story was made to raise money, perhaps for a building.

[In 1932] Brother M. L. Hollis came from Red Bay, Alabama to East Tupelo for a tent revival. Many local people had shown an interest in organizing a church . . . and the ladies decided to make a quilt to help with expenses. The name on the outer edge of each square is the person who made it, and each name inside donated five or ten cents to have their name placed in the square. After the quilt was finished, the church folk had an ice-cream supper. Everyone paid five cents for a cone of ice cream and a chance on the quilt. I only had one nickel, so I had one cone of cream. When the number was drawn, I had won the quilt.

I had gone to the ice-cream supper with my brother, Charlie, and his girlfriend. The next day, Charlie's girlfriend called me and wanted me to give the quilt back so they could give it to Brother Hollis. I didn't care for this girl Charlie was dating, so I would not give the quilt back. She called me several times to try and get the quilt back. I was just a selfish kid, and since I did not care for the girl, I kept the quilt.[2]

The raffle winner took good care of the quilt; it is in good shape some seventy years later, as clean and pristine as the day it was made (fig. 7.4). From the number of signatures, it appears to have been a successful fund-raiser; there are thirty squares, each with at least sixteen signatures in addition to that of the maker, and then there were all those five cent ice-cream cones that came with a chance on the quilt.

This was not the only time the plans for a fund-raising quilt did not turn out as hoped. A "Centennial Methodist Church Fund-Raiser Quilt" was organized by a tireless employee of the Methodist Church, Bessie Miller, whose first job in the 1920s was as a rural missionary in north Mississippi. The church group enjoyed great success in gathering names to be embroidered on the quilt, although the amount charged per signature is not known. The design of the piece was that of a four-block quilt, with the signatures forming the rays of a sunburst in each block. Unfortunately, when the quilt was finished, no one stepped forward to buy it, so Bessie Miller, as the person responsible, paid out of her pocket for it. It remains within her family.[3]

In some instances, the intention all along was to have people pay to sign the quilt, then present the quilt as a gift to the minister (apparently the plan of the East Tupelo congregation until a little girl refused to cooperate). The members of the Missionary Society of Hopewell, Tennessee, made a fund-raiser quilt which they presented to their minister, a circuit rider in the Memphis Methodist Conference in the late 1930s and early 1940s. This group charged the very high price of five dollars to have one's name put in the center yellow appliquéd fabric circle of the motif. Additional names, at twenty-five cents each, radiated from the circle like sun rays.[4] This quilt is now in Mississippi and has been since 1952, but whether it was brought in by the minister or by his daughter, who now owns the piece, is not known.

Although it might seem so, from the number documented, churches were not the only beneficiaries of fund-raising quilts. There was the example already given of one being made to raise money for a school's piano. Another was made in 1932 to raise money for an elementary school in Oakland (Itawamba County). It is one of the most inventive signature quilts documented; it is done in the "Snowball" design, and the signatures are carefully embroidered along the outer edges of the white "balls." It seems apparent that the designers of the project wanted their quilt to look like a regular quilt, with its pretty pieced four-pointed stars, so they devised a discreet way of including the names. Each ball contains four names, and the color of the embroidery thread was different for each name— either red, gold, blue, green, black, or purple— which adds yet another decorative element and furthers the goal of incorporating the names as an integral part of the quilt design.[5]

One fund-raiser quilt recorded by the documentation team (fig. 7.5) comes with an almost unbelievable tale of good luck. It was purchased by the current owner in 1990 at a Jackson flea market, and her mother and grandmother recognized the quilt; each name on the quilt is one of their rela-

tives: aunts, uncles, cousins, maternal grandmother, grandfather, aunt, and great uncle.[6] One patch has only a surname—the grandmother was pregnant with her mother at the time and paid the charge of twenty-five cents per name to have her new baby included on the quilt. With one hundred names on the quilt, it should have raised twenty-five dollars for the church.

Fig. 7.4. "Eight-Pointed Appliquéd Star with Signatures" made by ladies at East Tupelo Freewill Baptist Church, East Tupelo, Lee County, Mississippi, in 1932. Of all-cotton materials, with a combination of hand and machine piecing, appliqué (with buttonhole or blanket stitch), and embroidery, it is hand-quilted by the piece at 4 to 5 stitches per inch. It is 63 inches wide by 81 inches long. MQA quilt no. H-59. Collection of Linda Anglin Prater, daughter of raffle winner.

Fig. 7.5. "Washington Pavement" made by a church membership in Marion, Lauderdale County, Mississippi, as a fund-raiser in 1940. Of all-cotton materials, it is worked in a two-color scheme, backed with the same gold fabric as that of front, and hand-pieced and embroidered. Hand-quilted by the piece at 5 stitches per inch, it is 62 inches wide by 76 inches long. MQA quilt no. G-51. Collection of Melanie Mann, descendent.

Friendship Quilts

Affectionately known as friendship quilts are those in which the names are of a group of well-wishers who got together to make a quilt for a particular person, maybe for a wedding present or as a gift to someone departing the community, or as a memento of a special group of friends to one of their members. They were private, not public, endeavors.

While the great number of names on a fund-raising signature quilt required a pattern that would accommodate each inscription (resulting in some original designs, such as that of figure 7.1), friendship quilts were usually made of conventional patterns; and just about every conceivable patchwork design, including stars, baskets, churn dashes, and the like, was made into such a quilt. A particularly attractive patchwork friendship quilt was made of brightly colored scraps in the "Chicken Foot" pattern by friends of Mattie Meredith who "loved people," according to her granddaughter.[7] Each of the friends, who all lived in Independence (Tate County), Mississippi, signed their names, and a couple of them included the date, 1934. One person, possibly Mattie, embroidered a floral design in the center of the block rather than inscribing her name. Another quilt, in a "Crossroads" variation named "Flyfoot," was made for a friend who had lost everything in a fire—a generous gift from a group of girls to one of the children of the family. Each of the makers signed her name in her block.[8]

The design that is acknowledged to have been devised particularly for signatures, "The Autograph Cross," or "Album," which came into being about 1840, was made fairly frequently; but, this being Mississippi, where great pride comes from being different, it was not used for friendship quilts. One quiltmaker made the design up in a very nice red-and-white color scheme, leaving the "crosses" white, as they should be for signing, but she only embroidered in one of them, including the year the quilt was made, 1911, and the initials of Samuel Terry Dandrige, the son for whom she made the quilt.[9]

There were many mentions of women gathering to quilt, and some people remembered playing as children underneath quilting frames as ladies sat around them to stitch. Nannette Shipp Sissell, who brought in a lovely "Cake Stand" friendship quilt made by her mother and friends in 1934, remarked, "Ladies of the community had quilting bees. They made tops in groups and quilted quilts and sold them, with the money going to Taylor Methodist and Baptist Churches [near Oxford, in Lafayette County]."[10] Mary Abbott of Prentiss County wrote the following about her mother's quilting practices: "Neighbors would get together in homes and quilt.

The lady of the house would make lunch. They would quilt as many tops as she had ready, then go to another home."[11]

One can only guess what kind of social pressure this put on a busy farm wife, especially if she was in Mary's mother's situation. Gladys Wingo, who had two other children besides Mary, was widowed at the age of forty-two and left to run a farm by herself. She depended, no doubt, on the companionship of her quilting friends to help keep her spirits up during tough times. It was surely a great incentive to get her tops made if she knew she would have help getting them quilted. (See one of Mrs. Wingo's quilts in fig. 6.5, p. 132.)

Fig. 7.6. "A Friendship Block," or "Star and Cross," called "Churn Dash" by the family, made by Leila Jenkins and members of the Dossville community, Attala County, Mississippi, in 1936 as a wedding gift for Horace M. (son of the maker) and Lois Jenkins. Of all-cotton materials, it is hand-pieced, with embroidered names and some machine work, and hand-quilted in an all-over right-angle pattern at 5 to 6 stitches per inch. It is 64 inches wide by 75 inches long. MQA quilt no. H-45. Collection of Melba Washington, granddaughter.

Fig. 7.8. Amanda McKay, maker of "Old Home Friendship Quilt," circa 1935

Fig. 7.7. "Old Home Friendship Quilt," called "Schoolhouse Friendship" by the family, made by Amanda McKay of the Ellison Ridge community, Winston County, Mississippi, circa 1938. Of all-cotton materials, hand-pieced and hand-quilted by the piece and with straight lines in the background at 4 stitches per inch, it is 72 inches square. MQA quilt no. B-28. Collection of Louella Zell McKay Ray (Mrs. Ovin C.), daughter.

Two different "Groom's Quilts" were found. These objects were made when friends and family or young ladies of the neighborhood gathered to piece and sign quilt blocks for a young man who was marrying. One, a colorful quilt in the "Double Pyramid" or "Dove at the Window" pattern, was made about 1897 in Stewart (Webster County), Mississippi, by a group of the bride's friends as a gift for the groom. The bride herself made a square and initialed it "SBT," for Sallie Bell Turner. In this instance, one person, Ellen Proctor Landrum, the mother of the groom, did all the quilting.[12] In

another example, the mother of the groom held a quilting party to make the couple a wedding gift, and enough blocks were made for two quilts, although there is no record of the second quilt. Each woman signed her name: "Aunt Annie," "Aunt Eula," etc. (fig. 7.6).

A mother, Amanda McKay, organized a friendship quilt (fig. 7.7) as a special gift for her daughter, Louella McKay. Mrs. McKay (fig. 7.8) invited relatives and mothers of Louella's classmates to make individual blocks. Each maker either signed the block herself or got help from Mrs. McKay, who then embroidered the names and put the quilt together. Neighbors gathered to help quilt it.

Although all of the examples mentioned thus far were made with patchwork, at least one appliquéd friendship quilt was found in Prismatic, Kemper County, Mississippi, made in 1933 by Inez Mitchell and friends. The design, a variation of "Rose of Sharon" known as "Rose of Heaven," contains the embroidered names of those who worked on the quilt: Marion Sullivan, Roxie Williamson,

Fig. 7.9. "Delectable Mountains," or "Barrister's Block Friendship Quilt," made by members of the Carter family in Pontotoc County, Mississippi, on July 4, 1930. Blocks had been machine-pieced ahead of time by the sisters-in-law; during the family gathering on the Fourth of July, different names were embroidered on the blocks and quilting was begun. Of all-cotton materials, with machine assembly of the blocks, it is hand-quilted with diagonal lines at 4 stitches per inch. It is 73 inches wide by 76.5 inches long. MQA quilt no. N-46. Collection of Shannon Carter, family member.

Essie Fedders, Jessie Swearington, Alma Lisenke, Carrie Gunn, Everdee Stephenson, and Inez Mitchell.[13] It provides yet another glimpse into how a group of young ladies entertained themselves with quilting in the early 1930s.

A charming "Dresden Plate/Friendship Ring" was made for Bobbye Jasper Johnson by the Twentieth-Century Women's Cultural Club of Philadelphia, Mississippi, perhaps as a wedding gift. There are twenty blocks, each in different fabrics, all set on a muslin background and all signed. Some of the blocks just have a last name, "Ladd," "Wright," "Turner," while others have the first and last name, "Mary Moss." A couple show just a first name. Clearly, there was no pre-planned agreement among the group as to the signing of the individual block each made. The seamlines are quilted with a chain design, and this was one of the few documented quilts that contained a polyester batting, which led the documentation team to date it at 1945, although the family estimated it to be as early as 1920.[14]

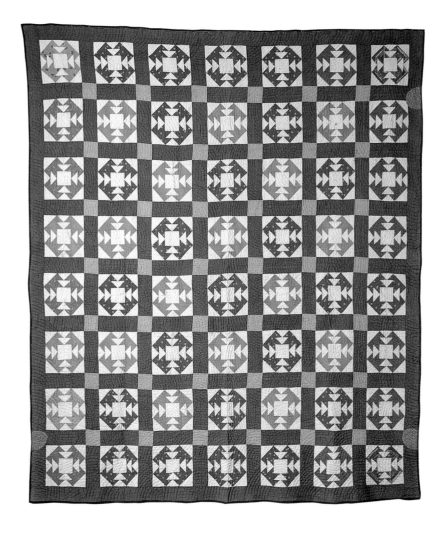

The Adkins quilt, spelled out each family member's entire name with individual letter blocks. Apparently paying little attention to the letter from which it was made, Mississippi quilters showed a great fondness for a quilt design that was known as "Capital T," "Four T Square," or "Double T" (fig. 7.10). It seems to have been regarded as just another nice patchwork design; the several quilts in this pattern had no obvious relation to a family name.

"Wheel" Quilts

The wheel, a motif that became a favorite for Mississippi quilters from the early nineteenth century on, seems to have first appeared as a plain, segmented circle. As the design became embellished with sawtooth edging and curved segments, it took on a variety of different names: "Pinwheel," "Wheel of Life," "Wheel of Fortune," and "Wheel of Time." In some of these variations, the swirls of the design met in the center, making them look exactly like a peppermint candy, especially when worked in red and white (fig. 7.11). Other wheels add a circle at the center, which can be either a tiny accent piece or a larger size, perhaps to suggest a hub or axle. Three different wheels from different time periods are shown here, and they are alike in two important ways. Each is stitched in a red, white, and green color scheme, and the swirled ball in each is done in red and white; it is fun to see how differently the quilts turned out.

A quilt called "Wheel of Time" by the maker has a tiny deep green circle, in the center of the motif, that matches the color of the background and has no sawtooth ring. This quilt is set with sashing that picks up the red of the two-colored swirls (fig. 7.12). It was made by Fannie Cobb, who

Single-letter Quilts

Fig. 7.10. "Double T" made by Carrie Stroud of Meridian, Lauderdale County, Mississippi, in 1907. Of all-cotton materials, the quilt is hand-pieced and hand-quilted in an all-over design of straight rows. It is 74.5 inches wide by 86.5 inches long. MQA quilt no. D-91. Collection of Marcia Shirley, great-great-niece.

One final type of inscribed quilt is the one in which the design is made of a single pieced letter, such as T or H (there were also Ws and Xs), that was repeated across the surface of the quilt in any number of clever settings. Usually, these quilts were made because that was the first letter of the family's surname, and, less often, the first letter of the given name of the recipient.[15] One unique piece, the

Fig. 7.11. "Pinwheel" made by Annie Norton in Mississippi in 1840 for her daughter, Sarah Joel Chivers. Of all-cotton materials, the quilt has fine, close quilting at 8 stitches per inch and is 78 inches wide by 89 inches long. MQA quilt no. G-41. Collection of Jane Johnston.

Fig. 7.12. "Wheel of Time" made by Fannie Cobb in Choctaw County, Mississippi, in the 1870–1900 period. Cotton materials are quilted by the piece, with grid pattern in sashing. It is 62 inches wide by 79 inches long. MQA quilt no. M-43. Collection of Bobbie Waycaster Wilson, great-niece.

Fig. 7.13. "Wheel of Fortune" by Virginia James Richardson Kinard, circa 1875. Of all-cotton materials and quilted by the piece, it is 76 inches wide by 75.5 inches long. MQA quilt no. D-34. Collection of Mary Kinard Cobb, granddaughter.

Fig. 7.14. *At left*, Virginia James Richardson Kinard stands with her sister, Harriet Ellen Richardson Palbert, in her garden in Lauderdale County, Mississippi. The land was homesteaded by Ransome C. Richardson, the sisters' father, in the early 1800s. His great-granddaughter and the current owner of the "Wheel of Fortune" quilt, Mary Kinard Cobb, resides on the property at this writing, 200 years after Mr. Richardson established ownership.

was a great quilter. She is known to have made twenty-five to thirty quilts during her lifetime, and the owner of this quilt has four others that Miss Cobb made.

One of the most wonderful things about the third "peppermint" quilt (fig. 7.13) is that the owner furnished a great photograph of the maker, Virginia James Richardson Kinard, and her sister in their sunflower patch (fig. 7.14), which is as close to a candid snapshot as possible from this time period. Virginia James Richardson was born on June 20, 1851, and died on December 19, 1936, having lived her whole life in Lauderdale County. She is said by her granddaughter, Mary Kinard Cobb, to have been "[s]trong-willed but loved by everybody. Made tea cakes and gingerbread cakes for community children, cutting the cookies on a flour sack."

In a version of this design made around 1910 to 1920 by Annie Mae Campbell Carney of Meridian, the exact same motif as the one on Mrs. Kinard's quilt is used, and the color scheme is the same, but it looks completely different. Only a tiny bit of white is used. The background of the quilt is teal green, and the swirls of the ball are teal green, alternating with red. A red-and-white diamond band surrounds the ball, and a white circle centers the motif. The twelve blocks of this quilt are set together with three-strip sashing, two reds and a green, and nine-patch blocks at the intersection of the quilt (the center square of the nine-patch is white). It is an impressive piece of work, and it is called the "Christmas Tree Quilt" by the family.[16]

The red, green, and white color scheme of the wheel quilts shown here was a favorite choice of quilters for their best quilts during the second half of the nineteenth century, no matter what the style of the quilt. Several other wheel quilts were documented with the same colors; one made in Georgia around 1850 used all three colors in the swirls to make a unique statement. So did one from Yantley, in Sumter County, Alabama, made by Mary Jane Watts Culpepper in the 1850–1870 period.[17]

Quilters were not restricted to the red, white, and green color plan for their wheel quilts, even though it might seem so with these myriad examples. Many scrap wheel quilts were documented, but even when a quilter worked with scraps, she clearly planned ahead so that the motif would not be compromised by faulty color placement. It is a sign of the difficulty of the pattern, perhaps, that such care was taken with each quilt. The most unusual color scheme can be found on a "Wagon Wheels Carry Me Home" quilt made by Rebeccah Phillips Smith (1866–1939) of Greasy Camp, Choctaw County, Alabama, in about 1930.[18] Teal green is the background; the spokes of the wheels alternate purple and teal green, and the rim of each wheel is orange. The set of this particular quilt requires a second block to join two wheels together; it is purple with a teal green X. The colors are as bright as the day it was made, and the quilt is a dazzling tour de force.

Surely one of the most charming stories to accompany any quilt was told about the "Cartwheel" or "Wheel of Fortune" quilt, made in Itawamba County by Lovie Ann Lollar.[19] She had this quilt in the frames, working on it, when the day arrived for the wedding of her daughter, Ophelia Louella Lollar, to Jim Ben Cockrell. The two wanted to marry in the room in which the quilting was taking place, so Lovie Ann just hoisted the quilt in the frames up near the ceiling, and the couple was married beneath it. It has descended through the happy couple's family to the present day.

Show Quilts

Quite a number of quilters at the beginning of the twenty-first century find themselves excited at the possibility of making a quilt that will be judged by people other than their family and friends. They love the idea of making a prize-winning quilt. The thought that their quilt might be selected for special recognition from a field of many others provides inspiration and incentive, and the work that results is sometimes mind-boggling in its complexity of design and perfection of execution. In some venues, the prize money awarded the top quilts is significant, although most quilters honestly compete for the recognition, not the money.

Historically, the idea that a person might feel a little bit too much pride in her quilting was not generally sanctioned. Quilting stitches that did not meet expectations, made by a well-meaning person at a quilting bee, were replaced in secret; several documentation forms confirmed this practice. Recognizing, however, that a competitive spirit could be a good thing, communities began to figure out ways to channel it to a positive end. The result was the making of exhibition quilts, as documented by a diary kept by Lucy Irion Neilson. Most of the references refer to the quiltmaking of her older sister, Cordele, who, in September of 1873, was making a quilt for exhibition at the Columbus Fair. Lucy, on the twenty-seventh and twenty-eighth of that month, remarked, "The gentlemen have gone to the trouble and expense of building a Floral Hall for the exhibition of ladies' handwork. It is a beautiful circular building, and is quite ornamental." She wrote again two years later, on September 27, 1875, of another quilt Cordele was working on for the fair, and again in 1877, with the comment that Cordele was temporarily at a standstill for lack of

scraps, and someone named Bess could not be persuaded to "give that blue satin Polonaise—stingy old thing!"[20] It is clear that Cordele found the making of quilts for exhibition to be a compelling activity, since she prepared an entry for three consecutive fairs, which apparently were held every other year.

The village of Washington, Mississippi, just outside Natchez, was an important town in the state's early years, serving as capital for a while. It held three fairs a year, in the spring, summer, and fall, on the grounds of Jefferson College, and the fairs attracted more than one thousand people.

Fig. 7.15. "Central Medallion" quilt thought to have been made by Liza Owens of Grenada County, Mississippi, in 1857. Of all-cotton materials, with appliqué work done in the *broderie perse* style and with fabrics from possibly as early as the 1800–1825 period, it is hand-quilted all over in custom designs, including feathered cables, at 8 stitches per inch. MQA quilt no. M-84. Collection of Margaret Mason, great-great granddaughter.

Fig. 7.16. "United States of America" made by Addie Edwards Van Hooser (1896–1936) in Neshoba County, Mississippi, in 1933. Of all-cotton materials, with a combination of techniques, including hand appliqué in blind stitch and buttonhole stitch, painting, and embroidery, the quilt has fine, close hand stitching at 11 to 12 stitches per inch. It is 84.5 inches wide by 88 inches long. MQA quilt no. I-03. Collection of Bobby Ruth Van Hooser Welsh, daughter.

Among the rare items offered for viewing in 1841 were "a locally-grown orange tree heavy with fruit, a new sort of 'comfort' to substitute for Negro blankets [one can only wonder], and two baskets 'made from the branches of the common swamp willow' by Mrs. J. F. H. Claiborne."[21]

The quilt documentation effort found early evidence of the competitive spirit in a *broderie perse* quilt made in 1857 as an entry for the Grenada County Fair (fig. 7.15). Family history says that the central medallion, or "quilt square," as they

called it, was sent over from England, and that is certainly possible. Motifs such as this were "at the peak of their popularity from about 1820 to 1840, both in Europe and in the United States."[22] Chintz, the fabric used for all the motifs on this quilt, was highly prized, especially if it was imported; and it is very possible that Liza Owens, or whoever made this quilt, hoarded the precious fabric until just the right use for it came along. The family says that the quilt won many ribbons, which have finally been lost, although they were passed down through several generations along with the quilt.

There were World's Fairs, in Chicago in 1933 and in New York in 1939, that influenced Mississippi quilters, three of whom created highly original designs to enter in the contests sponsored by the fairs, and another who made a duplicate of a winning Chicago entry. Sears, Roebuck and Company sponsored a "Century of Progress" quilt contest to coordinate with an exhibition of the same name that celebrated the one hundredth birthday of the city of Chicago; the city's centennial celebration was part of the 1933 World's Fair. Sears sponsored another quilt contest in 1935, called the "National Make It Yourself" contest, inspired, no doubt, by the overwhelming number of entries and accompanying favorable publicity resulting from the 1933 contest.

Addie Edwards married Arlie Van Hooser, a farmer, and they had one daughter and one son. Her life, however, was not that of a typical farmer's wife: during her brief lifetime, she worked as an artist's model and a sculptor. She designed her own quilts, many of which she gave to relatives. One extra-special quilt she made as an entry in the Sears "Century of Progress" contest (fig. 7.16). She must have felt very proud when it took a blue ribbon, an Award of Merit, in the contest.

Addie not only designed the quilt, she executed every aspect of it, including painting each state's flower onto the corresponding silhouette of the state. The painted flowers were then accented with embroidery, and the abbreviation for the state's name was discreetly added beneath the flower. The top of the map was surmounted by a pair of flags that wave gaily, although in opposite directions, from tricolor flagpoles that were finished with a gold-colored finial. Below the map, the letters U and S were appliquéd in the traditional tricolor scheme of red, white, and blue. The blue part was embellished with white stars. The family indicated that Addie believed that the judges somehow did not care for her work on the flags, and that prevented her taking a larger prize.

A second entry to the 1933 Sears "Century of Progress" contest took the blue ribbon as the best in the Memphis region. It was made by Mrs. E. E. Wilkins and her daughter, Mrs. J. A. Swanson, of Duck Hill. It is an exquisitely pieced and quilted "Carolina Lily" done in red, pink, and green on a white background. There is a scalloped border featuring a single lily motif at the top of each point of the scallops. Feathered wreaths and other decorative designs are incorporated into the extremely fine quilting.[23]

Mrs. Avery Burton of Duck Hill made up a completely original design and submitted it to the 1935 "National Make It Yourself" contest under the name "A Curiosity Bedspread" (fig. 7.17). Everything about the quilt is curious, to use her choice of words—the mix of designs, the choice of motifs, the insertion of a rather traditional red, white, and green appliquéd flower block, the overlaid embroidery on the seamlines. Perhaps the most uncommon feature is the inclusion of two human figures, a woman and a man, in early twentieth-century clothing. The depiction of human forms on quilts is so rare as to always be interesting. The

quilt is clearly a documentation of things in Mrs. Burton's life, in the same vein as the Gabbert crazy quilt mentioned in chapter 4 (p. 88), but Mrs. Burton's style is much more painterly. Every quilt submitted to the "National Make It Yourself" contest was awarded a green ribbon as a merit award, and Mrs. Burton's ribbon is still attached to the quilt. So is a paper label, used, no doubt, by Sears, Roebuck and Company for tracking this and all the other entries to the contest.

The sponsors of the New York World's Fair, which was held from 1939 to 1940, were surely cog-

Fig. 7.17. "A Curiosity Bedspread" signed and dated with the following information: "Made of Sears, Roebuck & Co. Goods in 1935. Made by Mrs. Avery Burton, Duck Hill, Miss., Age 68 years." The piece, of appliquéd cottons, is unquilted and is 74 inches wide by 75 inches long. Collection of the University of Mississippi. Photo courtesy of Shelley Zegart and the Quilt Digest Press.

Fig. 7.18. Mamie Lettie Moore Andrews in her mid-twenties, shortly after her marriage on August 19, 1902. Her marriage would endure for 37 years; her husband, Albert Hugh Andrews, died the same year she made the World's Fair quilt.

Fig. 7.19. "New York 1939" made by Mamie Lettie Moore Andrews (1879–1945) of McComb, Mississippi, in 1939. Of all-cotton materials, pieced and appliquéd, the quilt has fine, close hand quilting at 12 stitches per inch. MQA quilt no. P-114. Collection of Al (grandson) and Karen Andrews.

nizant of the great success of the "Century of Progress" quilt contest of the 1933 World's Fair in Chicago. Twenty-four thousand quilts had been entered! Accordingly, the 1939 World's Fair organization sponsored a contest named "America through the Needle's Eye," which was for all sorts of needlework, including quilts. It was subsidized throughout the East and West by department stores that ran preliminary contests and awarded prizes of more than three thousand dollars. Quilts could be either old or new, the latter being those made after the announcement of the contest.[24] *Good Housekeeping* magazine also sponsored a contest, with its subject the same as the theme of the fair: "Better Living in the World of Tomorrow." The contest was limited to only quilts based on the theme, and six hundred entries were submitted.[25]

A Mississippi woman, Mamie Lettie Moore Andrews (fig. 7.18) was about sixty years old and surely very forward-thinking (says her family, proudly) at the time she designed and made her entry for the fair (fig. 7.19). It contains towers with lightning bolts, representing, no doubt, the impact of rural electrification and the influence of technology on the future; there are also doves to represent peace. The structure in the center is based on one of the buildings at the fairgrounds, an image of which had surely been broadly circulated in the fair's promotional materials. Even more interesting than the motifs is the border, which is worked in strips and squares so that "New York" can be spelled out, with the same method used to make the four corner squares and center half-square on the bottom border. It is not entirely clear which contest Mrs. Andrews entered. Her theme would suggest that she was working with the *Good Housekeeping* rules; however, she took a blue ribbon, which could have been from a regional level of the "America through the Needle's Eye" contest.

Fig. 7.20. Lizzie Dunn, *nee* Elizabeth Beatrice Welch, was born on June 17, 1871, in Greensboro, Mississippi (now Choctaw County), the daughter of Dr. and Mrs. Thomas C. Welch. Her father died 5 months before her birth. She was educated in area schools and later became a teacher. When she married John Luther Dunn, a farmer and merchant, they settled in the Duck Hill area, where she continued to live after his death in 1935. She lived to be 100 years old and was piecing quilts when she died in 1971. The family estimates that Lizzie completed from 150 to 200 quilts during the course of her lifetime and gave most of them to family, friends, and newlyweds as gifts. Photo courtesy of Alice Sanford.

The "Century of Progress" quilt contest was a gold mine for Sears, Roebuck and Company. Not only did Sears reap a fortune in goodwill for the company from the publicity the contest generated, it also replicated many of the winning quilts in kits, complete with fabric, which it sold through its catalog and other outlets. The company also published and sold a book called *Sears Century of Progress in Quiltmaking*, which contained patterns for the prize-winning quilts and for pillows to match.[26]

Lizzie Dunn (fig. 7.20) of Choctaw County, Mississippi, purchased two Sears kits (through *Progressive Farmer* magazine) in 1934. One was a "Wheel of Mystery" design, the other was a "Rising Sun" (fig. 7.21), which she selected in yellow. It was also available in pink, blue, and lavender. The "Rising Sun" was a replica of a prize-winning quilt, which was itself a kit manufactured by H. Ver Mehren of Des Moines, from the "Century of Progress" contest.[27] The quilt entered into the Sears contest had more complicated quilting and

Fig. 7.21. "Rising Sun" variation, called "Sunburst" by the family, made by Elizabeth Beatrice (Lizzie) Dunn (1871–1971) in Duck Hill, Mississippi, in 1934 and 1935. The quilt, from a kit of all-cotton materials, is hand-pieced and hand-quilted. MQA quilt no. H-12. Collection of Alice Sanford, granddaughter.

stronger colors than did the kit that Sears eventually manufactured from it. This may be the only documented instance of one kit quilt inspiring another kit quilt.

Mrs. Dunn likely knew nothing of the background of her quilt design, although she was probably aware that it had been a winner in the World's Fair contest, which became the colloquial name for the "Century of Progress" contest. She bought both the kits to make quilts for her two granddaughters. One of the granddaughters offers the following eyewitness account of the quiltmaker:

This hardy homemaker enjoyed quiltmaking and crochet. Wives of the sharecroppers on the Dunn farm helped Lizzie put the quilt tops she pieced into the quilt frame that was always suspended from her bedroom ceiling. She taught many of these women the art of quiltmaking.

She was a prolific quilter who pieced quilts in the summer and quilted them in the fall and winter. She would race through her gardening, flower beds, cooking, and housekeeping duties, and then gratefully spend the rest of the summer day piecing scraps on a screened side porch. She would sit in a rocking chair with her quilt scraps in clean, bleached flour sacks stacked around her. Most of Lizzie's quilts were made from dress scraps or purchased scraps from Sears and Roebuck. She carded cotton batts from the cotton grown on the Dunn farm for the batting, and never used "store bought" batting.

In her drive to complete as many quilts as possible each year, Lizzie might shorten her creation, leaving users with cold noses or cold toes come winter![28]

Quilts Made Especially for Children

Quiltmakers in Mississippi from the antebellum period forward made quilts especially for their children. One of the earliest is a crib quilt from Ashburn plantation, from a family said to be among the first in Natchez. The quilt is in the "Broken Dishes" pattern, thought to have been made in the 1840–1850 period, but it could have been made even earlier (see p. 26 for more information). Another early crib quilt was made in the 1850s in a red-and-green "Nine-Patch" design, set with alternating white squares (fig. 7.22). It was the baby quilt of Charles Fife, of Vicksburg, who had grown to be a young man by the time of the Civil War; he sold cigarettes between the lines to the troops.[29] These two examples illustrate what was true of all early quilts made for children: they were not done in a juvenile theme; they were merely smaller quilts made in traditional patterns.

Regular patchwork patterns continued to be used for baby quilts into the 1930s and 1940s. A "Stars" or "Tumbling Blocks" was made by Lou Sikes Johnson (1868–1944) for her grandson, James E. Palmer, born in April 1936.[30] A "Four-Patch" design was chosen by Sadie Bain Cottman for the baby quilt she made to celebrate the birth of her niece in 1944. It contains scraps of fabric from the dresses of three generations of women.[31]

Far more popular for children's quilts, after the turn of the twentieth century, were those made with juvenile themes. It will come as a surprise to no one that the favorite design was, by far, "Sunbonnet Sue" (figs. 7.23 and 7.24), whose name was "Dutch Girl" in a great many Mississippi examples. One reason for her widespread acceptance was that patterns were available and easy to find—one pattern manufacturer, Ladies Art Company, had a

"Sunbonnet Sue" in production constantly from 1920 to 1925. Sears also sold the pattern, as did many other sources. There are at least fifteen different variations of the design, and lots of different names for it: "Sunbonnet Baby," "Sunbonnet Susie," "Little Dutch Girl," and even "Mary Ann" or "Mary Lou." (An enterprising quilter named Betty Hagerman won the Kansas State Fair in 1978 with a quilt called "A Meeting of the Sunbonnet Children," which depicted all the different versions of Sunbonnet Sue and Overall Sam.[32])

The origin of the figure of a sunbonneted child lost in a world of her own seems to be with a British illustrator of the 1870s, Kate Greenaway. In the United States, a book entitled *The Sunbonnet Babies Primer* was published in 1902 by Rand McNally. It was illustrated by Bertha L. Corbett, and read by more than one million first-grade children for nearly thirty years. Mrs. Corbett's little sunbonneted girls were produced as embroidery patterns by Frank's Art Needlework Company of St. Louis beginning in 1905, and, from that point on, patterns and different interpretations were offered by just about everybody in the business.[33]

Mississippi quilters loved Sue just like everyone else did. The general plan for a "Sunbonnet Sue" quilt seemed to be that she would wear a different outfit in each of the blocks on the quilt.

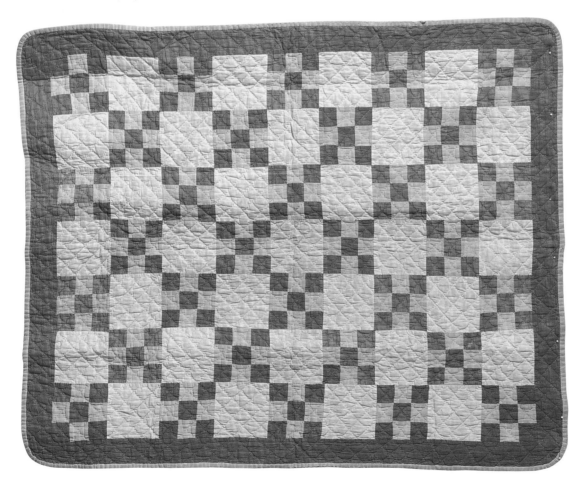

Fig. 7.22. "Nine-Patch" crib quilt, maker unknown, from Vicksburg, circa 1850. Of all-cotton materials, it is hand-quilted in an all-over design at 8 stitches per inch. It is 31 inches wide by 38 inches long. MQA quilt no. E-63. Collection of Elizabeth Clarke, granddaughter of Charles Fife, for whom quilt was made.

Fig. 7.23. "Sunbonnet Sue," called "Sunbonnet Girl" by the family, made by Georgia B. Currie of Mendenhall, Simpson County, Mississippi, in 1932 as a high school graduation gift for the owner. Of all-cotton materials, in a combination of hand-piecing and appliqué with a running stitch, and with embroidered flowers on bonnets, the piece is hand-quilted in an all-over crosshatch design at 7 to 8 stitches per inch. It is 68 inches wide by 84 inches long. MQA quilt no. I-52. Collection of Myerl Langford, niece.

Fig. 7.24. "Flower Girl," called "Dutch Doll" by the family, made by Inez Hudson May of Lodi, Montgomery County, Mississippi, in the 1930s. This pattern was offered through Sears, Roebuck and Company in 1934. Of all-cotton materials, it is hand-pieced and appliquéd with a blanket stitch, with some machine work. Hand-embroidered flowers are in the girls' hands, and it is hand-quilted in straight lines at 3 stitches per inch. The quilt measures 65 inches wide by 80 inches long. MQA quilt no. C-34. Collection of Sarah Landrum May, daughter-in-law.

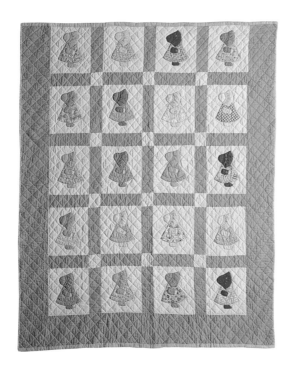

Usually there were twenty blocks, but some quilts contain thirty or thirty-six little girls. The blocks were usually mixed to get even distribution of color across the quilt, but one quilter put all the Sues in yellow dresses on one row, the ones in blue on another row, those in red on another, and so on. She used no sashing, so there is no other detailing to distract from the monochromatic rows.[34] Most of the time, Sue stood straight up in her block, but sometimes she was placed on the diagonal, which gave the impression that she was either falling forward or backward.[35] Quilters usually set the blocks together with sashing, often with cornerstones of a different color (pink and blue was a favorite combination). Sometimes stripped sashing and "Nine-Patch" cornerstones added nice finishing details.

One shouldn't assume that these quilts were always made for children—one was made as a wedding gift for Audrey Eakes, who married Douglas Green in 1932. Each maker of a block signed her name.[36] One of the Sues on Mrs. Green's quilt is turned in the opposite direction of all the others. In another quilt, one Sue is upside down. (This may be the introduction of the "deliberate mistake" that became a folk tradition of quilters. It was to show one's humility—only God is perfect, therefore one should not strive for perfection in a quilt.)

Ladies' Art Company had a pattern for a boy in overalls and a straw hat during the same period of time (1920–1925) as they ran "Sunbonnet Sue." They called their little fellow "Overall Bill." Frank's Art Needlework Company called theirs "Overall Boy," and others were "Farmer Boy," "Straw Hat Boy," "Sunny Jim," and "Overall Andy." There were even "Happy Jack," "Romper Boy," and "Dutch Boy." And there was also "Overall Sam" (fig. 7.25), which is the preferred name for the pattern in Mississippi. There were a few of

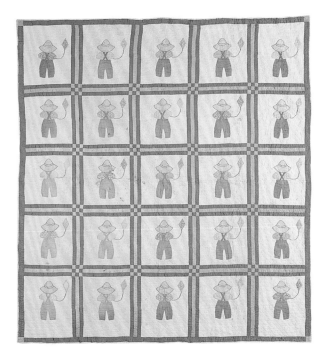

Fig. 7.25. "Overall Sam," called "Boy and Kite" by the family, made by Olivia Virginia Smith Cole of Lena, Leake County, Mississippi, circa 1932. (Quiltmaker was about 18 years old and may have been assisted by her mother, Cora Cole Smith, and her sisters Aldreen Smith Latham and Dorothy Smith Morland. Aldreen made a matching quilt at the same time.) Of all-cotton materials, it is hand- and machine-appliquéd, with hand stitching in blind and running stitch and embroidered details. It is hand-quilted by the piece around the appliqué and in an all-over crosshatch design in the background. It is 76.5 inches wide by 83.75 inches long. MQA quilt no. E-06. Collection of Jeanette Farmer, daughter.

Fig. 7.26. "Three Little Pigs" made by Hazel Chapman (Stanley), age 16, Frances Chapman, age 15, and Sue Chapman (LaCava), age 13, with a little bit of work by Mary Ellen Chapman (Howell), in Coffeeville, Yalobusha County, Mississippi, in 1932 and 1933. Of all-cotton materials, it is hand-pieced and appliquéd with a blind stitch, hand-embroidered, and quilted. It is 37.5 inches wide by 59 inches long. MQA quilt no. P-75. Collection of Kay Chapman Locke, sister.

these quilts made, but nowhere near the numbers of "Sunbonnet Sue" quilts. Pattern companies suggested that the two designs, the boy and the girl, be used as companions on a quilt (probably so they could sell two patterns rather than one), but Mississippi quilters didn't go for that idea. Their quilts were strictly unisex.

A "Sunny Jim" that was made in 1928 and 1929 by Bessie Fox Truly of Fayette, Mississippi, for her grandson, Tommy, was in constant use by him when he was a small boy. It has survived only because it was finally put away to be saved for posterity. Mrs. Truly was heard to say that "[h]er children were smart, her grandchildren very smart, and her great-grandchildren were brilliant."[37]

After "Sunbonnet Sue" and "Overall Sam," the next favorite motif for children's quilts was one based on fairy tales or nursery rhymes. The "Three Little Pigs" (fig. 7.26) was especially favored, in part because a Jackson newspaper in the early 1930s printed a series of patterns, one every Sunday for fourteen weeks. When all the squares were made up and put together, a child's quilt resulted. In the center is the wolf, dressed up in a bonnet, shawl, and skirt, with his old tail sticking out from underneath in the back. He is rendered in appliqué and embroidery; this panel is the length of two of the blocks that surround it. It is placed toward the top of the quilt; there is one row of blocks above the wolf, and two rows are beneath it. The rows and the blocks on either side of the panel are all based on the fairy tale. Each of the three pigs is given his own block; each of the different houses are featured; other blocks contain phrases from the fairy tale: "No! By th' hair," "Of my chin," "And I'll puff." The phrases begin with appliquéd letters and are finished with embroidery. It is a charming, playful piece, and several quilts from the pattern series were doc-

Fig. 7.27. "Nursery Rhymes/Lindbergh Baby" made by Velma Bentley Couch of Anguilla, Sharkey County, Mississippi, in 1932. Of all-cotton materials, the quilt has hand-appliqué with a buttonhole stitch, hand embroidery, some machine construction, and hand-quilting with a right-angle design in the blocks and straight lines elsewhere at 6 stitches per inch. It is 65 inches wide by 79 inches long. MQA quilt no. E-52. Collection of Lela C. Phillips, daughter.

Fig. 7.28. An embroidered picture of the Lindbergh baby was based on a photograph in a newspaper story.

umented, along with stories from the owners indicating how much the quilts meant to them. One owner's mother had stitched the quilt while awaiting her daughter's birth; another was made by the wife of a Primitive Baptist preacher and her daughter, who enjoyed working together; and a third was done by three sisters whose mother insisted that they do handwork each day. They decided to make the quilt from the newspaper, and they gave it to their baby sister, the last sibling, when she was born.

Velma Bentley Couch was making a quilt of nursery rhymes, taking her designs from books. She wanted to have twenty blocks, each portraying a different nursery rhyme: a piggy going to market, Jack jumping over a candlestick, the old lady who lived in a shoe, a dog running away with a bone, etc. She had made eighteen different blocks, but had run out of ideas for the last two. She made a big butterfly for one, and then she saw a picture of the missing Lindbergh baby. "That's it," she must have thought, and traced it onto a quilt square, which she embroidered, including the name "Lindy Jr." and the date, "1932" (figs. 7.27 and 7.28).

All the country was held in thrall at the kidnapping of the Lindbergh baby, but Mississippians, especially, had a special place in their hearts for Charles Lindbergh. He had spent several days in Maben (Oktibbeha County) in 1923, four years before his famous trans-Atlantic flight, as the result of a minor accident. The townspeople got to know him as a shy, sweet young man who took people up for rides, earning money to pay for the replacement parts he had had to buy for his plane. After the whole world knew him, he went back to Maben in the *Spirit of Saint Louis* and circled the boarding house where he had stayed and been treated so well, dropping a small gift out of the plane to his former landlady.[38]

A participant in the quilt documentation day at Natchez brought in a "Mother Goose" quilt that she had made at her mother's insistence when she was nine years old. It contains five picture blocks, executed in a combination of appliqué and embroidery, illustrating the tales of "Humpty Dumpty," "The Old Woman Who Lived in a Shoe," "Little Red Riding Hood," "Ride a Cock Horse to Banberry Cross," and "Little Miss Muffett." The picture blocks alternate with solid red blocks; the quilt is bordered in the same red. It is a doll-sized quilt and won a blue ribbon at the Mississippi State Fair in Jackson in 1929; the ribbon is still on the quilt![39] (One other doll quilt was found, a very pretty yellow and pale blue "One-Patch," made of one-and-one-eighth-inch squares. The square quilt measured thirty and one-half inches per side and was embellished with French knots on the binding.[40])

Nursery rhymes were also the subject of a sweet little six-block quilt (fig. 7.29) made by Emma Cummings for her first child in 1920. She graduated from Mississippi Normal College (later Mississippi Southern) and began teaching at age eighteen. She married just before her husband was shipped out to France in World War I; he returned in 1919. Their son was born on March 21, 1921. She must have decided to prepare for either a son or a daughter, because her scenes of "Jack and Jill" and "Little Jack Horner," as well as others, are sashed in both pink and blue.

Animals, naturally, were also chosen for baby quilts. One very inventive 1932 piece called "Peter Rabbit" by the family (called "Boy and Girl Rabbits" by the documentation team) was made by a kindergarten teacher for her son, using designs from a coloring book.[41] There was a crib quilt, from the 1930s or 1940s, of baby animals—rabbits, a lamb, ducks, and a puppy—made as a team effort: "Lois Bonner did the embroidery and Miss Molly

pieced and quilted it."[42] And there was at least one "Scottie" quilt, made from the widely circulated pattern inspired by President Franklin Delano Roosevelt's dog, Fala.[43] This particular quilt was made around 1940 and includes sixty-one little doggies, all marching one behind the other, except for one, who is deliberately turned vertically. The dogs are in subdued color schemes of solid-color fabrics, although some of the colors are not naturally found in the canine world—turquoise, for example. Each Scottie is wearing a little sweater carefully coordinated to his fur color.

There were other baby quilts, too many to be

Fig. 7.29. "Nursery Rhymes" made by Emma Jenkins Cummings of West Point, Mississippi, during 1920 and 1921. Of all-cotton materials, the quilt is hand-appliquéd with a buttonhole stitch; it has some machine work and is hand-quilted at 5 stitches per inch "in the ditch." It has a knife-edge finish on all four sides and is 35 inches wide by 50 inches long. MQA quilt no. O-19. Collection of Ruth Cummings Carter, daughter.

described. They are the most sentimental of quilts, akin in their emotional content to the diary-like crazy quilts. No better expression of the reason for the making of these quilts could be given than the following: "Feeling I would have a baby girl and love her so much—even before she was born—I wanted to make a quilt for her. This top was in Sears catalog. I ordered it in the fall of 1940 and my baby girl was born 17 April 1941. I made it by hand. . . . All a labor of love and God has blessed me with a beautiful, loving, precious daughter for 56 years now."[44]

Unique Techniques

The standard needlecraft methods for making a design on a quilt top are patchwork and appliqué, both of which involve the manipulation of colored bits of fabric to make a specified arrangement; sometimes embroidery is added to make accents, such as the stems of flowers. Members of the documentation team were intrigued whenever a quilt would appear that involved a different method for creating the design for the quilt top or for the quilt itself. Among the unique techniques displayed on the quilts brought in for documentation were painting, reverse appliqué, and unusual ways of working with fabric, such as folding or puckering. (These techniques are not necessarily unique to Mississippi; they are unique to quiltmaking in general.)

Puckering may not be exactly the right term for the technique that is used to make a great favorite of Mississippi quilters, the "yo-yo" spread. Whatever it is called, it involves placing a row of basting stitches along the outer edge of a fabric circle, then pulling on the thread to decrease the outer circumference so that the raw edge of the circle can be pulled to the wrong side of the fabric. The circle is then flattened down so that the entire circumference is finished with a fold. In some yo-yo quilts, the thread is pulled tightly so that the raw edges "pucker" in the center of the flattened circle; sometimes the puckered center is placed to the right side of the quilt to add an interesting texture.

The size of the fabric circles and the amount of puckering (or gathering) can vary widely from one yo-yo quilt to another, but most of the circles finish out to about one and one-half inches in diameter. Hundreds of circles are made, then connected to one another with a few whipstitches at equidistant points along the outer edges. In many instances, the "quilt" is considered finished when the last circle has been attached. Some yo-yo quilts are backed, but there is never a batting, and no quilting. For this reason, it is hard to say whether or not a yo-yo spread is actually a quilt, and many people specified that their piece was a coverlet, not a quilt.

There were thirteen yo-yo quilts brought in for documentation, and they exhibited a wide range of color placement. One was set in the popular "Trip around the World" design, in which rounds of color spread out from a center point (fig. 7.30). Others exhibited completely random placement of color (fig. 7.31); others were put together in block designs of nine to twenty-five fabric circles, with additional circles color-planned to form sashing. One of the most interesting was solid white, which most likely was made to be used over a colored sheet or blanket.[45]

Another type of bedcovering that is not considered a true quilt in some quarters is familiarly known as the "Biscuit Quilt." One such example made an appearance; it was constructed by stitch-

Fig. 7.30. "Yo-Yo Counterpane," set in a "Trip around the World" design, by Molly Warren Webb (d. 1943). Of all-cotton materials, it is 83 inches wide by 99 inches long. MQA quilt no. Q-96. Collection of Venita Ganett, great-great-granddaughter, and Sherry Westbrook, great-great-great-granddaughter.

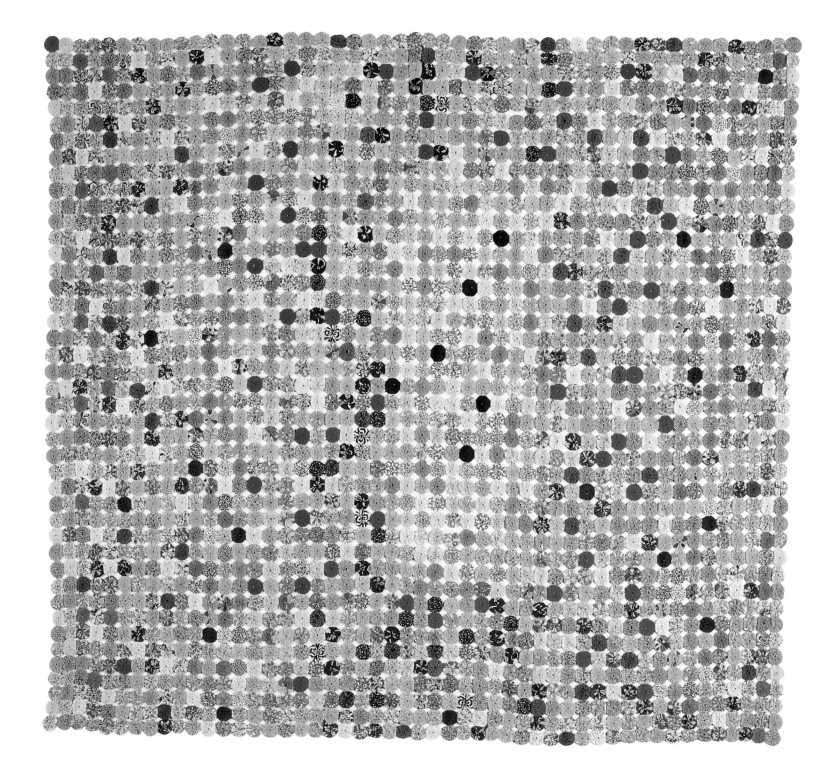

ing together small "pillows," each of which had been stuffed before being hand-stitched to the next one. The family called this quilt a "Silk Puff," an irresistible name for the piece, which was made of silks, satins, and taffetas and stuffed with wool.[46] It was backed with taffeta, and the borders, also of peach-colored taffeta, were quilted at five stitches per inch. Each "biscuit" had one quilting stitch, or a "tack," through its center.

One other type of quilt involved the manipulation of fabric in a way that is not a common practice in quiltmaking. Squares of fabric are cut, then folded twice so that two sides of the resulting smaller square are finished with folds. Working with a foundation fabric, the quilter arranges the folded squares so that overlapping circular rows are formed; each row is stitched to the base as it is laid in place. The finished motifs can be fairly large, as in the example shown in figure 7.32, or they can be much smaller; one quilt contained thirty motifs, rather than nine.[47] There are examples of this type work in which one motif is made of a size to cover the entire top.

Names for the quilt made of folded fabric squares range from "Target," to "Petal," to "Cockleburr," to "Pine Cone," to "Pineapple." No matter what it is called, nor how many motifs make up the top, it is very heavy, even though it is not quilted and contains no batting; a backing is usually applied.

Just as method of construction can be the unique feature of a quilt, so can the technique employed to make the decorative design of the piece. Several quilts were made with methods that are not unheard-of in the quilt world, but are certainly uncommon. One was done completely in reverse appliqué, which is a technique in which two or more layers of fabric are placed together and the uppermost layers are cut and turned under to reveal the layers beneath (fig. 7.33). It is a more exacting method than traditional laid-on appliqué, in which shapes are cut from fabric and placed where desired, then stitched down.

Painted quilts are rarer even than reverse appliqué quilts, especially ones from the 1940s and earlier. It is not, however, its singleness which makes the one painted quilt that was documented so exceptional; it is its beauty (fig. 7.34). Each of the twenty-five patterned blocks is painted with an original design of a flower, restrained and delicate in execution. Embroidery has been used sparingly, to outline the main shapes of each piece and to create details such as veining in the leaves. The pat-

Fig. 7.31. "Yo-Yo Spread" made by Agnes Willis Supple of Washington County, Mississippi, started in 1929, when she was seventeen years old, and finished in 1931. Coverlet of all-cotton materials is 80 inches wide by 90 inches long. MQA quilt no. C-49. Collection of Mary E. Clark.

Fig. 7.32. "Target," or "Pine Burr," provenance unknown, circa 1930. The quilt of all-cotton materials, made using folded fabric construction and pieced onto foundation fabric, is not quilted. It is 72 inches wide by 73 inches long. MQA quilt no. K-11. Collection of Bertha Carr, on loan to Mississippi Cultural Crossroads Center in Port Gibson.

Fig. 7.33. "Floral Appliqué," maker and provenance unknown, from the 1860–1870 period. Made with all-cotton materials, the quilt motif is of reverse appliqué executed with a blind stitch and a chain stitch. It is hand-quilted around each appliquéd piece and in an all-over grid pattern at 7 stitches per inch. It is 86 inches wide by 85.5 inches long. MQA quilt no. G-49. Collection of Betty Morrow.

Fig. 7.34. "Floral—Embroidered and Painted" made by Madie Angelitti Burch Permenter in Philadelphia, Neshoba County, Mississippi, circa 1940. Of all-cotton materials, it contains hand-painted and embroidered floral designs; it is hand-pieced, with some machine work, and is hand-quilted around the designs and in an all-over design of cross-hatching at 7 to 8 stitches per inch. It is 70.5 inches wide by 71 inches long. MQA quilt no. I-40. Collection of Ed (grandson) and Marlene Permenter.

terned blocks are set against dark blue setting blocks in a checkerboard pattern, and the quilt is bordered on all four sides with a design of a white picket fence placed against a dark blue background. The maker, Madie Permenter, a teacher and housewife, was innately gifted as well as inordinately skilled.

Some artists use embroidery floss rather than paint. A marvelous summer spread was made with alternating pale blue and cream-colored blocks, each of which are embroidered with what appear to be original designs of fruits, such as strawberries or cherries, and unusual flowers of all kinds—tuberoses, for example. It is a lovely, sentimental piece, reminiscent of *The Country Diary of an Edwardian Lady*, a popular book of several years back.[48]

There were several other quilts whose design was executed solely in embroidery; most of these appear to have been made with the help of transfer patterns, which were heat-sensitive sheets of inked paper with a design drawn in; when they were ironed onto a fabric, the lines that were to be stitched were transferred to the fabric. Other embroidered quilts were available as kits.

The Shaifer Quilts

Working with the Shaifer collection of quilts (see figs. 6.4, 7.36, 7.37. and 7.38) was one of the highlights of the entire documentation effort. Rarely does it occur that a collection of this size, more than fifty pieces, covering such a broad span of time remains together. It covers nearly one hundred years, from 1850 to 1950, and in its entirety affords a good overview of a century of Mississippi quiltmaking. The owner of the collection, Libby Hollingsworth, is a Mississippian through and through. Her father's people are the Shaifers of Port

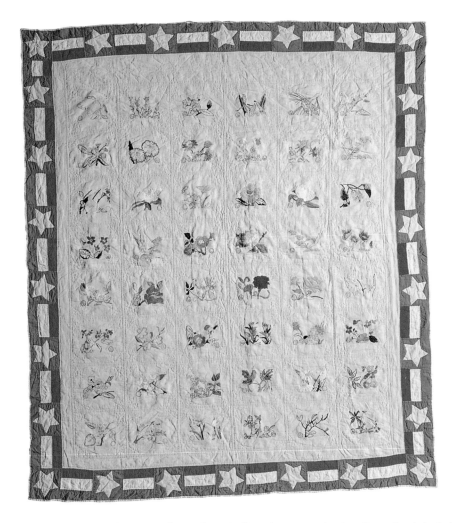

Gibson, and her mother's people are from Indianola in Sunflower County. Her mother's grandparents were from Biloxi and built the house now named Beauvoir, famous as the summer and retirement home of Jefferson Davis. When Mrs. Hollingsworth's great-grandmother, Virginia Brown Baker, was born there, the house was named Orange Grove. As an adult, Mrs. Baker made a crazy quilt from scraps of garments worn by her ancestors at the house. During a wedding reception held there in the late twentieth century for a great-great-granddaughter, the quilt was on display.

Fig. 7.35. "State Flowers" made by Carla Parr Bateman of Myrtle, Union County, Mississippi, in the 1920–1930 period. The quilt of all-cotton materials has motifs created with a combination of appliqué (done with buttonhole stitch) and fine embroidery. The quilt top is pieced with a combination of hand and machine methods; it has a border of stars and stripes and is hand-quilted to outline flowers and echo seam-lines with fine, close hand quilting at 12 stitches per inch. MQA quilt no. O-143. Collection of David Thomason.

Fig. 7.36. "Churn Dash" made by Mary Jane Wheeless of Port Gibson, Mississippi, in the 1875–1900 period. Of all-cotton materials, the quilt is hand-pieced and quilted in an all-over pattern of shells at 5 to 6 stitches per inch. It is 86.5 inches wide by 87 inches long. MQA quilt no. K-22. Collection of Libby Hollingsworth, great-niece.

Fig. 7.37. "Pinwheel" made by Amanda Guice Shaifer of Port Gibson, Mississippi, in 1890. Of all-cotton materials, the quilt is hand-pieced, with some machine work, and is hand-quilted by the piece and in a cross-hatch design. It is 80.5 inches wide by 83 inches long. MQA quilt no. K-29. Collection of Libby Hollingsworth, great-grand-daughter.

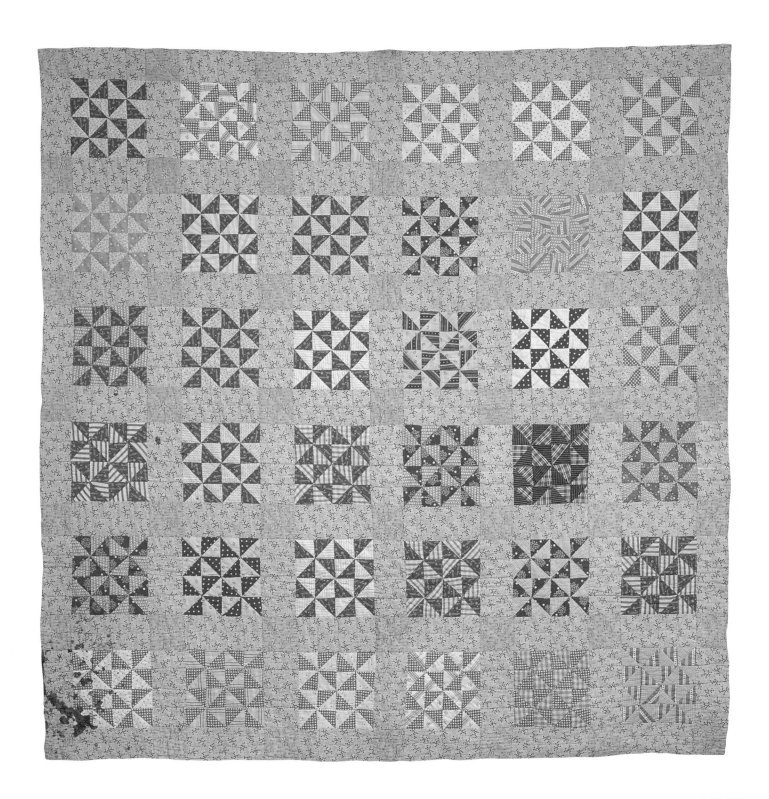

Fig. 7.38. "Three Tulips" made by Elizabeth Wheeless Shaifer and Laura Percy Shaifer of Port Gibson, Mississippi, in the 1920s. Of all-cotton materials, the quilt is hand-appliquéd with a blind stitch, with some machine work, and quilted by the piece and in a crosshatch design at 5 stitches per inch. It is 76 inches wide by 85 inches long. MQA quilt no. K-48. Collection of Libby Hollingsworth, granddaughter and niece.

The Shaifer story begins about 1813 and continues up through the twentieth century. Abram Keller Shaifer settled in the vicinity of Port Gibson sort of by accident. He was traveling from Tennessee to New Orleans on the Natchez Trace, intending to do some business with the partners who were floating seven flatboats down the Mississippi River as he traveled overland, when he fell dreadfully ill. He was forced to spend several weeks recuperating in Fayette with some friendly people who took him in and nursed him back to health. He recovered his strength and went on to New Orleans, only to discover that his partners had disposed of the merchandise they had delivered to the city, and five of the boats as well. They had left him two boats, which he sold for lumber before beginning his return trip to Pennsylvania back up the Trace.

He stopped over to pay a call on the kind friends who had tended him so well during his sickness, and decided that he liked the area so well that he would just stay there. The little town of Port Gibson was just getting started, and it was here that he settled; records show that he had purchased a commercial building there by 1815. To make a living, he chose to take a different tack than cotton farming; he began raising vegetables and fruits, especially melons, and exported his produce all over the country.

In 1817, he married Elizabeth Hannah Humphries and started the family whose daughters and granddaughters and great-granddaughters would be great needlework enthusiasts and quilters. Family diaries record the quilting activities of the daughters and their friends, such as the Wheeless girls, some of whom would marry Shaifer men. Of course, some of the Shaifer girls returned the compliment and married Wheeless men! Both names are intertwined, not only with one another, but with those of other area families in the generations that followed the marriage of Abram Shaifer and Elizabeth Humphries.[49]

CHAPTER EIGHT

The Tradition Continues
1945—2000

In today's world, if you're involved in quilting, you've found something that will let you cope with just about anything. If you're lonesome, you can reach out to another quilter; if you're sad, you can make yourself glad by looking at the beauty you're creating; if you're happy, you can share it by giving a quilt as a gift. Time will go okay if you can work with your hands.

—Martha Skelton

ALTHOUGH THE QUILT documentation effort limited the recording of quilts to those made before 1946, the members of the Mississippi Quilt Association believe that the enormous popularity of quiltmaking in the state at this time, the beginning of the twenty-first century, must be celebrated lest the reader have the impression that quiltmaking in the state has dwindled. Nothing could be farther from the truth. Since 1975, quilts across the nation have been made in quantities that dwarf even the numbers from the second half of the nineteenth century, which had always held the record for greatest creativity and production; and there is every reason to believe that quiltmaking in Mississippi has followed the national trend. However, if those quilts had been included in this first effort,

the documentation team simply could not have handled the volume. It is the hope of the volunteers from this first effort that the time from 1946 forward will form the basis for a second documentation project. It would be interesting to know if the state mirrored the national trend of lack of interest in quilting during the decades of the 1950s and 1960s. Also, there are indications that the number of quilts made by African Americans after 1946 could be substantially greater than the number from before 1946. It is almost a certainty that a second documentation effort will find many more practicing African American quilters and a substantial body of quilting work that will contribute to our knowledge in this area.

The Mississippi Quilt Association concluded

"Moons and Stars" made by Martha Skelton of Vicksburg, Mississippi. From an Aunt Martha's pattern created in the 1930s comes this variation on the "Man in the Moon" block. Of all-cotton materials, it is hand-pieced and hand-quilted. It is 80 inches wide and 93 inches long. Collection of Martha Skelton.

185

that the best way to establish that quiltmaking is thriving in Mississippi at the beginning of the twenty-first century is by recognizing a number of particularly outstanding quilters. The association wanted to recognize notable quilters whose work will be treasured by their families and admired by others fifty or a hundred years from now. To make such a selection (from so many possibilities) a committee was appointed and charged with choosing a cross section of quiltmaking styles. The final list of thirteen quilters was selected with no consideration given to the age of the person, the number of quilts she had produced, where she lived, or whether or not she had participated in the quilt search project.

The selection committee, after due deliberation, chose the following as representative of the different types of quiltmakers in Mississippi as the new century begins: Martha Skelton, sisters Martha Dubard and Sue Mitchell, Ginny Freeman, Martha Ginn, Ruth Vinson Irwin, Clara Ann Johnson, Ollie Jean Lane, Gwen Magee, Geraldine Nash, Barbara Newman, Suzanne Peery Schutt, and Hystercine Rankin. Many, perhaps most, of these Mississippi quilters identify themselves as traditional quilters, in that they continue to practice the style and workmanship of their grandmothers and prefer to work with time-honored designs, perhaps deviating from the standard with a distinctive detail or color scheme. At the same time, many contemporary Mississippi quilters are trying new possibilities, turning out pieces that are expressions of that quiltmaker's particular and individual design aesthetic. Mississippi's quiltmaking heritage is doubly enriched by the contributions of both types of artists. At this, the beginning of the twenty-first century, it is safe to say that the future of quilting in the state is in good hands.

Martha Skelton

Because Martha Skelton (fig. 8.1) has been such an influence on so many of the state's quilters, including several featured here as her contemporaries, she could be considered the benevolent spirit of quiltmaking in Mississippi. In fact, it has been said that she is responsible for the survival of quilting in the state,[1] although this self-effacing gentlewoman will acknowledge only that she was quilting when she came to the state from Oklahoma in 1947, and that she has never stopped. "I was the only person I knew who was quilting in the late forties and the fifties," Martha says.[2] She was a young wife and mother then, with the attendant duties of those roles as defined in that pre-feminist era: cook and hostess for her husband's business dinners and luncheons, Sunday school teacher, PTA mother, garden club member, and community volunteer.

Alan Skelton, Martha's husband, had been asked by the U.S. Corps of Engineers to relocate from Oklahoma to Vicksburg to join the Waterways Experiment Station, established after the record-shattering 1927 flood to explore methods of preventing another such disaster. Martha says that Mississippi was very different from Oklahoma, primarily because the place she left behind was so "new," not having been granted statehood until November 16, 1907. One of the biggest differences for the young woman, however, was that she was separated from her kindred quilters. Martha grew up in an extended family that included her maternal grandmother and an aunt, who, in addition to quilting, practiced many other fabric arts: crochet, knitting, tatting, and embroidery. The textile arts were an ingrained part of daily life in Martha's upbringing, and so it seemed natural to her to continue quilting, even as she moved to a place where she knew of no one else who shared her interest.

When pressed to say what she learned from her mother, grandmother, and aunts about quilting, Martha replied that she had been taught simply how to cut out the pieces and put them together, and how to quilt them—in other words, the techniques required to assemble a quilt. Her family members did not spend much time with her on color planning, but along the way someone told her she had an "intuitive sense of color," so she hasn't spent a lot of time worrying about tints and shades and contrast and value and brights and muddies in her quilts. She has just followed her intuition. Her first quilt, started when she was fifteen years old, was a little six-pointed star, set with muslin. (Always the teacher, Martha explained that the muslin came from a flat bolt, one on which the number of yards could be measured off for purchase by counting the number of folds of fabric.) That little star quilt has long since worn out, which is actually a point of pride with Martha, who loves quilts on a bed and wants hers to be used, a point of view that is based on the role quilts played in her early life.

Martha kept on stitching through the "Dark Ages" of quilting—the fifties, sixties, and early seventies. She was delighted when the "quilt revival" (still happening) began in the 1970s because she finally had the opportunity of helping others learn the craft she had loved her whole life. As more and more people developed a new interest in quilts, many began to want to learn how to make them. As the demand for classes grew, Martha was there to fill the need for a teacher, at first in classes sponsored by university extension services, and later as a volunteer teacher in department stores. She would eventually teach in shops, guilds, and quilt organizations all over Mississippi, making it almost impossible to find a quilter in the state today who has not taken a class with her.[3] She initiated the Mississippi State Fair's first quilting bee in the early 1980s, at the request of then Agricultural Commissioner Jim Buck Ross, and coordinated the quilting bee for thirteen years. She has been a regular supporter and judge of the Mississippi Cultural Crossroads show in Port Gibson, which contrasts African American and European styles of quilting.

Martha's teaching renown reaches far beyond the borders of the state; she has taught in Alabama, Florida, and Texas. A true highlight in an event-filled life was being the featured quilter at the Smithsonian Festival of American Folk Art in 1974, mostly because it provided her with an early opportunity to show people how to do it, which she has always loved. (She returned as a featured quilter to the festival in 1997.) "I learn from every class I teach," she says, with characteristic modesty. "Every student has something to offer, which I can benefit from in my own work."

Even though acclaim continues to be heaped upon her, this teacher remains a student. Martha Skelton, who has been acclaimed as "Mississippi's Finest Quilter,"[4] and to whom many attribute their dedication to the art, strongly believes in taking classes herself. She has attended sessions led by Nancy Pearson, Jeanna Kimball, Elly Sienkiewicz, and Jenny Beyer, among others. She also spends a great deal of time reading quilting books and studying techniques. "I've been fortunate to be able to build a very extensive library of quilt books," she remarks, adding that she reads broadly and enthusiastically, trying to absorb as much about techniques and quilt history as is available. She does not believe that she has been influenced in her work by any one particular person she has read or studied with, but by all of them. "There's always something out there to learn," she points out, and fervently declares, "I hope I never get to the point where I feel like there's nothing left to learn!"

Fig. 8.1. Martha Skelton of Vicksburg stands next to her "Mariner's Compass" wall hanging. Photo by Barbara Newman.

The perpetual student was, at the time of this writing, completing a Hawaiian-style quilt, for which she cut one big quilt-sized appliqué to make the design of the top, in the manner typical of Island quilts. Continuing in the Hawaiian style, she echo-quilted the piece (that is, she placed multiple lines of quilting to duplicate the shapes of the appliqué). Martha admits to a real love of appliqué, and it is a subject she particularly enjoys teaching. "People are scared of appliqué, and I like to help them get over that fear and learn to love it like I do," she says.

Because the Hawaiian-style quilt is the one she is just finishing, it is her favorite of the moment. The quilt she is currently working on is always her favorite; the same goes for the stage of quilting she likes the most—it is whatever she is doing at that particular moment. She doesn't even complain about binding, although she realizes that step is the least favorite of most quilters. "When it's done, you've finished a quilt, and that's something to be happy about. So I like binding!" remarks Martha, with irrefutable logic.

Although she loves many different kinds of quilts, Martha confesses to having a special place in her heart for star quilts, and she has made lots of star variations. Usually not one to make the same quilt design more than one time, she allows that she may have made the same star more than once, although she would not be interested in exactly replicating one of her earlier quilts. The quilts she *is* interested in replicating are wonderful old traditional quilts. Her work with the state documentation project gave her inspiration for several quilts, one of which was a star design she has already reproduced. (Martha was a committed project volunteer, spending many, many hours helping to identify quilt patterns and evaluate quilts. "We worked very hard," she admitted.)

"I'm more interested in making quilts the way they were made in the beginning," Martha says, in defining what qualities define a traditional quilter, a term she uses to describe herself. After verifying that she does most of her work by hand, and that she still keeps a healthy, up-to-date scrap bag fed with the remains of dressmaking, she turns to the question of time. She believes that a traditional quilt requires a solid commitment of time; she doesn't believe in the "quilt in a weekend" idea for her own work. She doesn't care for "cookie cutter" quilts, those that have the same look; she believes that a traditional quilt "doesn't look like everyone else's." Accompanying her definition of what makes a traditional quilter is a great respect for proficient technique and excellence in workmanship.

"I have a lot of respect for superior craftsmanship, because I know what it takes. [In looking at fine old quilts,] you have to admire someone who was so careful and respectful of what she was doing. Along with making good fabric and color choices, she went on to develop the skill. She had the discipline to develop the skill," explains Martha, whose excitement at finding outstanding examples of skilled needlework was expressed by the stars and exclamation points she drew on the documentation forms for those quilts. Martha also commented about the quilters who were documented in the survey, "I've gotten to know lots of people in this state through my teaching. Most of them are much like the women I grew up with in Oklahoma—farm women who never had much, who made do with little. They were good, strong women. Those were the women who made the quilts we documented."

Like every quilter, Martha has dreams of what she wants to make in the future. She says that every New Year's Day she sits down and makes one list of quilts she has in progress and another list of the ones she might want to do next. She would surely find it very rewarding to also list what she accomplished during the year just past, for this woman has made an estimated two hundred or more quilts, quilts with an investment of time and technique. "A lot of them have been used up, and lots have been loved a lot, although not used up," she chuckles.

Martha Skelton's quilts hang in the permanent collections of the American Quilt Museum in Paducah, Kentucky, in the Mountain Mist Collection in Cincinnati, Ohio, and in the Old Capitol Museum in Jackson, Mississippi. Her quilts have traveled to the Netherlands, Germany, and Japan. Her work has been published in many quilt books and magazines, and she has been featured on numerous television shows and in countless newspaper articles. When asked to name which, of all the awards and recognition she has received, was the most meaningful to her, she couldn't single one out as most special. Instead she said, "I've taught a lot of people."

Martha Skelton quilts for the purest of motivations—the absolute love of it and what it represents. When asked how she would like to be remembered, this self-effacing practitioner of the art of quilting replied that she would like for people to say about her, "If somebody needed something, I'd help them."

Martha Dubard and Sue Mitchell

Two sisters from Louisville, Mississippi, Martha Dubard and Sue Mitchell (fig. 8.2), come from a family of quilters, as did Martha Skelton. Sue, who admits being the older of the two, remembers their grandmother making string quilts, using pages from the old Sears Roebuck catalog as a foundation, and she remembers selecting the pink fabric for a flower garden quilt her grandmother made for her. Martha has in her possession a pieced full-blown tulip quilt from their paternal grandmother, who had inherited it from her mother, who had pieced it about the time of the Civil War.

Early in her life, Sue developed an interest in quilting. "In 1951 I bought a magazine that contained pictures of four quilts, including a quilt like the 'Tulip' quilt in our family and a 'Nine-Patch' variation," she said. "My first quilt was the 'Nine-Patch,' and I recently began work on a 'Pineapple' quilt featured in that magazine. I still have the magazine."

Sue's interest in and love of quilting eventually inspired her sister to begin quilting. "Sue had been quilting for a long while," Martha said, "and when I retired from teaching about ten years ago, I began to take quilting classes. It has now become almost an addiction. I love to see the finished product and sometimes begin another quilt before I completely finish with one."

Martha keeps a quilt diary and has recorded nineteen bed-sized quilts and fourteen wall hangings. Sue has completed approximately fifteen quilts and ten wall hangings but admits to having "at least that many more ready to quilt."

Between the two quilting sisters, they have won blue ribbons in several area quilt shows. However, it is perhaps as teachers that they are best known throughout the state, having taught classes on precision piecing at gatherings of the Mississippi Quilt Association for several years. During some years, Martha teaches and Sue assists, and at other times the roles are reversed. "We like to teach this class on basic quilting," Martha says, "because careful, precise piecing with each small unit is the key to a successful project."

Another aspect of the sisters' quilting, one that

Fig. 8.2. *Left*, Martha Dubard and, *right*, Sue Mitchell. The Kirkpatrick sisters learned to quilt from their grandmother.

makes them popular in their hometown, is their willingness to share their skills. They are frequent teachers at the local quilt guild and go into their area schools to assist teachers with projects, using quilts as a basis for learning.

Sue is an advocate of the "lard can" philosophy of quilting. She has several of these tin cans with unfinished projects stored in them. "If I never get around to finishing them," she says, "just think how much my family will enjoy finding them some day." Martha, on the other hand, feels compelled to finish a project once it is begun. A friend said of Martha, "If she is standing in her driveway waiting for someone to pick her up, she has that needle going while she's waiting, even if it's just two minutes."

Ginny Freeman

One of Mississippi's quilting treasures is not a Mississippian. Ginny Freeman resides in Slidell, Louisiana, but for many years has been an integral part of Mississippi quilting. Known for her execution of miniatures, Ginny comes from a quilting family which included both of her grandmothers, some great aunts, her grandfather, four aunts, numerous cousins, a sister, and even her mother-in-law.

"As a child, I cut out pieces for my mother and grandmother," Ginny remembers. "But as a young adult I didn't quilt. When quilting became popular in the late 1970s, I decided to make a cathedral window and just progressed from there."

As a teacher, Ginny has taught organized classes in appliqué, dimensional appliqué, *broderie perse,* and rosemaling. She has taught quilting to school children, patiently working with them on a weekly basis for months at a time, passing along to them the craft she learned to love as a child. How-

Fig. 8.3. Although she lives in Louisiana, Ginny Freeman has been claimed as one of their own by Mississippi quilters.

ever, it is as a one-on-one teacher that she has made her greatest impact. One Mississippi quilter tells the story of being on a bus to the American Quilt Society show in Paducah, Kentucky, with Ginny.

Ginny was kept busy the entire trip moving from one seat to the next, teaching others in the group. "I wanted to learn to make a small 'Cathedral Window,'" a member of that group remembers, "and since Ginny works so much in miniatures I knew she could teach me. Neither one of us had any fabric, so she borrowed a tiny little piece and used that. The result was indeed a tiny 'Cathedral Window.'"

One of Ginny's passions is making yo-yo quilts, or spreads. Some of her yo-yos are the size of a dime but always perfect. Another of her skills is making tiny "Sunbonnet Sues" to be worn as lapel pins. When two quilters meet, one can often be heard to say, "Oh, I see you are wearing one of Ginny's pins." She also makes angels, Santas, needle cases, yo-yo necklaces, and other miniature pieces. Ginny prefers making miniatures to making full-sized quilts, but her projects are so intricate and detailed that there is as much work involved in one of her miniature quilts as there would be in a bed-sized quilt.

A humble person who prefers supporting others to being a leader, Ginny has won a number of awards in quilt challenges, including a regional award in the Hoffman Challenge. She estimates that she has completed approximately fifteen miniature quilts, about thirty small quilts, twenty wall hangings, seven or eight full-sized quilts, and six baby quilts—a notable number for a lady who seems to spend most of her time helping others master the art which she loves so well. When asked for her best quilting tip, Ginny said, "Perseverance, patience, accuracy—but most of all, enjoy!"

Fig. 8.4. Martha Ginn with her "This Is My Story, This Is My Song" quilt.

Martha Ginn

Martha Ginn proves the old adage, "If you want something done, get a busy person to do it." A quilter for some sixteen years, Martha has completed approximately one hundred pieces, including miniatures, wall quilts, children's quilts, and full-sized quilts, not to mention vests and jackets. She began her quilting career by making traditional quilts, but "the longer I quilt," she says, "the more daring I become with design and color. I enjoy the challenge of something new, and I want my quilts to represent my ideas."

Martha remembers growing up with quilts on all the beds in the house, and she just assumed that all families quilted. Although she was an accomplished seamstress as a young adult, Martha's early interests leaned more toward embroidery and cross-stitching. Slowly she began to develop a deeper appreciation for quilts her grandmother had made. Her first quilting experience was a cross-stitch sampler pattern. The blocks proved to be too beautiful to be quilted by a non-quilter, so she left her daughter to stitch the blocks while she learned to quilt.

An active person involved in a variety of church, choral, civic, gardening, and team tennis activities in Hattiesburg, where she has lived for the past thirty years, Martha often has to juggle responsibilities with her many interests. She likes to be productive and wants something concrete to show for the time involved. "Quilting represents the quiet, peaceful, introspective person in me; at other times it is joy shared with other quilters, a way to make a connection," she confides. And quilting enables Martha to enjoy all aspects of sewing: designing, creating, and playing with colors and fabrics, as well as using sewing skills. "Quilting allows me to be artistic in a medium that lavishes time and energy on the work," she says.

In addition to having won numerous awards from viewer's and judge's choice to honorable mention in local and regional shows (including the Gulf States Quilt Association's prestigious show in New Orleans, where Martha has won first and second place awards and a coveted "Viewer's Choice" award), she has also had quilts accepted in the American Quilter's Society Show in Paducah, Kentucky, and the International Quilt Association Show in Houston. Two of her most rewarding experiences were in designing and leading in the making of a quilt featuring children's book characters for the new Hattiesburg Public Library and in helping to create two large wall quilts for her church's sanctuary.

Like most master quilters, Martha is in demand as a teacher, having taught all levels of quilting to all ages of quilters. Also, like other quilt artists, it is difficult to get Martha to say which of her quilts she likes best; but judges and other quilters point to her "This Is My Story, This Is My Song" quilt as possibly her best. This Baltimore album-style appliqué quilt, begun in 1990 and completed in 1995, required approximately one thousand hours for planning, drafting, and appliquéing the top and another five hundred hours for quilting and binding.

Of this quilt, Martha states, "After making several traditional album blocks from patterns by Elly Sienkievicz, Nancy Pearson, and Pat Andreatta, I began designing my own blocks to commemorate important events in my life." The quilt includes, for example, the Texas state seal for Martha's native state and the magnolia logo of the Mississippi Quilt Association to commemorate her involvement in and her two terms as president of the association.

"This Is My Story" also includes the "Double Happiness" symbol to celebrate the love for special Chinese friends and a cotton boll for her beloved adopted state of Mississippi. "Five years is a long time to work on one quilt," Martha observes, "but the journey was as sweet as the destination. I remember when and where I worked on each of the blocks. They take me back to many memories with quilting friends and quiet times at home with Roy [her husband] or in a room alone with just quilting and music."

While Martha has won several awards and has been featured in national quilting magazines, she says, "Recognition is nice, but I find the greatest satisfaction not in competition, but in knowing that I have helped numerous people become quilters. I find the joy of sharing quilts with others gives far more lasting satisfaction than seeing my name or my quilts in print."

Ruth Vinson Irwin

One of Mississippi's most prolific and talented quilt artists is Ruth Vinson Irwin of Meridian. Ruth began quilting in the early 1970s and since that time has crafted more than 250 quilts. She loves "painting with fabric and the wonderful texture achieved by hand quilting." Ruth is a "full-time quilter," working out of her home in Meridian. "I'm drawn to both art and traditional quilts," she says. "In my more recent past, I have preferred creating works with one hundred percent cotton, hand-dyed fabrics, paints, fabric crayons, and various threads."

Ruth began quilting in a rather unusual way. In 1974, while working as a seamstress for a company producing baby strollers, she suggested that the backs of the seats in the strollers would be more comfortable if they were quilted. The company took her advice and business improved. Her idea took seed within her as she began taking leftover scraps of fabric home from work, piecing simple blocks with two or three colors, and quilting them by machine.

From that beginning, she has progressed through a long series of learning and sharing to exhibitions, competitions, and award-winning quilts. She recalls one early exhibition, held at the Texas Museum of Natural History and titled "Materializations: New Life from Old Traditions," as a unique blend of past and present, or as a "tree

Fig. 8.5. An artist who works in fabric, Ruth Vinson Irwin also makes traditional quilts.

of quilting that continues to grow." Her picture quilts are truly known from America to Australia. In the early 1990s while living in Austin, Texas, she and a fellow quilter represented the Austin Area Quilt Guild in their sister city of Adelaide, Australia.

Ruth's early honors as a quilter include "Lisa's Quilt," which appeared in Jennifer Amor's *Flavor Quilts for Kids to Make.* This quilt is a fabric crayon design of her friend Lisa Beaman's house and family. Ruth designed the mice which ran through a maze in her favorite teacher, Cathleen McCrady's, quilt "The Great Scrap Quilt Maze." This quilt appeared in the American Quilt Society's 1993 Quilt Engagement Calendar.

She moved to Meridian in 1992 after having been away almost twenty years. "When I left Austin and the quilt guild of more than four hundred members who had taught me so much, I knew I had to find other quilters in the area. Placing an ad in the newspaper, I located fifteen interested women." As their first project, these quilters completed a number of crib quilts which were donated to the children of "Peavy House," the local children's shelter.

This gesture filled not only the hearts of the children who received the quilts, but Ruth's heart as well. She next made a special picture quilt for the shelter, incorporating not only the house into the design, but the first names and ages of all the children who have been through the shelter home. The shelter children have also assisted Ruth in her quilting by sketching the patterns for food items incorporated into the design of a quilt for "Love's Kitchen," which serves meals to those persons who are not able to provide for themselves. Another of her "caring" quilts is the quilt she made for Care Lodge, a center which is dedicated to those who have died as a result of domestic violence. Ruth

also quilts for the Church of the Mediator, which each year raffles one of her works of art to raise funds for church projects.

At this time, Ruth makes both traditional and art quilts, incorporating either hand or machine quilting. Her style of art quilting is attributed to her aunt, who encouraged her to draw and use colors at an early age. Although an innovative quilter in both design and technique, Ruth indicates that she feels "very much in touch with pioneer quilters. I thank them in my own way with every quilt I complete."

Since returning to Mississippi, Ruth has taught quilting classes and has shown her work in area exhibitions, museums, and libraries. She continues to design her own quilts and also works on commission. She encourages others to try quilting. It is her belief that quilting not only helps the individual but makes a difference in a community. One look at her work shows not only the care given to her quilts, but also the manner in which she gives her heart to those around her.

Clara Ann Johnson

Long known in Mississippi as both an excellent and a prolific quilter, Clara Ann Johnson says of herself, "I can't *not* quilt. I'm a quilter; that's what I do." This statement seems to sum up Clara Ann's life as a quilter. She remembers "helping" her grandmother select colors and fabrics for her quilting before Clara Ann was six years old. From that time, although she didn't really get heavily involved in her art until her three children were grown, she considered herself a quilter.

Every type of quilt appeals to Clara Ann. She enjoys pieced and whole-cloth quilts as well as appliqué. Like many quilters, she quilts for her family. If a grandchild or some other family mem-

Fig. 8.6. Clara Ann Johnson began choosing colors for quilts with her grandmother before she was 6 years of age.

ber mentions wanting a particular quilt, Clara Ann goes to work on it. In all, she has made a total of about seventy-five quilts, including full-sized and small quilts.

For a number of years before her death, Clara Ann's mother was a victim of Alzheimer's disease. One spring, Clara Ann saw a Mother's Day card with a beautiful flower wreath on it. She decided to make a quilt using the picture as an inspiration; the resulting quilt, "I Remember Mama," is considered by many to be her best work.

Clara Ann is seldom without a quilt project in her hands. When she and her husband, James, visit their son in the Dallas area, she pieces or appliqués all the way there and back. "It is amazing how much you can accomplish while riding along. And it doesn't make me nervous if James's driving isn't really good," she says. Trips to quilt gatherings, whether near or far, find Clara Ann stitching away if someone else is willing to drive.

According to other quilters who have learned from her, Clara Ann's greatest attribute is patience. The level of skill of the learner is not a factor with her. "She taught me to tie a knot," one friend remembers. And that level of patience translates to her quilts. It is not uncommon for her to put hundreds of hours of quilting into one quilt, and, as others observe, "she makes it look so easy."

Clara Ann is not an intensely competitive quilter. She has entered a few local shows, usually at the insistence of others, and each time she was rewarded with first place ribbons, judge's choice awards, or viewers' choice awards.

Her best quilting tip? "Just get started. You don't always have to know how you are going to finish before you begin. Some of my best quilts have just developed after I started them."

Perhaps the greatest compliment a quilter can receive was given to Clara Ann by a fellow quilter who said, "Clara Ann can take an idea, form it in her mind, then execute the project with the ease and skill of a true artist."

Ollie Jean Lane

In 1987, when Ollie Jean Lane of Yazoo City retired at age fifty-five, she remembered her long-felt desire to own a beautiful quilt, preferably an appliqué quilt. "I decided to make quilting my primary hobby, and I began by trying to teach myself," the former Extension home economist states. "However, I wasn't happy with the quality of my work and I began looking around for quilt groups and classes." The rest, as they say, is history.

Like many others who begin quilting, Ollie Jean did not know that it would become such an important part of her life. Following retirement, she struggled with her parents' failing health and her husband's illness. Carry-along projects fit nicely into the lifestyle she found herself living, and at the same time it was excellent therapy. The fact that her family appreciated her quiltmaking and encouraged her added to her sense of fulfillment in her work.

Like many Mississippi quilters, Ollie Jean comes from a family whose members quilted, either for necessity or pleasure. She remembers two of her mother's quilts, a "Wild Goose Chase" and a "Flower Garden," which were carefully planned, as opposed to being made from scraps and feed sacks for utilitarian purposes. Her mother sold eggs a few at a time and saved the money to buy muslin at nine cents per yard. When the top was finished, neighbors came to quilt, and Ollie Jean remembers playing under the quilt.

Perhaps it was the conversation around the quilt, or the pleasure the women seemed to take in

Fig. 8.7. Although she has a degree in home economics, Ollie Jean Lane's professional life didn't lead her to quilting; it was her appreciation of the beauty of quilts.

the process of quilting, which seeped through the quilt to a little girl playing under the frame. Whatever it was, the result is one of Mississippi's most prolific and excellent quilters. "I like creativity and I like busy hands," Ollie Jean says. "Quilting offers a challenge in choice and expression of ideas and feelings. It gives a sense of accomplishment which is both useful and beautiful. And a visit to a quilt shop just to 'feel' the fabric can brighten a gloomy day."

And how many quilts has Ollie Jean made? The numbers are impressive, especially considering the exacting standards she has set for herself: thirty full-sized quilts, fifteen single-bed quilts, thirty wall hangings, fifteen baby quilts, fifteen table and pillow covers, and ten miniatures. Ollie Jean is a quilter who enjoys being surrounded by her quilts. She uses full-sized quilts, wall quilts, quilt books, and even a full-sized quilt frame as part of the decor in her home.

One interesting aspect of Ollie Jean's quilting, one which she recommends to other quilters, is that she makes extensive notes on every phase of a quilt, from the original idea, through selecting the fabric, to the finished piece. A scrapbook records a picture and details of each quilted piece.

One of the moving forces in the organization of a statewide quilt association in the early 1990s, Ollie Jean enjoyed the enthusiastic support of her husband, Jim. His membership in the Mississippi Quilt Association, although he was not himself a quilter, proved an invaluable asset when Ollie Jean served in leadership positions, including state president. Until failing health prevented his doing so, Jim attended meetings with Ollie Jean and often served as registrar-accountant for the meetings. During Jim's illness, Ollie Jean pieced several quilt tops while he was waiting to see his doctors or while he was a patient in the hospital.

Ollie Jean's quilts have hung in the American Quilt Society show in Paducah in four different years, and her work has appeared in Robert Shaw's *Quilts: A Living Tradition.* She has received a number of local, regional, and national awards. When asked the secret of her success, she gave her best advice to quilters: "Give yourself time to quilt at least two hours a day. Something else might have to be left undone, but quilting takes time, and a commitment to that time is a key to being successful."

Gwendolyn A. Magee

Roland L. Freeman, author of the recent and well-received book *A Communion of the Spirits: African-American Quilters, Preservers, and Their Stories,* has this to say about one of the quiltmakers included here, "Of the thousands of quilters I've met over the past twenty-five years, Gwendolyn A. Magee is among a select few who has successfully expanded the perimeters of traditional quilt making and now has brilliantly shifted, almost exclusively, to art quilts with a new and refreshing vision that stuns the imagination. Her creativity has placed her on the cutting edge of today's contemporary quilt makers."

Jackson quilter Gwen Magee has been quilting since 1989. She became involved in quilting because she wanted to make something very special for her daughter to take to college, something that would be symbolic of home and family. She decided that a quilt would be the perfect gift, so she enrolled in a quilting class. That was ten years ago, and she never anticipated that quilting would so quickly become the primary outlet for her creative expression. To date, she has completed twenty-one quilts. The two daughters, Kamili and Aliya, for

Fig. 8.8. Through quilting, Gwendolyn A. Magee has found a means of expressing an innate sense of color and form. Photo by Roland Freeman.

Fig. 8.9. "Full of the Faith" by Gwendolyn A. Magee. Photo by Judy Smith-Kressley.

whom she created her first quilts, along with her husband, D. E. Magee Jr., have remained her greatest inspiration as well as her strongest supporters. In the short ten years since Gwen began quilting, she has become a nationally recognized quilter, garnering awards and recognition for her abstract and representational art quilts.

From her earliest childhood, Gwen was fascinated by color, and she particularly was interested in intense, vibrant colors. It was not until she became a quilter, however, that she found a medium in which she was able to develop the ability to manipulate color to achieve the types of patterning and effects which had always appealed to her.

As a busy professional woman, Gwen has had to make time to quilt. Her position requires her to travel, a situation which complicates the desire to quilt. However, her desire to quilt and the artistic nature of the quilts she has produced have resulted in some amazing accomplishments. She was featured in quilt collector and photographer Roland Freeman's book and traveling exhibit *A Communion of the Spirits: African-American Quilters, Preservers, and Their Stories.* Her work also appeared in Carolyn Mazloomi's *Spirits of the Cloth: Contemporary African-American Quilts* and numerous quilt periodicals, including *Quilts Japan* (1993 and 1997).

Gwen's quilts have hung in a number of prestigious exhibits, notably in the Mississippi Museum of Art, the American Quilter's Society Museum in Paducah, the Museum of Fine Art at Spelman College in Atlanta, the Atlanta History Museum, the Smithsonian Institution, the Mint Museum in Charlotte, North Carolina, and the San Diego Historical Society Museum. Three of these exhibits featured one of Gwen's quilts on the brochure cover.

Fig. 8.10. Geraldine Nash has become a prolific quiltmaker in the 12 years since she learned the art, making more than 150 quilts. Photo by Evelyn Ann Palmer.

Geraldine Nash

When the 2000 Governor's Awards were presented in March, the Heritage Award went to the quilters of Mississippi: Cultural Crossroads. Much of the credit for the success of that quilting group goes to Geraldine Nash.

Geraldine went to work in 1988 as a baby-sitter for Mississippi: Cultural Crossroads. During the early years of the program, there were few children to watch, so Geraldine joined the quilting group. Working under master quilter Hystercine Rankin, Geraldine quickly found that quilting seemed a natural extension of herself. Her mother had been a quilter and taught some of her children to quilt. "I first started with my mother," she says, "but I did it more because she felt I needed to sit down and learn to quilt, not because I wanted to."

Now, Geraldine quilts because she enjoys the opportunity the art affords for her to be creative. It also affords her a chance to relax and rid herself of daily stress. One of the biggest pleasures, however, is the opportunity to talk with other quilters in the Cultural Crossroads group and to learn new techniques.

In the twelve years she has been quilting, Geraldine has made approximately 150 quilts. And her efforts have not gone unrewarded. She was selected to be a featured quilter at the Festival of American Folklife at the Smithsonian Institution and at the Cultural Olympiad in Atlanta. She has also received folk artist fellowships for her work with traditional patterns, scrap improvisation, small pieces, and small narrative quilts. Asked for her best quilting tip, Geraldine emphasized the importance of keeping an iron and ironing board nearby.

Barbara Newman

One of Mississippi's most prestigious quilters began her career as a quilter with these words, "OK, I'll go to the meeting, but I won't learn to quilt." The quilt world is a richer place as it begins the new century because Barbara Newman broke that resolve.

Barbara Dukes Newman began her quilting endeavors only nine years ago at the urging of long-time friend Peggy Randolph, who was starting a night quilting group. Barbara joined the group with the understanding that she would not quilt. However, she soon became interested and began studying quilting with Martha Skelton, who became her good friend, mentor, and inspiration.

"Quilting," Barbara says, "fulfills my need to create, gives me a way to release stress, and keeps me from having to do housework." Described by her friends as "always operating in fast-forward," Barbara worked for forty-five years as a banker, rising to senior vice president in charge of several departments at Deposit Guaranty National Bank. A feature in a Jackson newspaper in 1997 described Barbara's daily routine of piecing on squares as her

husband drove the two of them to work each day. Her lunchtime was devoted once again to working on hand-pieced designs. The degree to which she has succeeded in mastering her art can be seen in the impressive awards her quilts have received.

Barbara's first full-sized quilt, "Reflections of Martha," was named in honor of Martha Skelton. Martha was Barbara's first quilting teacher and a continuing inspiration. "Reflections of Martha" was juried into the American Quilter's Society Show in 1994 and won Honorable Mention, Founder's Award for the Best Use of Fabric, in the International Quilt Association's show in Houston, Texas. It also won Best Amateur Entry in the Pennsylvania National Quilt Extravaganza and Best of Show in the Gulf States Quilt Association's show in New Orleans, Louisiana.

Completed in early 1996, "There Are No Snakes in My Garden" is viewed by many to be her definitive work. It collected more acclaim than Barbara's first quilt. It won many local, state, regional, and national awards, including Viewer's Choice, Judges' Choice, and Best of Show. "No Snakes" won one of its most prestigious awards, the Robert S. Cohan Master Award for Traditional Artistry, in the International Quilt Show in Houston, Texas, in 1996. It was named one of the 382 finalists in the Ultimate Quilt Search to find the twentieth century's one hundred best American quilts. As part of the Silver Star Exhibit, "No Snakes" hung in the 1999 International Quilt Festival and Market in Houston, Texas, and in the Patchwork and Quilt Expo 2000 in Strasbourg, France.

"There Are No Snakes in My Garden" was made in honor of Barbara's mother, who loved birds and flowers. Barbara remembers, "As a young girl, Mother made me work in her garden. I was very afraid of snakes, but my mother would say, 'Honey, don't be afraid; look at the beauty because there are

Fig. 8.11. "Memory Square" by Geraldine Nash. Photo by Patricia Crosby.

Fig. 8.12. Meticulous quilter Barbara Newman displays "Lisa's Legacy, from Baltimore to Brandon," one of three prize-winning quilts stitched by the former banker.

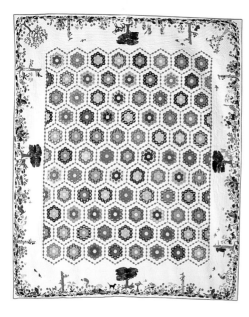

no snakes in my garden.' What else could I name my 'Flower Garden Quilt?'" This quilt was made for Barbara's oldest daughter, Debbie. It is bordered with a garden path filled with memories of her life, such as her son riding his bike and her husband playing golf. The label shows Debbie sitting at the garden entrance holding her Yorkie.

Barbara's third full-sized quilt was created for her youngest daughter, Lisa. The Baltimore Album squares of "Lisa's Legacy, from Baltimore to Brandon" depict phases of Lisa's life. Some of the originally designed squares capture memorable scenes, such as the church where she and a friend played dolls on the steps as a child, her marriage, the birth of her children, and Lisa as a school teacher. "Lisa's Legacy" was completed in 1999 and received First Place, Traditional Appliqué, in the International Quilt Festival in Houston, Texas, and Third Place, Professional Appliqué, in the American Quilt Show in Paducah, Kentucky, in 2000.

Barbara's quilts have appeared in numerous quilt-related publications, with all three full-sized quilts selected for the American Quilt Calendar featuring quilts from the International Quilt Association.

Full-sized quilts are not the only type of quilt Barbara enjoys making. Three of her smaller quilts, "Block and Roll," "North Jackson All Star," and "Cherries Jubilee Celebration," have also been prize winners.

Barbara has been married to Johnny Newman, her biggest fan, for forty-five years. He has been very supportive in her endeavors, creating specially designed items to assist in her quilting. When Barbara is trying to meet a quilting deadline, Johnny takes on many household duties. "He teases me sometimes," Barbara says, "but he is my biggest supporter." Barbara and Johnny have two daughters and three grandsons.

Barbara describes herself as an overachiever. She is one of nine children, the daughter of a country Baptist preacher. Her mother was legally blind, so she was taught to work from a very early age. In years to come, the quilting world will look at the legacy left by this Mississippi quilter and be glad that she worked hard.

Suzanne Peery Schutt

One Mississippi quilter tells stories of her past with her quilts. The daughter of a novelist-newsman, Suzanne Peery Schutt says that she expresses the literary leanings she inherited from her parents through her quilts. Her father, James Robert Peery, who was a news director for radio and television, wrote two novels, *Stark Summer* and *God Rides a Gale,* both published by the company that is now HarperCollins in the 1930s and 1940s; her mother was a schoolteacher. When Suzanne was a young girl, the family lived with her grandmother in a big old Victorian house in Eupora, Mississippi. Years later, Suzanne documented her memories of that happy time in a quilt she named "Childhood Enchanted." (The quilt was the Mississippi winner in *Good Housekeeping*'s 1994 All-American Quilt Contest and was later documented in "Quilts and Quiltmaking in America," an on-line presentation from the Library of Congress and the American Folklife Center at the Smithsonian.)

Suzanne's professional life involved a stint in the 1970s at the Mississippi State Department of Archives and History, during which time she remembers seeing in the galleries there a one-woman quilt show by Martha Skelton. Ten or so years later, she decided she wanted to leave the business world, simplify her life, and learn how to quilt. Her first teacher was Martha Skelton, whose work she vividly recalled from a decade earlier. In the years since, her relationship with Martha has blossomed into a marvelous friendship based on their shared love of quilts. She remembers talking about her desire to tell stories through her quilts with Martha and being reassured, "Whatever you feel in your head, you can express in fabric."

That encouragement went a long way toward sparking the budding artist's enthusiasm for story quilts, a genre that does not have many practitioners. "I think of quilting as a creative art," says Suzanne. "It's no different from writing a book or painting a picture." She keeps scrapbooks of ideas and designs that she plans to incorporate into future quilts and mentioned a quaint Russian village in a printed advertisement for vodka that caught her eye. Even when Suzanne works with a traditional pattern, she makes it her own. She tells about a patchwork quilt she made in blue and white, to which she added a stenciled portrait of a general and a grouping of soldiers. The name of the design is "Burgoyne Surrounded."

Suzanne is intrigued by research. For her "Burgoyne Surrounded" she went to the library to look up the correct coloring for her soldiers' uniforms. She discovered that they wore black boots, yellow-gold trousers, and blue jackets. Even though she stresses that her figures are more folk art than fine art, she wants them to be accurate. When she designed "A Book Lover's Album," she used her family's favorite quotes, from *The Rubáiyát of Omar Khayyám,* to John Mayfield's "I must go down to the sea again," to Shakespeare, a favorite of her mother's.

The first quilt Suzanne made was a "Trip around the World," through which she learned the technique of patchwork. Her second quilt was "Childhood Enchanted," in which she learned appliqué. Then she made a "Mariner's Compass," so she could learn how to work old blocks into a new quilt. She has found that she loves learning new techniques. Asked her favorite aspect of quilting, she says she loves "thinking them up," although she admits she can design many more in her mind than she can get around to making. Suzanne is one of those rare quilters who doesn't start a new quilt until she finishes the one she's got in progress. "I'm the queen of finishing," she laughs, when a comment is made about how unusual this habit of hers is. "I'm a child of the Depression, and my grandmother taught me to finish what I start." Disciplined though she is, Suzanne loves her hobby. "When quilting stops being fun, that's when I'll stop quilting," she declares.

Hystercine Rankin

Hystercine Rankin is a wife, a mother, a grandmother, a community leader, a quilter, and a living

Fig. 8.14. "Papercuts and Patchwork" is the name Suzanne Peery Schutt gave this quilt, which she planned to have the look of an antique.

Fig. 8.15. One of the legends of Mississippi quiltmaking is Hystercine Rankin, who is known far beyond the state's borders as a quilter of outstanding renown.

Fig. 8.16. Members of the quilt search documentation team in the middle of a long day. Clockwise from the upper left: Cindy Milton, Carol Vickers, Miriam Rice, Joan Alliston, Nancy Welsch, Martha Ginn, Evelyn Palmer, Martha Skelton, Carol Gieger, Nancy Braswell, Ollie Jean Lane.

legend. Long recognized as one of the nation's premier quilt artists, Hystercine has been declared a master artist by the Mississippi Arts Commission, and her quilts have spread as far away as England, Frances, Germany, Canada, and Guam. One of her quilts is on display at the Smithsonian Institution in Washington, D.C., and during the 1996 Summer Olympics in Atlanta, the Folk Art Park, a permanent tribute to southern folk art and artists, selected one of her quilt patterns to be duplicated on a large scale for the world's visitors to enjoy.

Taught by her grandmother to quilt, Hystercine has been quilting since she was twelve years old. All of her aunts and great aunts quilted, but during her early years, the quilting was done "because in those days people had to provide cover to help keep the family warm."

Probably the most famous of Hystercine's quilts are her story quilts, or memory quilts, as she likes to call them. "These quilts are all my creations. I think up an idea, cut the pieces, appliqué

them, and then quilt the quilt," she states. Memories recorded in the memory quilts range from walking to school to milking cows, bringing in firewood, and picking cotton.

One of those instrumental in beginning the quilting project at Mississippi: Cultural Crossroads, Hystercine has influenced countless others younger than herself to become good quilters. She has sold a number of her quilts to quilt lovers from all over the world. She admits that the money helped at the time, especially with putting her children through college. Having reared fourteen children, as well as helping to rear five of her brothers, a niece, and a nephew, Hystercine finds quilting to be a relaxing pastime.

And what advice does she give them when they begin? "Start quilting on a four-inch square. Practice making your stitches small and follow a simple pattern." It would be difficult to argue with that advice, given the admiration which Hystercine Rankin's quilts continue to evoke.

APPENDIX

Booneville

Batesville

Tupelo

River

Sunflower River

River

Big

Tombigbee

Starkville

Greenville

River

Black

Big

Philadelphia

Yazoo

Ridgeland

Meridian

Clinton

Brandon

Vicksburg Jackson

Mississippi

Port Gibson

Pearl

Leaf

Chickasawhay

River

Natchez

Hattiesburg

River

McComb

River

Pascagoula

River

Bay St. Louis

Quilt Search Day Locations

MISSISSIPPI QUILT ASSOCIATION
QUILT DOCUMENTATION PROJECT

Date_____ ID #_____ Location_____

Interviewer_____

MQA Code_____

Copy of Documentation desired __Yes __No $5.00 paid_____

PRESENT QUILT OWNER INFORMATION

NAME_____

ADDRESS_____

CITY, STATE, ZIP_____ PHONE_____

To the best of my knowledge, this quilt was made prior to 1946. Permission is given for Mississippi Quilt Association to use the photograph of the quilt and the information given on this form for purposes of research and education. The Mississippi Quilt Association is not responsible for any loss or damage to quilts submitted for documentation or for any inconvenience to the owner or representative.

Would you be willing to allow this quilt, if selected, to be used in an exhibit? __Yes __No

Signature_____ Date_____

QUILT HISTORY

1. Quilt name or pattern used by family/owner_____
2. Owner's relationship to quiltmaker (daughter, granddaughter, son, etc.) _____
3. Why was this quilt made?

       __Dowry   __Income   __Gift   __Personal use   __Fund raising

       __Birth   __Death   __Marriage   __Anniversary   __Historical event

       __Other; explain_____
4. Where and when was the quilt made?

       City_____ County_____ State_____ Year_____
5. If the quilt was made out of state, when was it brought to Mississippi?_____
6. Did the quiltmaker __design __piece __appliqué __quilt __tie the quilt?
7. If you know of others who worked on this quilt, please give names and role they played:

_____

_____

_____

8. Give any stories, customs, other interesting information about this quilt:

_____
_____
_____

9. Has this quilt been exhibited or displayed? Explain_____

_____
_____

10. Has this quilt won prizes? ___ Yes ___ No List dates and events_____

11. Has this quilt been restored? __ Yes __ No Describe work done and by whom_____

ID # _____

QUILTMAKER'S HISTORY

1. Name of quiltmaker_____ Occupation_____

2. Date of birth_____ Place of birth_____

3. Date of death_____ Place of death_____

4. Quiltmaker's spouse's name_____ Occupation_____

5. Number of children_____

6. Highest school grade attained by quiltmaker_____

7. Did the quiltmaker grow up in an __urban __rural area?

8. Where quiltmaker lived most of life_____

9. Where quiltmaker lived when quilt was made_____

10. Quiltmaker's age at time quilt was made_____

11. Where did quiltmaker get patterns or quilting designs?_____

12. Why did the quiltmaker quilt?

    __Income   __Pleasure   __Church   __Gifts   __Necessity

    __Other; explain _____

13. Did the quiltmaker make other quilts? __Yes __No Approximately how many?_____

Where are they? _____

14. Did the quiltmaker participate in group quilting activities? yes no don't know

15. Do you know if any of the following exist?

    __Quiltmaker's diary   __Letters   __Scrapbook   __Photos of quiltmaker

    __Family Bible   __Will   __Patterns   __Sewing tools

    __Awards/ribbons   __Newspaper clippings   __Photo of quilt

Where are they?_____

16. Anything else we should know about the quiltmaker? _____

_____

17. Has this quilt or any other quilt made by this quiltmaker been registered in a quilt documentation project in another state? __Yes __No Where?_____

18. Do you know of any other quilt owners or quiltmakers that should be included in this project?
__Yes __No   Please give name(s) and address(es):

_____
_____
_____
_____
_____
_____

Other interesting information about the quiltmaker:

_____
_____
_____
_____
_____
_____

**Thank you for taking part in the Mississippi Quilt Association Documentation Project.
We appreciate your sharing this quilt with us.**

ANALYSIS

ID #_____

MQA Analyst_____

Pattern_____ Brackman Identification #_____

Size _____" Length   x   _____" Width   Estimated date of construction _____

_____**Quilt**   _____**Top Only**

TYPE
__ Pieced   __ Appliqué
__ Comb. Pieced/App.   __ Whole cloth
__ Crazy
__ Other_____

CONSTRUCTION
__ By hand
__ By machine
__ Combination of both

SETTING
__ Straight block to block
__ Straight with alternate blocks
__ On point block/block
__ On point with alternate blocks
__ Sashed
__ Medallion
__ Other _____

PIECED
__ Block   __ Strip   __ String
__ One patch   __ All over   __ Other

APPLIQUÉ
__ Blind stitch
__ Buttonhole or Blanket
__ Running stitch
__ Machine appliqué
__ Other_____

BORDERS __Yes __ No
If Yes, answer the following:
__ Single   __ Multiple
__ Piecing   __ Appliqué

On how many sides? __ 4 __ 3 __ 2 __ 1
__ Fabric used in quilt
__ Different fabric

BINDING
Applied binding __ Yes __ No
If Yes, answer the following:
__ Single fold
__ Double fold
__ Straight grain
__ Bias grain
__ Backing brought to front
__ Front brought to back
__ Knife edge

FIBER/COLORS
Top: __ Cotton   __ Silk
             __ Wool   __ Combination
             __ Other_____

Fabric of top: __ Solid __ Print __ Combination

Predominant colors of top (check all that apply)
             __ Red to pink   __ Orange to peach
             __ Yellow to gold   __ Green
             __ Blue   __ Purple to lavender
             __ Black to gray   __ Brown to tan
             __ White/muslin   __ Multicolor/scrap

Value: __Pastel __ Dark to medium

Backing: __ Cotton__ Wool __ Flour/feed sack
             __ Check or plaid
             __ Other_____
             _____

Fabric of backing: __ Solid __ Print
__ Combination

Predominant colors of backing:
__ One of fabrics used in quilt top
__ Contrasting fabric to quilt top
__ White or muslin

QUILTING

__ Hand quilted   __ Machine quilted
__ Tacked (tied)   __ Blind tacked
__ Unquilted   __ All-over
__ By the piece   __ In blocks
__ In alternate blocks   __ In sashing
__ In borders   __ Utilitarian quilting
__ Fine, close quilting
__ Stitches per inch_____

BATTING

__ Cotton   __ Wool
__ Blanket   __ Other_____
_____

CONDITION OF QUILT

__ Excellent   __ Good   __ Faded
__ Worn   __ Moderate use   __ Damaged
__ Unwashed   __ Restored

Describe restoration

_____
_____
_____
_____
_____
_____
_____
_____
_____
_____

NOTES

Chapter One:
Mississippi Quiltmaking before 1825

1. Clarke and Guice, *The Old Southwest, 1795–1830,* 21.

2. Ibid.

3. Cox, *Mississippi Almanac, 1997–1998,* 3.

4. Clinton, *The Plantation Mistress,* 166, quoting William B. Dabney writing to Williamson Barnes, 4 September 1823, Barnes Collection, College of William and Mary, Williamsburg, VA.

5. Clinton, *The Plantation Mistress,* 166, quoting Nancy Robinson, January and April 1833, Robinson Collection, Mississippi State Archives, Jackson, MS.

6. Clinton, *The Plantation Mistress,* 166, quoting "Grandma Finley" in the Archer Collection, North Carolina State Archives, Raleigh, NC.

7. Cox. *Mississippi Almanac 1997–1998,* 2.

8. Ibid., 2–3.

9. Clarke and Guice, *The Old Southwest, 1795–1830,* 183.

10. Ibid., 110.

11. Ibid., 183.

12. Ibid., 184.

13. Ibid., 185.

14. Ibid., 225.

15. Kiracofe and Johnson, *The American Quilt,* 86

16. Martha Polk Douglas, MQA Quilt Documentation Form J-66, September 14, 1996.

17. Thomas L. Wallis, MQA Quilt Documentation Form O-41. The quilt brought in for documentation is a red-and-white "Double Irish Chain" made by Mrs. Black when she was 81 years old, as a gift for her grandson during his eighteenth year. *His* grandson, Mr. Wallis, now owns the quilt.

18. Marcia White Beeson, MQA Quilt Documentation Form L-040, January 11, 1997, and Betty Redus White, MQA Quilt Documentation Form L-041, January 11, 1997, both descendants of quiltmaker Martha Hutton Redus, about whom story is told.

19. Montgomery, *Printed Textiles,* 281.

20. Ibid., 279.

21. The reason this is so common is that black is the color the dyer went to when a first color didn't turn out as planned; therefore, the yarn has been dyed twice, and it has been weakened. Dyeing is a very caustic process and damages the fabric, even as it makes it more beautiful.

22. Eanes et al., *North Carolina Quilts,* 39.

Chapter Two:
Antebellum Quiltmaking in Mississippi, *1825–1861*

1. Cox, *Mississippi Almanac, 1997–1998,* 8.

2. Ibid.

3. Burner et al, *An American Portrait,* 271.

4. McKee et al, *Mississippi,* 327.

5. Reps, *Cities of the Mississippi,* 132, quoting Joseph Hold Ingraham, *The Southwest, By a Yankee* (New York: Harper & Bros., 1935), 1:37–38.

6. Clark and Guice, *The Old Southwest, 1795–1830,* 84.

7. McKee et al, *Mississippi,* 72–73.

8. Ibid., 73, 77.

9. Clark and Guice, *The Old Southwest, 1795–1830,* 204, quoting from Gideon Lincecum, "The Life of Apushimataha," *Publications of the Mississippi Historical Society* 9(1906): 415–85.

10. Documentation form mailed to Quilt Documentation Project by Susan Turner Price Miller, of Pella Iowa, November 13, 1997. The quilt this information accompanies may be seen in figure 2.2. It is an unusual example of the *broderie perse* style of quiltmaking.

11. "Special Places in Mid-Mississippi," *Mississippi Travel Guide* (summer/fall 1998): 60–61.

12. Alice Elizabeth Hamer Sanford, MQA Quilt Documentation Form H-15, July 13, 1996.

13. Burner et al, *An American Portrait*, 271.

14. Ibid.

15. Alice Evans Hairston Evans, MQA Quilt Documentation Form N-54, April 5, 1997. The quilt is known as "Henry's Quilt" in the family because it belonged to her great-grandfather, a survivor of the Civil War who came home to marry the widow of another Confederate States of America soldier.

16. Freeman, *A Communion of the Spirits*, 39–40.

17. Lorenz and Stamper, *Mississippi Homespun*, 25.

18. Ibid., 26.

19. Susan Turner Price Miller, MQA Quilt Documentation Form, submitted by mail with no number, November 13, 1997.

20. Christine Whitehead, MQA Quilt Documentation Form P-70, August 23, 1997.

21. Susan Peterson, MQA Quilt Documentation Form M-15, March 22, 1997.

22. Teresa Smith and Barbara Haigh, MQA Quilt Documentation Form F-87, April 22, 1996. See also newspaper clipping from *Catahoula News Booster*, of Jonesville, Catahoula Parish, LA., owner not sure about date, c. 1994–1995.

23. Mamie Smith Hammett, MQA Quilt Documentation Form F-51, May 22, 1996.

24. Monica A. Kirk Bristow, MQA Quilt Documentation Form P-152, August 23, 1997.

25. Winnie Hellum Sykes, MQA Quilt Documentation Form M-37, March 22, 1997.

26. Ida Fitzpatrick Wallace, MQA Quilt Documentation Form O-68, May 10, 1997.

27. Ruth Kendall, MQA Quilt Documentation Form O-75, May 10, 1997.

28. Jacquelin Tennyson, MQA Quilt Documentation Form M-56, March 22, 1997.

29. Willie Faye White (granddaughter of quiltmaker), MQA Quilt Documentation Form Q-83, September 20, 1997.

30. Kathryn Martin (Mrs. Lowrey T.), MQA Quilt Documentation Form Q-75, September 20, 1997.

31. Ruby W. Anders, MQA Quilt Documentation Form Q-61, September 20, 1997.

32. Joyce C. Lewis, MQA Quilt Documentation Form M-75, March 21, 1996.

Chapter Three: Quiltmaking during the Civil War and Reconstruction, 1861–1875

1. Burner et al., *An American Portrait*, 361.

2. Cox, *Mississippi Almanac, 1997–1998*, 9.

3. Hoehling, *Vicksburg*, 49.

4. Ibid., 126–27.

5. Ibid., 40–41.

6. Burner et al., *An American Portrait*, 363.

7. Cox, *Mississippi Almanac, 1997–1998*, 9.

8. Hague, *A Blockaded Family*, 23.

9. Cox, *Mississippi Almanac, 1997–1998*, 9.

10. Hague, *A Blockaded Family*, 115.

11. Ibid., xxi.

12. Cox, *Mississippi Almanac, 1997–1998*, 10.

13. Hoehling, *Vicksburg*, 39.

14. Hague, *A Blockaded Family*, 106–7.

15. Ibid., 107.

16. Ibid., 59.

17. Lorenz and Stamper, *Mississippi Homespun*, 6.

18. Ibid.

19. Howell, *Mississippi Scenes*, 135.

20. Mrs. John T. Turfit, MQA Quilt Documentation Forms N-25, N-26, N-28, N-29, April 2, 1997. The maker of the quilts was a Mrs. Von Peet, and the quilt designs are a grouped eight-pointed star with nine stars per block and 16 blocks, a scrap quilt in a pattern known as "Providence," a "Nine-Patch String," and an "Anvil" variation known as "Wagon Tracks."

21. Burner et al., *An American Portrait*, 375–76.

22. Ramsey and Waldvogel, *Southern Quilts*, 54–57.

23. Researched and written by Joyce Tucker, daughter-in-law of present owner of "Drunkard's Path" quilt, Lydia Smith Tucker.

24. Hague, *A Blockaded Family*, 158.

25. Hoehling, *Vicksburg*, 104.

26. Laurel Horton, "South Carolina Civil War Quilts," in *Uncoverings 1985* (Mill Valley, CA: American Quilt Study Group, 1986), 61.

27. Sherra W. Owen, MQA Quilt Documentation Form O-157, May 10, 1997.

28. Lelia Ruffin Henry, undated handwritten note accompanying quilt, MQA Quilt Documentation Form L-03.

29. Gail M. Stables, MQA Quilt Documentation Form P-66, August 23, 1997. See also MQA Quilt Documentation Form Q-59 for a beautiful four-block appliqué quilt,

c. 1850, in an unknown pattern, owned by Hope Cutrer and documented on September 20, 1997.

30. Shirley H. Johnson, MQA Quilt Documentation Form P-85, August 23, 1997.

31. Letter from Mrs. William R. Eades, Memphis, TN, to Carol Vickers, Decatur, MS, May 6, 1997.

32. Martha W. Bailey, MQA Quilt Documentation Form O-129, May 10, 1997.

Chapter Four:
Postbellum Quiltmaking in Mississippi, 1875–1900

1. Willard Glazier, *Down the Great River*, 367–68, 374, quoted in *Cities of the Mississippi*, by Reps, 142.

2. McKee et al., *Mississippi*, 263.

3. Cox, *Mississippi Almanac, 1997–1998*, 14.

4. McKee et al., *Mississippi*, 130.

5. Cox, *Mississippi Almanac, 1997–1998*, 14.

6. Joy Rushing, MQA Quilt Documentation Form C-95, November 4, 1995.

7. Mrs. F. W. Alexander, Quilt Documentation Form L-35, January 11, 1997.

8. Kiracofe and Johnson, *The American Quilt*, 178. *The Progressive Farmer* began a woman's column in 1902 but did not begin selling quilt patterns until the 1930s.

9. Joyce Everett, document attached to MQA Quilt Documentation Form D-38, January 13, 1996.

10. Rubye M. Harrison, MQA Quilt Documentation Form D-43, January 13, 1996.

11. Robert N. Jenkins, letter with MQA Quilt Documentation Form D-133, undated.

12. "Rolling Star" and "Morning Star" from Sarah Rawlings, MQA Quilt Documentation Forms D-35 and D-36; "Eight-Pointed Star" from Mattie Malone, MQA Quilt Documentation Form O-77, May 10, 1997, who was referring to her grandmother, Sarah Buse (1852–1934) of Lee County, MS.

13. "Chips and Whetstones" from Rosemary Comer, MQA Quilt Documentation Form P-131; "World Without End" from Sue K. Honeycutt, MQA Quilt Documentation Form P-59; example of a "Sunburst" is from Juanita McVay, MQA Quilt Documentation Form O-142. A "Rising Sun" example is from Susan Miller, whose quilt was made by Lula Roberts when she was sixteen years old as a wedding gift for her oldest brother, near Riceville

in Amite County. The year was 1894, and the MQA documentation form was mailed in from Pella, Iowa.

14. Emma Lee May, MQA Quilt Documentation Form P-31, January 13, 1996.

15. Lora E. Cook, MQA Quilt Documentation Form O-14, May 9, 1997. Author interview with Ed and Marlene Permenter in Jackson, MS, January 22, 1999.

16. Ibid.

17. Hazel Milner and Janice Harrison, MQA Quilt Documentation Form I-97, August 24, 1996.

18. Costelle Morrow and Odell Dulaney, MQA Quilt Documentation Form O-54, May 10, 1997.

19. Ruby Graham, MQA Quilt Documentation Form O-62, discussing her grandmother, Margurette Carpenter, May 10, 1997.

20. Mary Ann Rouse Thomas was the grandmother of Dr. Robert Cargo, noted Alabama quilt collector and scholar. He donated the pair of quilts, along with many other made-in-Alabama quilts, to the Birmingham Museum of Art in 1997.

21. Jean C. Eady, MQA Quilt Documentation Form I-112, August 24, 1996.

22. Mildred D. Viverette, MQA Quilt Documentation Form I-98, August 24, 1996.

23. Fred Day Smith, MQA Quilt Documentation Form Q-58. The quilt was made in Franklin, Lincoln County, MS, by his great-grandmother, Lydia W. Day.

24. The four diamonds and the triangle base are all made of the same fabric in this pattern. An example brought in by Dorothy Gilbert of McComb was made from leftover scraps of indigo-blue fabrics that her mother had used to make dresses for Dorothy and her sister when they were children. MQA Quilt Documentation Form Q-62; quilt made by a Mrs. Long (1886–1972) in Raymond, Hinds County, MS, in the 1890s. Another "Dove in the Window" was called a "Groom's Quilt" because it was made by a group of ladies, including the bride, as a gift for the groom in 1897. Each young lady initialed her block, and the one with the letters "SBT" stood for the bride. It was quilted at 11 stitches per inch by Ellen Proctor Landrum. (See "Crown of Oaks" quilt, figure 4.17, for an example of Ellen Landrum's work.) Sarah Landrum May, Quilt Documentation Form C-33, November 11, 1995.

25. Martha V. Underwood (Mrs. J. W.), in a letter dated November 15, 1999, to Carol Vickers, Chairman, MQA Heritage Quilt Search Project.

26. Two outstanding examples of the "Carolina Lily" came from the 1930s: a red, white, and green one with

"Wild Goose Chase" sashing and borders, made by Mary Jane (Jenny) DeWees in Neshoba County (MQA Quilt Documentation Form I-55); and a dark blue (almost black), pink, and green example with pink checked sashing made by Fannie Love Reynolds in Lodi, Montgomery County (MQA Quilt Documentation Form C-116); she signed the quilt and put her age (70) on it in 1932.

27. Lena Lou Kleinpeter, MQA Quilt Documentation Form Q-89, September 20, 1997.

28. Lena Lou Kleinpeter, MQA Quilt Documentation Form Q-90, September 20, 1997.

29. Ibid.

30. Gladys Grimer, MQA Quilt Documentation Form Q-71, September 20, 1997, in reference to a quilt made by her husband's grandmother. This quilt also has a reel design in the center, but contains four leaves and four buds. It is worked in pink, gold, and green on a white background. It is machine appliquéd and heavily echo-quilted.

31. Betty N. Byrd, MQA Quilt Documentation Form B-15, September 23, 1995.

32. Doris Gray, MQA Quilt Documentation Form D-81, January 13, 1996.

33. Myerl Langford, MQA Quilt Documentation Form I-53, August 24, 1996.

34. Louise McGahey Doolittle Edmondson, MQA Quilt Documentation Form I-24 and accompanying letter, August 24, 1996.

35. Mildred Jennings, MQA Quilt Documentation Form F-31, April 20, 1996. This beautiful quilt was made by Mary Elizabeth Perry, born in Georgia in 1833 and died in Atlanta, Arkansas, in 1881. Her great-granddaughter brought the quilt to Mississippi in 1969.

36. Belle Savell Brown, MQA Quilt Documentation Form I-09, August 14, 1996.

37. Rosemary Comer, MQA Quilt Documentation Form P-132, August 23, 1997.

38. Mary Irene Carter Murry, MQA Quilt Documentation Form P-68, August 23, 1997.

39. Jackie Bailey, MQA Quilt Documentation Form C-108, November 4, 1995.

40. Sara Whitehead, MQA Quilt Documentation Form D-19, January 13, 1996. The quilt featured twelve red four-point stars with tan centers and tan and red feathering, set onto a chrome orange background. It is a stunning piece, made by Miss Ethel Street in Meridian in the fourth quarter of the nineteenth century.

41. Emma Lee May, MQA Quilt Documentation Form D-30, January 13, 1996. The maker of the quilt was

Sarah Jane Ledlow of Decatur, MS. Date of quilt is around 1875.

42. Elizabeth Carr, MQA Quilt Documentation Form E-67, March 2, 1996, granddaughter of the maker, Florence Butler Jackson; grandfather was Maurice Henry Jackson.

43. Written documentation of this quilt was submitted to MQA by Annabelle and Bob Meacham of Senatobia, MS. An undated letter was accompanied by numerous color snapshots of overall quilt and details. MQA Quilt Documentation Form M-01, March 22, 1997.

44. Ida Fitzpatrick Wallace, MQA Quilt Documentation Form O-72 and accompanying information, May 10, 1997.

45. Mary Ester Huber Walker, MQA Quilt Documentation Form C-136, November 4, 1995.

46. Mrs. Albert King (Frances), MQA Quilt Documentation Form H-20, July 13, 1996.

Chapter Five: Early Twentieth-Century Quiltmaking, 1900–1930

1. McKee et al., *Mississippi*, 134, 196.

2. Cox, *Mississippi Almanac, 1997–1998*, 17.

3. Theda Brown, great-great-granddaughter of Carrie Butler Brown, MQA Quilt Documentation Form I-27, August 23, 1996.

4. Millie Smith, MQA Quilt Documentation Form I-23, August 24, 1996.

5. Robert L. Lence, MQA Quilt Documentation Form O-27, May 10, 1997. The quiltmaker was Mrs. J. J. Hudspeth of Ashland, in Benton County. She made the quilt around 1900.

6. McKee et al., *Mississippi*, 263.

7. Ibid., 16.

8. Cox, *Mississippi Almanac, 1997–1998*, 17.

9. Ibid.

10. McKee et al., *Mississippi*, 154.

11. Cox, *Mississippi Almanac, 1997–1998*, 16.

12. Barry, *Rising Tide*, 278.

13. Ibid., 206.

14. Ibid., 363.

15. Ibid., 366.

16. Cox, *Mississippi Almanac, 1997–1998*, 15–16.

17. Floyce Adams, MQA Quilt Documentation Forms

H-46 through H-50, July 13, 1996.

18. Fanny Bergen, "The Tapestry of the New World," *Scribner's Magazine,* September 1894, 361–62, quoted in *The American Quilt,* by Kiracofe and Johnson, 207–8.

19. Lorenz and Stamper, *Mississippi Homespun,* 70.

20. William Milton Myers and John Lamar Myers, MQA Quilt Documentation Forms E-17 and E-81, March 2, 1996.

21. D. O. Thoms, MQA Quilt Documentation Form J-40, September 13, 1996.

22. Betty Y. Bingham, MQA Quilt Documentation Form J-58, September 14, 1996.

23. Author interview with Roy S. Huff, Mobile, Alabama, April 23, 2000. Mr. Huff remembers distinctly that he and his mother quilted three quilts in one four-month period during the winter of 1930.

24. Jean C. Eady, MQA Quilt Documentation Form I-114, August 24, 1996.

25. Carl Benjamin Spence, MQA Quilt Documentation Form I-125, August 24, 1996.

26. Lois Kilgore, MQA Quilt Documentation Form N-36, April 5, 1997.

27. Laura Windham Cartwright, MQA Quilt Documentation Form P-134, August 23, 1997.

28. Jane I. Sturdevant, for Mrs. Mildred Nick, daughter of quiltmaker, MQA Quilt Documentation Form F-56, April 20, 1996. Another name for this pattern was found to be "Cross Road to Jericho."

29. Marcia Shirley, MQA Quilt Documentation Form D-93. Three other Carrie Stroud quilts were documented in Meridian on January 13, 1996.

30. John Lamar Myers, MQA Quilt Documentation Form E-81, March 2, 1996.

31. Cindy Williams, MQA Quilt Documentation Form D-26, January 13, 1996; the maker was Irene May, her grandmother, of Decatur, MS.

32. Joyce Tucker, MQA Quilt Documentation Form D-76, January 13, 1996. Quilt was made in Dekalb, Kemper County, MS, circa the 1900–1920 period, by Martha Susan Harvin Gully.

33. Marie Upton, MQA Quilt Documentation Form C-20, November 4, 1995. Quilt was made by Lulu Gwin Collins, her grandmother.

34. Diann Greer, MQA Quilt Documentation Form Q-48, September 20, 1997. Quilt was made in Minden, Webster Parish, LA, by the owner's grandmother, Pink Adams Lary, and her great-grandmother, who was named "Louisiana Savannah Moscow America Almond Strickland Adams." Quilt is dated 1918, which makers remember because the grandfather was serving in World War I under General Pershing at the time.

35. Betty H. Eason, granddaughter-in-law of the maker, MQA Quilt Documentation Form H-39, July 13, 1996.

36. Charlotte Kunkle, MQA Quilt Documentation Form F-49, April 20, 1996. This piece was made in Ink, Arkansas, for Charlotte in 1944 as a baby quilt. It incorporates fabric from the dresses of her great-grandmother, her great-aunt, her mother, and three aunts.

37. Shirley A. Smith, MQA Quilt Documentation Form E-86, March 2, 1996. The quilt was made in Yazoo City, MS, in the 1930s.

38. Lois Clingon, MQA Quilt Documentation Form P-88, August 23, 1997. The quilt was made by her mother-in-law, Emma Clingon, in Belmont, Tishomingo County, MS. The family name for it is "Fence Rail."

39. Betty R. White, granddaughter of maker, MQA Quilt Documentation Form L-42, January 11, 1997.

40. Glenn D. Adkins, MQA Quilt Documentation Form D-157, January 13, 1996.

41. Gwen Marston, unpublished manuscript on string quilts, Beaver Island, MI, April 2000.

42. Weytha Nunley, MQA Quilt Documentation Form P-89. August 23, 1997, daughter of quiltmaker.

43. Mary M. Jones, MQA Quilt Documentation Form C-66, November 4, 1995, great-granddaughter of quiltmaker.

44. Benberry, *Always There,* 49–50, 92.

45. Author interview with Ponjola Posey Andrews, Jackson, MS, January 22, 1999.

46. Ibid.

47. Mattie Davis, MQA Quilt Documentation Form D-104, January 13, 1996.

48. Sarah Thomas, MQA Quilt Documentation Form H-31, July 13, 1996.

49. Robbie Martin, MQA Quilt Documentation Form A-10, attached handwritten note, August 19, 1995.

50. Ibid.

51. Elizabeth Richter McCleary, donor of the Mississippi Friendship Quilt to the New England Quilt Museum, handwritten notes in museum files, circa 1988.

Chapter Six:
The Golden Age of Mississippi Quiltmaking, 1930–1945

1. McKee et al., *Mississippi,* 165 (author's emphasis).

2. Burner et al., *An American Portrait,* 614–15.

3. Cox, *Mississippi Almanac, 1997–1998,* 18.

4. Estabelle Reid, in a letter attached to MQA Quilt Documentation Form I-104, submitted by Clara R. Dunn, daughter, August 23, 1996.

5. Cox, *Mississippi Almanac, 1997–1998,* 18.

6. Kiracofe and Johnson, *The American Quilt,* 190–95.

7. Mildred Fountain, MQA Quilt Documentation Form Q-01, September 20, 1997.

8. Cox, *Mississippi Almanac, 1997–1998,* 19–20.

9. Ibid., 20.

10. Cathryn Edwards, writing about her grandmother, Kate Lott, of Columbia in Forest County, who left a legacy of fifteen beautiful quilts from this era and later, MQA Quilt Documentation Form J-10, September 14, 1996.

11. Kiracofe and Johnson, *The American Quilt,* 233, quoting Erma H. Kirkpatrick in "Quilts, Quiltmaking, and the *Progressive Farmer*: 1886–1935," in *Uncoverings 1985* (Mill Valley, CA: American Quilt Study Group, 1986), 142.

12. Lettie Daniels, attachment to MQA Quilt Documentation Form P-10, August 23, 1997.

13. Ibid.

14. Sue Fountain, daughter of Caddie Hudson Butts, MQA Quilt Documentation Forms F-36 through F-40, April 20, 1996.

15. Jeanne Walters, MQA Quilt Documentation Form A-2, August 19, 1995, with a quilt from Aleatcher Brown of Hinds County, circa 1935.

16. Winnie Hellums Sykes, MQA Quilt Documentation Form M-38, March 22, 1997.

17. Lois Ford, granddaughter of quiltmaker, MQA Quilt Documentation Form I-141, August 24, 1996.

18. Author interview with Lavada Rushing Brewer and Janet Sturdivant, January 22, 1999.

19. Betty Bohannon, MQA Quilt Documentation Form P-143, August 23, 1997.

Chapter Seven:
Special Quilts

1. Naomi McNeely, daughter of the minister, MQA Quilt Documentation Forms H-25 and H-26, July 12, 1996.

2. Linda Anglin Prater, quoting her mother, Frances Lamb Anglin, attachment to MQA Quilt Documentation Form H-59, July 13, 1996. Linda Prater remarked to one of the documentation team that her mother's judgment was keen: "Charlie didn't marry that girl."

3. Betty Fletcher, MQA Quilt Documentation Form E-73, March 2, 1996. See also letter from Yvonne Brunton to Martha [Ginn?], February 29, 1996.

4. Helen Fesmire, MQA Quilt Documentation Form Q-37, September 20, 1997.

5. Jack N. Murphree, MQA Quilt Documentation Form O-116, May 10, 1997.

6. A similar thing happened with quilt Q-67. A "Roman Cross" design, it was made by and for members of the McComb First Baptist Church, circa 1930s. It stayed in the possession of Mrs. Hugh (Mary) Middleton until 1996, when it was sold in a garage sale. A sharp-eyed shopper, Andrea A. Sanders, noticed her father-in-law's name among those on the quilt and purchased it for him as a Christmas gift. "A grand surprise," says the owner, Dr. Henry J. Sanders. MQA Quilt Documentation Form Q-67, September 20, 1997.

7. Prudie M. Moss, MQA Quilt Documentation From M-79, March 22, 1997.

8. Vera Downs, daughter of the recipient, MQA Quilt Documentation Form P-08, August 23, 1997.

9. Amanda G. Murphy, MQA Quilt Documentation Form P-110, August 23, 1997. She adds that the family is descended directly from Martha Washington and that Mr. Dandrige celebrated his 100th birthday on March 4, 1991.

10. Nannette Shipp Sissell, MQA Quilt Documentation Form M-11, March 22, 1997.

11. Mary Frances Abbot, MQA Quilt Documentation Form J-04, September 14, 1996.

12. Sarah Landrum May, great-granddaughter of quilter and granddaughter of the man for whom it was made, MQA Quilt Documentation Form C-33 and attachment, November 4, 1995.

13. Clarie Murphy, niece of Inez Mitchell, for whom the quilt was made, MQA Quilt Documentation Form D-151, January 13, 1996.

14. Mary Grace Johnson, MQA Quilt Documentation Form I-91, August 24, 1996.

15. Two "letter" quilts were brought in that seemed to have been made simply because the pattern appealed to the maker: an "H" quilt by Janeiro Lorene Cranage of Union (MQA Quilt Documentation Form I-99, July 24, 1996), who calls it a "4-Hs Quilt"; and a "W" quilt by Emma Calaway Vickers of Louisville, in Winston County (MQA Quilt Documentation Form I-130, July 24, 1996). There may have been other letter quilts made simply for the appeal of the design; there were a number of "T" quilts, for example: MQA Quilt Documentation Forms E-54 (March 2, 1996), F-43 (January 13, 1996), and D-91 (April 20, 1996) record three.

16. Cheryl Shannon, MQA Quilt Documentation Form D-146, January 13, 1996.

17. Frances Dupont, MQA Quilt Documentation Form L-14, January 11, 1997; and Mary Partridge, MQA Quilt Documentation Form D-42, January 13, 1996.

18. Jo Ann Bonner, MQA Quilt Documentation Form F-93, April 20, 1996.

19. Wilma Grammer, MQA Quilt Documentation Form F-03, April 20, 1996.

20. Lorenz and Stamper, *Mississippi Homespun*, 71.

21. Thomas Affleck, editor of *Western Farmer and Gardener*, quoted in *Mississippi Scenes*, by Howell, 291.

22. Bullard and Shiell, *Chintz Quilts*, 36.

23. Interview by Carol Vickers with Mrs. J. A. Swanson, Duck Hill, MS, February 19, 1999.

24. Woodard and Greenstein, *Twentieth-Century Quilts: 1900–1950*, 24.

25. Waldvogel, *Soft Covers for Hard Times*, 47.

26. Ibid.

27. Waldvogel and Brackman, *Patchwork Souvenirs of the 1933 World's Fair*, 39. Waldvogel and Brackman reveal that the H. Ver Mehren "Sunburst" design was available in preselected fabrics in three grades and in three colorations: in addition to yellow, the shopper could choose from pink, blue, or orchid (Sears would offer the same color choices). The fabrics could be pre-stamped with the pieces that would be needed to construct the quilt, or one could purchase stamping powder and do it themselves; it was even possible to order the fabric pieces already cut. Waldvogel and Brackman do not specify which version of the kit the maker used, but they do say that "Mrs. Carpenter [the winner] did not design her pattern, blend her fabrics, or mark the cutting lines. Her genius was in the choice of a show-stopping design and the feat of finishing a complex pattern from kit to bound quilt in about a month. The family does not recall if she quilted the top alone (she used H. Ver Mahren's quilting designs) but she must have had help with the intricate quilting to have met the deadline at the Philadelphia Sears mail-order house." Incidentally, Mrs. Carpenter's quilt won $210 for her, which must have been a windfall in the depression days of 1933. Because her brother had encouraged her to enter the contest and had bought the fabric and batting for her, she gave the quilt to him.

28. Alice Elizabeth Hamer Sanford, MQA Quilt Documentation Form H-12, July 13, 1996.

29. Elisabeth M. Clarke, MQA Quilt Documentation Form E-63, March 1, 1996. Ms. Clarke is the granddaughter of Charles Fife, for whom the baby quilt was made. It measures 31 inches wide by 38.5 inches long.

30. Carolyn Palmer, granddaughter, MQA Quilt Documentation Form I-79, August 24, 1996. Family name for the quilt is "Blue Star."

31. Charlotte Kunkle, MQA Quilt Documentation Form F-49, April 20, 1996.

32. Woodard and Greenstein, *Twentieth-Century Quilts, 1900–1950*, 30.

33. Ibid., 31.

34. Leigh Wilson, MQA Quilt Documentation Form E-47, March 2, 1996.

35. Frances Johnson, MQA Quilt Documentation Form D-11, January 13, 1996; Emily Harrell, MQA Quilt Documentation Form I-145, July 24, 1996.

36. Audrey Eakes Green, MQA Quilt Documentation Form I-73, August 23, 1996.

37. Bettye Groome, MQA Quilt Documentation Form G-54, May 11, 1996.

38. Howell, *Mississippi Scenes*, 169–70.

39. Ruth Emrick, MQA Quilt Documentation Form F-47, April 20, 1996.

40. Martha Lemmons, MQA Quilt Documentation Form D-14, January 13, 1996.

41. Claire Corona, MQA Quilt Documentation Form F-21, April 20, 1996.

42. Jo Ann Bonner, MQA Quilt Documentation Form F-95, April 20, 1996. Called "Dee Dee's Quilt" by the family, it was made by Jo Ann Bonner's grandmother and her friend.

43. Lloyd Mayatt, MQA Quilt Documentation Form I-01, August 24, 1996, great-great grandson of maker, Leah Kirkpatrick, who was helped by her daughter Odell Dean of Laurel, MS.

44. Written by Dorothy Roberts for MQA Quilt Docu-

mentation Form P-07, filled out by JoAnne R. Bradley, the daughter and owner of the embroidered "Overall Sam" quilt, August 23, 1997.

45. Jane Weathersby, MQA Quilt Documentation Form H-36, July 13, 1996.

46. Jessie M. Everett, MQA Quilt Documentation Form D-130, January 13, 1996.

47. Mrs. J. H. Craig, MQA Quilt Documentation Form F-18, April 20, 1996. Mrs. Craig bought her quilt for one dollar at a junk shop in Nashville before 1943; she has since seen information that said the design originally came from Germany, and the pattern was called "Sunburst."

48. Mary Grace Johnson, MQA Quilt Documentation Form I-90, August 24, 1996. The quilt was made by Bobbye Johnson in Coldwater (Neshoba County), MS, in 1905. Edith Holden, *The Country Diary of an Edwardian Lady* (1906; reprint, New York: Holt, Rinehart and Winston, 1977).

49. Notes from undated Carol Vickers interview with Libby Hollingsworth.

Chapter Eight:
The Tradition Continues, 1945–2000

Quotes from the quilters are taken from the Mississippi Quilt Association's interview guide and from conversations with friends and acquaintances of the quilters, unless otherwise noted.

1. Paula Maniscalgo, "Stitchin' History," *Mississippi*, September/October 1995, 52.

2. All quotes from Martha Skelton taken from author telephone interview with Martha Skelton, June 20, 2000.

3. Barbara Newman, "Mississippi's Number One Teacher," *Traditional Quilter*, March 1995, 43.

4. Maniscalgo, "Stitchin' History," 52. See also Newman, "Mississippi's Number One Teacher," 43.

BIBLIOGRAPHY

Amor, Jennifer. *Flavor Quilts for Kids to Make.* Paducah, KY: American Quilt Society, 1991.

Barry, John M. *Rising Tide: The Great Misssissippi Flood of 1927 and How It Changed America.* New York: Touchstone Books, 1997.

Benberry, Cuesta. *Always There: The African-American Presence in American Quilts.* Louisville: Kentucky Quilt Project, 1992.

Blum, Dilys, and Jack L. Lindsey. *Nineteenth-Century Appliqué Quilts.* Philadelphia: Philadelphia Museum of Art, 1989.

Brackman, Barbara. *An Encyclopedia of Pieced Quilt Patterns.* Vols. 1–8. Lawrence, KS: Prairie Flower Publishing, 1984.

Brackman, Barbara. *Clues in the Calico: A Guide to Identifying and Dating Antique Quilts.* McLean, VA: EPM Publications, 1989

Brackman, Barbara. *Quilts from the Civil War: With Designs and Patterns from Terry Clothier.* Layfayette, CA: C & T Publishing, 1997.

Bullard, Lacy Folmar, and Betty Jo Shiell. *Chintz Quilts: Unfading Glory.* Tallahassee, FL: Serendipity Publishers, 1983.

Burner, David, Elizabeth Fox-Genovese, Eugene D. Genovese, and Forrest McDonald. *An American Portrait: A History of the United States.* New York: Charles Scribner's Sons, 1985.

Carney, Bob. *The Other Mississippi: Especially the 1920's and 1930's.* Bay Minette, AL: Lavender Publishing Co., 1994.

Clark, Thomas D., and John D. W. Guice. *The Old Southwest, 1795–1830: Frontiers in Conflict.* Norman: University of Oklahoma Press, 1989.

Clinton, Catherine. *The Plantation Mistress: Woman's World in the Old South.* New York: Random House, 1984.

Cox, James L. *Mississippi Almanac, 1997–1998: The Ulimate Reference on the State.* Yazoo City, MS: Computer Search & Research, 1997.

Eanes, Ellen Fickling, et al. *North Carolina Quilts.* Chapel Hill: University of North Carolina Press, 1988.

England, Kaye. *Civil War Study: A Nation Divided.* Indianapolis: Kaye England Publications, 1998.

Freeman, Roland. *A Communion of the Spirits: African-American Quilters, Preservers, and Their Stories.* Nashville, TN: Rutledge Hill Press, 1996.

Gilbert, Jennifer. *The New England Quilt Museum Quilts, Featuring the Story of the Mill Girls.* Lafayette, CA: C & T Publishing, 1999.

Haigh, Janet. *Crazy Patchwork.* Chicago: Quilt Digest Press, 1998.

Hague, Parthenia Antoinette. *A Blockaded Family: Life in Southern Alabama during the Civil War.* Boston: Houghton, Mifflin, and Company, 1888. Reprint, University of Nebraska Press, Bison Books, 1991.

Hoehling, A. A. *Vicksburg: Forty-Seven Days of Siege.* Mechanicsburg, PA: Stackpole Books, 1969.

Horton, Laurel, and Lynn Robertson Myers. *Social Fabric: South Carolina's Traditional Quilts.* Columbia, SC: McKissick Museum, University of South Carolina, 1985.

Howell, Elmo. *Mississippi Scenes: Notes on Literature and History.* Memphis, TN: self-published, 1992.

Johnson, Mary Elizabeth. *Star Quilts.* Lincolnwood (Chicago), IL: Quilt Digest Press, 1997

Johnson, Mary Elizabeth, ed. *Times Down Home: Seventy-Five Years with the Progressive Farmer.* Birmingham, AL: Oxmoor House, 1978.

Kiracofe, Roderick, and Mary Elizabeth Johnson. *The American Quilt: A History of Cloth and Comfort, 1750–1950.* New York: Clarkson N. Potter, 1993.

Locklair, Paula W. *Quilts, Coverlets, and Counterpanes: Bedcoverings from the MESDA and Old Salem Collections.* Winston-Salem, NC: Old Salem, 1997.

Logan, Marie T. *Mississippi-Louisiana Border Country.* Rev. ed. Baton Rouge, LA: Claitor's Publishing Division, [sic], 1980.

Lorenz, Mary, and Anita Stamper. *Mississippi Homespun: Nineteenth-Century Textiles and the*

Women Who Made Them. Jackson: Mississippi Department of Archives and History, 1989.

Mazloomi, Carolyn. *Spirits of the Cloth: Contemporary African-American Quilts.* New York: Clarkson Potter, 1998.

McKee, Jesse O., Velvelyn Foster, Dennis J. Mitchell. J. Jessee Palmer, Thomas J. Richardson, Stephen Young, and Daniel C. Vogt. *Mississippi: A Portrait of an American State.* Montgomery, AL: Clairmont Press, 1995.

McMorris, Penny. *Crazy Quilts.* New York: E. P. Dutton, 1984.

Montgomery, Florence. *Printed Textiles: English and American Cottons and Linens, 1700–1850.* New York: Viking Press, 1970.

Ramsey, Bets. *Old and New Patterns in the Southern Tradition.* Nashville: Rutledge Hill Press, 1987.

Ramsey, Bets, and Merikay Waldvogel. *Southern Quilts: Surviving Relics of the Civil War.* Nashville: Rutledge Hill Press, 1998.

Reps, John W. *Cities of the Mississippi: Nineteenth-Century Images of Urban Development.* Columbia, MO, and London: University of Missouri Press, 1994.

Shaw, Robert. *Quilts: A Living Tradition.* Shelburne, VT: Hugh Lauter Levin Associates, 1995.

Sibley, Marlo. *Mississippi off the Beaten Path: A Guide to Unique Places.* Old Saybrook, CT: Globe Pequot Press, 1997.

Trestain, Eileen Jahnke. *Dating Fabrics: A Color Guide, 1800–1960.* Paducah, KY: American Quilter's Society, 1998.

Waldvogel, Merikay. *Soft Covers for Hard Times: Quiltmaking and the Great Depression.* Nashville: Rutledge Hill Press, 1990.

Waldvogel, Merikay, and Barbara Brackman. *Patchwork Souvenirs of the 1933 World's Fair.* Nashville: Rutledge Hill Press, 1993.

Woodard, Thos. K., and Blanche Greenstein. *Twentieth-Century Quilts: 1900–1950.* New York: E. P. Dutton, 1988.

INDEX